Tim Burton: The Monst

Tim Burton's films are well known for being complex and emotionally powerful. In this book, Helena Bassil-Morozow employs Jungian and post-Jungian concepts of unconscious mental processes along with file semiotics, analysis of narrative devices and cinematic history to explore the reworking of myth and fairy tale in Burton's gothic fantasy world.

The book explores the idea that Burton's lonely, rebellious 'monstrous' protagonists roam the earth because they are unable to fit into the normalising tendencies of society and become part of 'the crowd'. Divided into six chapters the book explores:

- the child
- the monster
- the superhero
- the genius
- the maniac
- the monstrous society.

Tim Burton: The Monster and the Crowd offers an entirely fresh perspective on Tim Burton's works. The book is essential reading for students and scholars of film or Jungian psychology, as well as anyone interested in critical issues in contemporary culture. It will also be of great help to those fans of Tim Burton who have been searching for a profound academic analysis of his works.

Helena Bassil-Morozow has been teaching Film, Drama and Literature in various further education institutions and in private practice for over five years.

Tim Burton: The Monster and the Crowd

A Post-Jungian Perspective

Helena Bassil-Morozow

Routledge
Taylor & Francis Group

LONDON AND NEW YORK

First published 2010
by Routledge
27 Church Road, Hove, East Sussex BN3 2FA

Simultaneously published in the USA and Canada
by Routledge
270 Madison Avenue, New York, NY 10016

Routledge is an imprint of the Taylor & Francis Group, an Informa business

Typeset in Times by Garfield Morgan, Swansea, West Glamorgan
Printed and bound in Great Britain by TJ International Ltd, Padstow,
Cornwall
Paperback cover design by Andrew Ward

This publication has been produced with paper manufactured to strict
environmental standards and with pulp derived from sustainable forests.

British Library Cataloguing in Publication Data
A catalogue record for this book is available from the British Library

Library of Congress Cataloging-in-Publication Data
Bassil-Morozow, Helena Victor, 1978-
    Tim Burton : the monster and the crowd, a post-Jungian perspective /
Helena Bassil-Morozow.
        p. cm.
    Includes filmography.
    Includes bibliographical references and index.
    ISBN 978-0-415-48970-6 (hardback) – ISBN 978-0-415-48971-3 (pbk.) 1.
Burton, Tim, 1958—Criticism and interpretation. 2. Monsters in motion
pictures. 3. Fantasy in motion pictures. I. Title.
    PN1998.3.B875B37 2010
    791.4302'33092–dc22
                                                                2009032724

ISBN: 978-0-415-48970-6 (hbk)
ISBN: 978-0-415-48971-3 (pbk)

For my parents

Contents

Preface

Growing up in the Soviet Union, in the predominantly collective mentality which presumes that the individual's life, both personal and social, belongs to the community, I always felt a strong pressure to conform. Communal societies, no doubt, have their own benefits – family support, emotional openness, easily accessible friends. An individualist who dares to insist on his or her emotional or intellectual independence is regarded by the group as a truly strange person, an outcast. When I saw *Edward Scissorhands* for the first time, I recognised the familiar theme, the universal metaphor for the individual–society conflict: the monster and the crowd.

Of course, Tim Burton makes films about artistic Western individualists who fight against the tenets of the bland, unimaginative, provincial or metropolitan middle-class mentality. In his case, the crowd is predominantly petit bourgeois, and the monster is anyone who wants to pursue an alternative lifestyle: a bohemian, a Goth, a punk, an artist or an anarchist. But it is not as simple as that. The monster versus the crowd is an age-old feud; it is deeper and more archetypal than the usual avant-garde rebellion against the various limitations to personal freedom ingrained in capitalist culture.

The conflict is linked to the process which Jung called *individuation* – developing into an autonomous individual, separating your ideas from the accepted norms of your community. It is the kind of conflict in which the minority, consisting of those who 'want to create', takes a stand against the majority, the common people who 'just want to live'. Imagination versus stagnation. And this is how Tim Burton sees it too, making films about the mad, creative monsters and the 'normal' people in the crowd.

Foreword

Dr Luke Hockley

Professor of Media Analysis, University of Bedfordshire

There is something of the trickster about this delightful book. The beguiling impression from the title is that the reader is going to be treated to a biography of Tim Burton. However, this is not to be. Nor is this a chronological account of Burton's films. Instead, Helena Bassil-Morozow's is a thematic approach to Burton's cinematic worlds which takes us on a heady journey though childhood, fantasy and the disappointments of adult life. Behind the cinematic surface she reveals a central problem in the films – how is it possible to live in a society where you don't feel you belong? This is a question which speaks to the heart of Jungian psychology.

What this book succeeds in offering is a classically Jungian view of the corpus of Burton's work. Don't worry if you're not that familiar with the films, as this book stands on its own. The only downside is that if it has the same effect on you as it did on me, you'll want to renew your acquaintance with the extraordinary filmic worlds of Tim Burton and you're in for many hours of viewing. Undertake this journey with this book beside you and you'll have a great tour guide as your companion. It ably indicates points of interest, reveals potential pitfalls and offers panoramic views into Burton's films as it takes us behind the scenes and deep into the thoughts of actors, composers and, of course, Tim Burton himself.

While the book rightly eschews notions of psychobiography it still offers glimpses of Burton the man, and illuminating they are. Readers are able to reflect for themselves on the relationship between the creative and collective act of filmmaking and how it is that a director who undertakes deeply personal projects to which he is fully committed brings his vision to life on the screen. You can rest assured that his forthcoming film *Alice in Wonderland* will be Tim Burton's *Alice* not Lewis Carroll's.

Helena's deep-rooted understanding of film theory is worn lightly throughout – occasional references are made here and subtle allusions there. In this way theory succeeds in permeating the book and it provides a certain security in the topsy-turvy, inside-out and upside-down films of Burton. In her writing Helena also brings something that is reminiscent of how films are edited. Ideas are juxtaposed, shot following shot, and as readers we are alternately drawn into the narrative and then jolted out of it, as ideas arise from the collusion of images and concepts. This gives the book a profoundly playful quality.

The book is timely too. Jungian film theory is a broad church in which authors exist in dialogue with each other. A dialogue which is not necessarily harmonious. This book adds a very welcome voice, graced as it is with a sensitivity to the nuances of Jung's ideas, supported by a solid appreciation of the last hundred years of film theory.

Acknowledgements

I would like to thank everyone who supported me in my heroic struggle with the hydra of copyright: the staff at Warner Bros., Walt Disney and Faber and Faber; John August – for being so professional yet accessible (he has his own online workshop!); and Jonathan Gems for his friendly and quick reply.

A special thank you goes to Ann Cummings at Brunel University Library for her understanding and support.

I am also extremely grateful to: my publisher, Kate Hawes, and assistant editor, Jane Harris, for the incredible support they provide to their authors; Christopher Hauke – for writing inspirational and insightful books; my teachers, Professors Avril Horner and Irina Kabanova, for their painstaking work on the corpus of my knowledge; my students – for providing me with real intellectual challenge; Alexey – for being the very patient testing ground for my ideas; . . . and to I. K., who knows the correct spelling of the word *dop·pel·gäng·er*

Permissions

I am very grateful to the following authors, companies and publishers for the permission to quote from their work:

The Collected Works of C.G. Jung (CW), edited by Sir Herbert Read, Dr Michael Fordham and Dr Gerhardt Adler, and translated by R. F. C. Hull, London: Routledge; Tim Burton and Mark Salisbury, *Burton on Burton,* published by Faber and Faber; Warner Bros. Productions Ltd; Twentieth Century Fox Productions Ltd; The Walt Disney Company Ltd; Columbia Pictures Corporation Ltd.

Introduction

The child with a thousand faces

'A poet has the imagination and psychology of a child, for his impressions of the world are immediate, however profound his ideas of the world may be,' says Andrey Tarkovsky in his self-exploratory book, *Sculpting in Time*. If the benchmark for true artistic creativity is purity of imagination, a certain naivety of outlook, freshness of vision and a stubborn faith in one's own work, then Tim Burton passes the test with top grades. His 'creative child', however, is much younger than that of Tarkovsky, in whom the wide-eyed search for meaning is veiled with mature perspicacity and gravitation towards graceful existentialist symbolism. By contrast, Burton's inner *puer* has not grown up into a fully fledged *auteur*. He has never mastered some of the indispensable principles of cinematic auteurism: the depth and complexity of concepts, the refinement and originality of cinematic movement or the stringent control over the narrative. The majority of his films have vague, myth-like structures, and are so conceptually 'uncluttered' (yet visually rich) that they can be enjoyed by children and adults alike. Besides, his films often *are* about children; to be more precise – about one child, a misunderstood being whose inability (or refusal) to grow up puts him into a conflict with the 'sensible', but senseless, society. What makes the puer different, and unique, is the ability to create new worlds – something that 'normal' people do not possess.

This 'outcast' image can appear in various forms in Burton's movies: the persecuted monster, the mad genius, the maniac, the unfinished young man living in his own Gothic dreamworld, and the disturbed superhero who fights his evil alter ego. These guises overlap and amalgamate ('the child' is also 'the monster', etc.), weaving a complex picture of the typical Burtonian male character – a strange little boy who grows up to be a weird, but talented, misfit. The misfit invariably has a dark imagination, is never accepted by the common people, and is sometimes even hunted down by them (Batman, Edward Scissorhands, Willy Wonka). Surprisingly, despite his 'introverted pariah' reputation, Burton enjoys great commercial success with the very 'crowd' of which his characters are so wary.

This book is about Tim Burton's use of the different guises of the image of the 'dark child' in his films, including the monster, the genius, the superhero, the maniac and the trickster. Thus, Chapter 1 ('The Child') traces the mythological, literary and psychological roots of the image that dominates Burton's films. Jungian (mainly Jung and Erich Neumann) and post-Jungian theories are my principal tools in this chapter, which deals with the child archetype in mythology and psychology of the individual (my justification of the choice of Jung over any other psychologies will appear later in the Introduction).

Chapter 2 is devoted to the 'monster' guise of the child, and covers *Edward Scissorhands*, *Frankenweenie*, *Batman Returns* and *Sweeney Todd*. It explores the psychosocial aspects of the monster figure (introversion, nonconformity, disability, hatred and rejection by society, abandonment by father/God, borderline personality qualities); its religious, philosophical and mythological implications (the son–father/man–God relationship and its breakdown and representation of this relationship in world mythology and religions); and the cinematic and fictional freaks that had impressed Burton in his youth (Boris Karloff as the Frankenstein monster, King Kong, Godzilla, etc.).

Chapter 3 is about Tim Burton's 'superheroes'. The superhero part of the Burtonian male character, quite predictably, wants to free the world from evil. His twofold inner/outer fight with what he perceives as evil in his culture and his own psyche is a crucial part of his quest for psychological unity. Since *Batman Returns* (1992) the individuation of the male character in Burton's films became enhanced by encounters with charismatic (but menacing) anima figures – Corpse Bride, Catwoman and Jenny/the witch in *Big Fish*. The hero's adventures will be analysed using the spiritual quest, *doppelgänger*, anima and father/God motifs. I will also discuss Burton's infantile superheroes – the Stainboy and Paul Reubens's original creation, Pee Wee from *Pee Wee's Big Adventure* (1985).

Chapter 4 mainly concerns the 'genius' guise of Burton's male characters (Vincent, Victor from *Frankenweenie*, Ed Wood and Willie Wonka). Burton's freaks grow up to become raw talents. As a rule, their creativity expresses itself in rather ambitious Frankensteinesque activities such as, for instance, monster-making. Vincent Malloy dreams of creating 'a terrible zombie' out of his dog Abercrombie; little Victor from *Frankenweenie* realises this dream – he actually revives his dog Sparky, who had been hit by a car, and turns him into a little 'doggy' version of the Frankenstein monster; Ed Wood, a mad Hollywood director, makes painfully bad horror movies; and Willy Wonka, the virtuoso chocolatier, possesses a collection of weird wax dolls and produces monstrosities out of various edible substances. 'The dark child' of Burton is invariably gifted, lonely, and perceived as insane by the hyperbolically 'normal' people surrounding him. Following the footpath of the traditional Frankenstein narrative, Burton puts a lot of emphasis on the unique abilities of the creator, his overwhelming ambition, his difference from the crowd, and his strong association with the hideous freak to whom he gives life.

The demonic side of Burton's freaks is examined in Chapter 5 ('The Maniac'). It picks up where the previous chapter left off, and focuses on the anti-hero, the *doppelgänger* (or the shadow, to use Jungian terminology). In Burton's films it usually manifests itself in the villainous ('Mr Hyde') side of the Burtonian hero – the dangerous psychopath. These characters illustrate the evil, unstable, perverted, totally asocial and antisocial side of 'the genius'. The chapter will incorporate Burton's first commercially successful features, *Beetlejuice*, *Sweeney Todd: The Demon Barber of Fleet Street*, *Batman* and *Batman Returns*.

Burton's two famous tricksters, Michael Keaton's Betelgeuse and Jack Nicholson's Joker, could have been discussed either under the 'monster' or 'the maniac' title, but I have chosen to put them in the latter category because of the aggressive nature of these characters. Betelgeuse is a trickster-like creature who oozes danger; he is rough, mad, evil and uncontrollable. Nicholson's Joker is even darker than Keaton's Betelgeuse, and uses his sinister creativity to torture and murder people.

Chapter 6 is devoted to the much-criticised *Mars Attacks!* and *Planet of the Apes*. These films are exceptions from Burton's 'the monster and the crowd' routine. They are not about the usual outcast's struggle for acceptance by society, and they are not built around the main character's internal fight with the personal *doppelgänger*. Instead, in these films Burton attempts to go further in his investigations of the conflict between individualism and collectivity, and focuses on society itself, on its dark, authoritarian and inhuman aspects. In *Mars Attacks!* and *Planet of the Apes*, the collective shadow takes the form of an outside invader (Martians or humanoid apes) and attempts to eliminate the human race. In this chapter I will try to explain why Burton's attempts to make films about the personal shadow usually earn critical acclaim and have great commercial success, while his renditions of the collective shadow are seen as 'over the top' and superficial.

Of course, I could have organised the book diachronically rather than synchronically, i.e. examined Burton's films in chronological order. This would have given me the opportunity to study his 'technical' progress as a film director, as well as examine the development of themes and motifs in his films. This is how it has been done by most of my predecessors[1]: Mark

---

1 Except Alison McMahan, author of *The Films of Tim Burton* (2005), who discusses Burton's works in terms of genre and stylistic features.

Salisbury (*Burton on Burton*, 1995; 2000; 2006); Le Blanc and Odell (*Tim Burton, pocket essential series*, 2005); Jim Smith and Clive Matthews (*Tim Burton*, 2007); and Edwin Page (*Gothic Fantasy: the Films of Tim Burton*, 2007). However, my opinion is that in Burton's case, the classic career-overview approach is not very effective – simply because his style, methods and themes do not change significantly throughout his directorial career. My choice of the synchronic layout is based on the assumption that the thematic range of Burton's films is more interesting to examine than his evolution as a director. Jungian psychology, with its propensity towards syntagmatic analysis of myths and a certain lack of respect for paradigmatic systematisation, is always handy for the investigation of thematic ranges.

Besides, I still use diachrony – but of a different kind. Burton's films traditionally deal with cultural and psychological issues pertaining to modern Western societies, from the end of the eighteenth century to the present day. While the synchronic approach breaks the unity of Burton's *oeuvre*, and the continuity of his protagonist, into many fragments (the different faces of the Burtonian child), I can nevertheless pull the fragments together by putting them onto the diachronic scale of modernity, thus establishing a new kind of continuity. This new diachrony reveals the face of the modern man as Burton usually depicts him – broken into pieces, then sewn together, and struggling to find a stable centre within himself – the centre which would help him not to fall apart again.

The question of style

Tim Burton has a singular vision, now confused with highbrow directing, now with mainstream commercialism – and yet he steadily remains in a league of his own. He is certainly not your typical 'artistic' filmmaker; he is not a 'camera and montage' person, breaking down, storyboarding each shot down to the finest detail, and then torturing his team and actors in an existential attempt to recreate his unique but ephemeral vision. Unlike for Hitchcock, who famously used to storyboard every shot in his films, or Spielberg, whose narratives are so very neat and smooth, narrative perfection would be completely out of place in Burton's works. In a Tim Burton film you will not find a long take choreographed with surgical precision, nor encounter an iconographic horse or a marble lion suddenly squeezed in between two other shots – so as to invoke complex references or highlight a higher idea. Neither will you stumble upon an elegant conceptual dissociation between the different cinematic codes and sub-codes (for instance, a first-person camera moving about in an empty flat while the invisible intradiegetic voice on the phone is having a seemingly banal conversation with his mother) in order to emphasise the deceptiveness and transience of reality: the irreparable gap between the 'inner' and the 'outer'.

No, Burton does not aim at this level of theoretical and conceptual complexity, and does not combine the cinematic means of expression in unexpected, groundbreaking ways, to achieve it.

And this is, perhaps, for the best. In fact, experimental tracking shots, lions, horses, clever camera angles and avant-garde points of view would not be suitable for his creative purposes. Growing up inspired by the style of Dr Seuss ('the rhythm of his stuff spoke to me very clearly', Salisbury, 2006: 19), avidly watching Ray Harryhausen's work and devouring horror B-movies from around the world, Tim Burton developed a unique personal style whose essence can be described as 'grand effect by simple means' (of course, one can also call it popular). He remains firmly democratic in his use and combination of cinematic devices. In many of his films he tells a fairly simple story, which, thanks to its straightforward sequentiality and uncluttered symbolism, is immediately accessible for the spectator regardless of his or her age or background. A Burton story is traditionally illustrated with beautiful pictures which are far more eloquent than any words can be. Films like *Edward Scissorhands* or *Charlie and the Chocolate Factory* have at their core the childlike naivety, pain and anger aimed at the insensitive crowd of adults who have long ceased to see the world in fresh colours. Despite being clear, his message is emotionally deep. To render the suffering and confusion of his immature protagonists, Burton cannot use the elaborate sequential and combinatorial devices that are traditionally employed to show the complexity, multiplicity and unpredictability of the adult world – intricate montage, 'philosophical' long takes with a series of complex compositions, freeze frames, rhythmic punctuation, logical discrepancies between picture and sound, clashes between the extradiegetic and intradiegetic planes, etc. Any 'grown-up' instruments would only obscure the message, and the purity of youthful vision would be lost.

Instead, Burton chooses to create an impact using different methods. At stake are not sequential editing or the position and movement of the camera but the quality and detailedness of the picture and its emotional correlation with music. In this sense, he is far less 'cinematic' than many directors. Burton is more of a '*mise-en-scène* director' who has always been praised for his extraordinary visual sense. His grand imagery seems to be slapped onto narrative canvases like blobs of dark matter, like some unexplainable and invincible forces, which effectively belittle both protagonists and antagonists. Burton's marvellous, powerful visuals are not organised into perfect arrangements. How the shots work as a sequence (either 'classic' or 'avant-garde') has never been of much importance in his films. In cine-semiotic terms, he is not as interested in the higher structural (syntagmatic) level as, for instance, such an extreme 'syntagmatic' director as Alfred Hitchcock. Most of Burton's directorial effort is put into single frames (morphemes); shots at most (words) – but not 'cleverly constructed' sequences (sentences, paragraphs, chapters). Experimental montage and other forms of 'authoritative' editing (Tarkovsky's 'camera montage', for example) are indicative of a certain desire to control the narrative as a whole, of the venture to achieve the solidity of the text. Burton, however, does not support such authoritarianism. Here is, for instance, his perception of storyboarding: 'I used to [storyboard] but I don't do as much anymore. In fact, I am getting anti-storyboard. I pretty much stopped on *Beetlejuice*. You storyboard things that need effects. I still do it to some degree. But certainly after the first *Batman*, I really stopped. And now, I can't even come up with – I'm getting twisted about the whole thing. There is something about being spontaneous and working shots out. [. . .] There's an energy and there's a working through things with people' (Fraga, 2005: 82).

As for editing, it is a very melancholy process for Burton. One of his interviewers, David Edelstein, notes: 'When I suggest to Burton that editing does not express him the way other parts of the process do, he muses that after a shoot ends, it's like breaking up with someone – he edits in depression, which somehow gets incorporated into the film' (Fraga, 2005: 33). In another interview, conducted by David Breskin, Burton admits to not paying much attention to shot sequences: 'When I look at rushes [unedited footage] I sometimes get chills because it reminds me of shooting. But editing? What can I tell you? I don't slap them together, but I'm not going to win any editing awards. It's okay. It's fine' (Fraga, 2005: 83). He is not, by his own admission, going to 'create some kind of trendy or hot editing' (Fraga, 2005: 33).

His deliberate emphasis on *mise-en-scène*, and noticeable disregard for the specific cinematic codes, won the heart of Anton Furst, who was hired as the production designer for *Batman* (1989). Furst said in an interview with Alan Jones that he had never felt so naturally in tune with a director – 'conceptually, spiritually, visually, or artistically' (Fraga, 2005: 22). Such a unique connection happened because the two shared the same philosophy of moviemaking. Both Furst and Burton are primarily concerned with creating visual impact, with delivering a powerful image. The impact lies not in camerawork but in the basics, in the first impression: 'When we first met, we both independently mentioned how sick we were of the ILM[2] school of film-making [. . .] We both agreed the best special effect we could ever remember seeing was the house in *Psycho* because it registers such a strong image. Impact, that's what films are about – not effects. I felt much better after that conversation, knowing he was totally uninterested in camera tricks and the clever, clever approach' (Fraga, 2005: 22). But Tim Burton is a 'clever, clever' director in the sense that he knows how to capture mass audiences without 'cheapening' his films on the one hand, and

---

2 George Lucas's brainchild, Industrial Light and Magic – a motion picture visual effects company.

how to create highly original works without resorting to mind-blowing complexity on the other.

A different kind of *auteur*

Despite his lack of ambition to control the narrative – both its textual and cinematic constituents – Burton is universally hailed as one of the most important contemporary Hollywood *auteurs*. Which is, in a way, paradoxical, because he cannot be further from an omniscient intellectual operating in riddles (like David Lynch) or an ace at complex, tonal montage (*à la* Jim Jarmusch).

Before trying to decide whether Tim Burton deserves the nebulous *auteur* title, let us remind ourselves what this title implies. *La politique des auteurs*, since its emergence in France in the late 1940s, and throughout its long life as a half-formulated concept, never managed to become a fully fledged theory. True, compared to André Bazin and François Truffaut's applications of the filmic authorship idea, Andrew Sarris's translation of it boasted more shape, but still lacked a quotable definition. As Sarris himself admitted, 'the auteur theory is not so much a theory as an attitude, a table of values that converts film history into directorial autobiography' (Sarris, 1968: 30–34). Even so, despite the lack of definition, the term is as popular as ever and its common usage is constantly growing. Any 'decent' *auteur* is required to possess any (or preferably both) of the following features:

1. Control over all or most of the processes involved in making a film

This is a slightly utopian requirement because of the so-called 'noise' (scriptwriter, editor, producer, cameraman, composer, the actors). According to the British film theorist Peter Wollen, the directorial factor is only one of the many different contributions in the moviemaking process, 'though perhaps the one which carries the most weight' (Wollen, 1969–1972: 104). The scriptwriter, for instance, can be very 'noisy', for his vision of the film's style, structure and meaning can be very different from that of the director. A very possessive *auteur*, Andrey Tarkovsky argued that the film author's wholeness of vision should be placed higher than any creative contributions coming from the support team:

> When a writer and a director have different aesthetic starting-points, compromise is impossible. [. . .] When such conflict occurs there is only one way out: to transform the literary scenario into a new fabric, which at a certain stage in the making of the film will come to be called the shooting script. And in the course of work on this script, the author of the film (not of the script but of the film) is entitled to turn the literary

scenario this way or that as he wants. All that matters is that his vision should be whole, and that every word of the script should be dear to him and have passed through his own creative experience. For among the piles of written pages, and the actors, and the places chosen for location, and even the most brilliant dialogue, and the artist's sketches, there stands only one person: the director, and he alone, as the last filter in the creative process of film-making.

(Tarkovsky, 1989: 18)

Undeniably, the biggest 'noise' of all comes from the people in charge of the budget (which Tarkovsky, as a young film-school graduate, quickly realised when his films began to suffer at the hands of Soviet censorship). Andrew Sarris recalls an old Hollywood anecdote which involves the studio head Samuel Goldwyn and a reporter. The latter 'had the temerity to begin a sentence with the statement ". . . when William Wyler made *Wuthering Heights*". The reporter never passed beyond the premise. "*I* made *Wuthering Heights*," Goldwyn snapped, "Wyler only directed it"' (Sarris, 1968: 8). Leaving the Hollywood studio system, or indeed any system that controls the financial base of the film, seriously narrows the gap between 'unlimited' and 'limited' control over the project.

The intrinsic complexity of the filmmaking process, in that it involves various people at different levels, makes it difficult to attain the goal of 'absolute control'. Authorship can only be approximate; it can only be shared – to a different degree in each individual case, of course – because 'writers, actors, producers and technicians challenge [the director] at every turn' (Sarris, 1968: 12).

2. A distinct 'voice' (recurrent themes, motifs, characters, techniques, stylistic features)

There is no doubt that Tim Burton has a unique cinematographic style. 'A distinct voice' sounds ambitious, but this is much easier to achieve than the 'sole authorship' prerequisite. The British film scholar Geoffrey Novel-Smith argued that recognisable motifs are one essential corollary of the *auteur* theory: 'The pattern formed by these motifs . . . is what gives an author's work its particular structure, both defining it internally and distinguishing one body of work from another (Caughie, 1981: 137).

Just like any work of art, a film should be original, recognisable and have an 'identifiable' maker's mark 'in the corner'. Originality, the covetable distinct style, can be further subdivided into formal (montage, *mise-en-scène*, camera angles, punctuation, sequential organisation of the narrative, etc.) and thematic. Like in a literary text, the two, the form and the content, intertwine and support each other. Quite often, film critics seem to equate 'originality' with formal complexity. Tricks like 'hot editing' (Burton's term), unusual POV (think of the 'soup's point of view' from Guy Ritchie's *Lock, Stock and Two Smoking Barrels*), and convoluted narratives (the multi-layered, twisted, nightmarish plot in Lynch's *Mulholland Drive* is a good example) are traditionally seen as part of the *auteur* culture and intellectual moviemaking. Technical virtuosity, stubbornness and a certain inescapable elitism are traditionally associated with the concept of directorial 'autership'. Also, there is always a danger that the desire to 'express oneself entirely in a film' is interpreted as a sign of egotism and vanity, the desire to 'play God' and be the centre of attention.

True, it would not be easy to squeeze Tim Burton into any of the *auteur* stereotypes. As a director, he is an oxymoron, or, as Le Blanc and Odell put it, 'a Hollywood contradiction' (2005: 11). Whatever aspect of his creative life you examine, there is always a paradox lurking in the background. Consider, for instance, the issue of unlimited control over one's work. On the surface of it, Burton is firmly rooted in the studio system. His career began at Disney, where he found himself after the California Institute of the Arts, a training school created by Walt Disney in the 1960s. Eight of his films, including *Batman, Charlie and the Chocolate Factory* and *Sweeney Todd*, were produced by Warner Brothers; *Edward Scissorhands* was financed by Twentieth-Century Fox, and *Big Fish* is a Columbia Pictures production. At the same time, he has always had a tempestuous relationship with the studio system, aiming to preserve his unique vision while keeping to the studio's budget. He regularly sounds disdainful when he speaks of his experience of dealing with the studio system, the phrase 'F**k your system' being one of the most expressive of his opinions (Fraga, 2005: 57).

And from the very start the fateful 'system' intermittently hindered and pushed forward Burton's directorial career. He considered himself lucky to be picked by the Disney Review Board out of the crowd of ambitious contenders at Cal Arts, but soon realised that 'the dream ticket' would only lead him to a dead-end: 'Disney and I were a bad mix [. . .] they want you to be an artist, but at the same time they want you to be a zombie factory worker and have no personality. It takes a very special person to make those two sides of your brain coexist' (Salisbury, 2006: 9–10). He found the atmosphere so stifling and 'anti-auteur' that he eventually left the studio in the middle of the 1980s after *Frankenweenie*, his black and white short, was deemed by Disney too 'dark' for children's audiences (it was subsequently shelved until 1992).

Tim Burton's instinctive ability to appeal to the mass audience can easily be confused with an acute sense for marketable cinematic products. It is obvious that the studio system, despite its notorious habit of preferring successful entrepreneurs to creative recluses, has successfully exploited Burton's Gothic fantasies – which happen to sell well. Having watched so many horror films as a child, and consequently having absorbed all the basic principles of a marketable mass movie – simplified narrative, big drama, emotional symbolism, hyperbolised visuals, high stylisation, rich artificiality of sets, costumes and make-up – Burton undoubtedly gained a sharp sense of 'product' that would appeal to a mass audience (something that is quite unusual in an *auteur* aspirant). And anyway, Burton is known as a director who is prepared to fight for his creative vision. He chose Johnny Depp over Tom Cruise as Edward Scissorhands at a time when Depp was no more than a teen 'novelty idol' and Cruise was already a confirmed superstar. Depp was eventually given the role – apparently after much fighting and debate on the part of the director. The actor could not believe his ears when his agent rang him weeks after the initial meeting with Burton: 'I put the phone down and mumbled those words to myself. And then mumbled them to anyone I came in contact with. I couldn't f**king believe it. He was willing to risk everything on me in the role. Headbutting the studio's wishes, hopes and dreams for a big star with established box-office draw, he chose me' (Salisbury, 2006: xi). Burton's side of the story looked like this:

> They are always saying, here is a list of five people who are box-office, and three of them are Tom Cruise. I've learned to be open at the initial stage and talk to people. He certainly wasn't my ideal, but I talked to him. He was interesting, but I think it worked out for the best. A lot of questions came up – I don't really recall the specifics – but at the end of the meeting I did feel like, and even probably said to him, 'It's nice to have a lot of questions about the character, but you either do it or you don't do it'
>
> (Salisbury, 2000: 91)

Burton feels justified in arguing with studio executives over 'details' like the choice of actors and film endings – but not like some touchy, capricious *auteur* with a systematic vision *à la* Adam Kesher in *Mulholland Drive*. Burton, in his elated stubbornness, resembles a child prophet who believes that he has seen an apparition of the Virgin Mary, and is now adamant that the visitation was absolutely genuine. 'If *Beetlejuice* turns out to be successful,' he said in one of his early interviews, 'I will be so happy, and so *perversely* happy. I'm for anything that subverts what the studio thinks you have to do' (Fraga, 2005: 15).

This amazing obstinacy, the force that bends even the pillars of the studio system, made the film critic Jonathan Romney label him as 'Hollywood's pet maladjusted adolescent' (Woods, 2002: 170). The 'adolescent', however, knows how to deal with those sensible, reasonable adults:

> . . . they don't know what you go through with studio people and executives, and they take their cue a lot from critics, and the feeling is

that 'Tim can't tell a story out of a paper bag'. [. . .] And every time, when they're developing a script and you're talking to the studio and you have these stupid meetings with them, I can say that if there is a problem with the movie it is *nothing* that you discussed. [. . .] And *Beetlejuice* was kind of the one movie that gave me, again, that feeling of humanity, that *F**k Everybody!* That made me feel very good, that the audience didn't need a certain kind of thing. Movies can be different things! Wouldn't it be great if the world allowed David Cronenberg to do his thing and people could tell the difference! And criticism would be on the whole other level! And the world be on the whole other level!

(Fraga, 2005: 57)

'The difference', one might assume, lies in the amount of 'noise' that gradually creeps into the film in the process of its evolution from the initial concept to the final product. All the while, and rather contrastingly, Burton has respect for the people who hand out the cash, and willingly acknowledges the financial responsibility for his creations: 'I've never taken the attitude of the artiste, who says I don't care about anything, I'm just making my movie. I try to be true to myself and do only what I can do, because if I veer from that everybody's in trouble. And when there is a large amount of money involved, I attempt, without pretending to know what audiences are all about, to try and do something that people would like to see, without going too crazy' (Woods, 2002: 51). Tim Burton is not a purist; he had always had an eye on the commercial side of the movie business. In some of his interviews he expressed rather anti-auteurish opinions: 'I care about money, which is why I get so intense when these people are on my case saying I don't make commercial movies, because I've always felt very responsible to the people who put up the money. It's not like you're doing a painting. There is a large amount of money involved, even if you're doing a low-budget movie, so I don't want to waste it (Salisbury, 2006: 51). It is his attempt to achieve the 'golden middle', the ideal position in the triangle consisting of the director, the studio and the audience, that makes him simultaneously accessible and, surprisingly, sophisticated.

Burton's visual style is extremely recognisable despite the fact that he does not harbour ambitions to produce avant-garde works and 'explore new artistic territories'. Most of his creative efforts seem to be aimed at the elements that are not exclusive to cinema, or, to use Christian Metz's term, at 'non-specific cinematic codes' (for instance, soundtrack and codes of visual iconicity shared with painting) (Metz, 1974: 224–235). Burton is at his most confident with the components that traditionally determine 'the main impression', or the general atmosphere of a film: visual-iconic elements, lighting, music and story (but not plot). At the same time, he does not worship specifically cinematic properties such as sequentiality, *movement of the image* (camera) and *movement in the image* (actors).[3] The fact that the 'picture' *moves* is an additional benefit rather than the main property of Burton's creative product – the movement allows him to tell a story, without foregrounding itself as a stylistic element. Much of his effort goes into the initial impression from the shot, hence the heightened attention to the static elements of the *mise-en-scène* (the ones which cinema shares with photography): setting, decorations, texture, colours, lighting, framing, make-up and costumes. They make Burton's works highly atmospheric. His relative neglect of camera movement and editing gives his films a charming imprecision – which is perfect for Burton's artistic purposes as this kind of background emphasises the magnificent, luminous symbolism of his films.

Burton's status in Hollywood is so ambiguous that some critics have altogether grouped his works with contemporary action movies, confusing his lack of narrative and stylistic precision with an interest in the action aspect of the film. Alison McMahan, in a book entitled *The Films of Tim Burton*, coins the term *pataphysical film*, and irrevocably attributes Burton's style to this genre. In her view, all *pataphysical* films have in common the following features:

- An alternative narrative logic
- Use of special effects in a blatant way
- Thin plots and thinly drawn characters, 'because the narrative relies more on intertextual, nondiegetic references'.

(McMahan, 2005: 3)

Examples of such movies include, for instance, *Van Helsing* (2004) and *Hulk* (2003). It appears that the movies labelled *pataphysical* by Alison McMahan are predominantly commercial. They privilege action over narrative and quite blatantly serve as a recycling factory for anything previously done in cinema, both stylistically and textually, mixing high and low, old and new; randomly combining genres, plots and recycled famous sequences from other films. For instance, the seven-minute sequence at the beginning of *Van Helsing*, incorporating segments from over 70 years of *Draculas* and *Frankensteins*, is not just an ironic statement, a reference that 'got out of control'. It is – decidedly – an integral part of the movie. McMahan places the roots of this genre in the days of early cinema and animation, Jules Levy's *Les Art Incohérents*, and in the visual and ideological legacy of Surrealism. She argues that the eccentric works of the first animator, the French science teacher Emile Reynaud,[4] with their fluidity of transformations, influenced contemporary pataphysical films.

---

3 The last two are Metz's terms (Metz, 1974: 232).
4 The director of *Fantasmagorie* (1908), *The Hasher's Delirium* (1910), etc.

The inherited traits include, in McMahan's view, dependence on 'excessive' special effects (which bring with them 'a change in narration and a flattening of the emotional aspects of the characters'), non-realistic narrative, and tongue-in-cheek attitude (McMahan, 2005: 15). She also insists that these films are not meaningless; rather, they 'have come to mean differently, to mean in new ways' (2005: 3). Unfortunately, the author does not explain what these news ways of meaning are, or what exactly constitutes 'the alternative narrative logic' which the 'pataphysical films' appear to follow.

Films like *Hulk, Van Helsing, Brothers Grimm* and *The Matrix* are blatantly lowbrow, populist and allusive to the point of non-stop recycling. Being fast-paced and powerfully visual, they are openly aimed at the spectator with a short attention span. Their creators deliberately macerate, mix and match other films and cinematic traditions in order to make the product more digestible and superficially attractive. People who make them know that they are producing a nakedly commercial product.

McMahan's belief that Burton's *oeuvre* belongs to the bulk of the 'pataphysical style' is understandable. His films contain some formal attributes of the aforementioned group, such as schematic plots and characters, interfilmic references and allusions, as well as 'in your face' special effects (of which the freakish, DIY effects from *Beetlejuice* are a good example). Burton, a self-confessed fan of classic horror movies, is especially reliant on allusions: 'Because I never read, my fairy tales were probably those monster movies. [. . .] I mean, fairy tales are extremely violent and extremely symbolic and disturbing, probably even more so than *Frankenstein* and stuff like that, which are kind of mythic and perceived as fairy-tale like' (Salisbury, 2000: 3). True, *Frankenstein*, in James Whale's realisation, was an important source of inspiration for Burton. *Frankenweenie* (1984) is bursting with direct references to both *Frankenstein* (1931) and *The Bride of Frankenstein* (1935), almost to the point of direct translation of Whale's vision into the children's pet story, in which Boris Karloff is replaced with a little monster dog, who dies but gets 'resurrected' by a boy genius. Some filmic allusions that Burton inserts into his films are smaller and less obvious. For instance, the slowly melting dolls' heads in *Charlie and the Chocolate Factory* (2005) is a tribute to André de Toth's *The House of Wax* (1953) with Vincent Price.

The misunderstood introverted punk Edward Scissorhands is an original creation – unlike many of his other powerful motifs and characters. In fact, it appears that only the characters who directly reflect Burton's own psychology – like Vincent and Edward – are entirely original. The rest are borrowed from a variety of literary and cinematic sources and can be traced to their roots in popular culture and literature. The popular borrowings include, for instance, the superhero Batman, the brainy green Martians from *Mars Attacks!*, the demon barber Sweeney Todd, who made his debut in 1846 in the penny dreadful series entitled *The String of Pearls: A*

Romance, and Ed Wood's circus of freaks and ghouls, including Bela Lugosi and Vampyra. Burton's (undeniably mediated) literary influences, are, too, many and diverse: Mary Shelley's *Frankenstein* and its numerous cinematic reworkings; Washington Irving's *The Legend of Sleepy Hollow*; Daniel Wallace's *Big Fish: A Novel of Mythic Proportions*; Roald Dahl's *Charlie and the Chocolate Factory*; Pierre Boulle's *Planet of the Apes*; and Lewis Carroll's *Alice in Wonderland*.

Knowing that Tim Burton likes to reuse aspects of old films, can we really tell the difference between 'pataphysical' references and 'important' references? Or, in other words, can one employ heaps of popular allusions in a meaningful manner?

Action, symbol, introspection

My argument is that associating Burton's works with commercial, fast-paced, action-packed films steeped with music-clip-like montage and random narrative citations, would be a mistake. The 'pop' nature of Burton's films is more of a lucky by-product of his creativity than an intended outcome. First of all, he is not an action director – both objectively and self-confessedly – and hence cannot be compared to Stephen Sommers, Roland Emmerich, James Cameron or the Wachowski brothers. His action sequences in *Batman* and *Planet of the Apes* are limp, clumsy and lacking in agility. 'I've seen better action in my day' is Burton's view of his own action-making skills (Fraga, 2005: 78). Ever the true nonconformist, he declares: 'If you want it to be a James Cameron movie then get James Cameron to do it. Me directing action is a joke; I don't like guns. I hear a gunshot and I close my eyes' (Salisbury, 2006: 114).

Still, it would be unfair to expect a perfect handling of fast sequences from a predominantly introspective director. The *action* Burton is trying to express is more of a psychological than a 'real' phenomenon. Even on the visual level, the 'quest' motif in his films, along with its principal battles and challenges, lacks the 'physicality', brutality and (pseudo)realism of traditional action movies. It is the 'inner', not the 'outer' movement that Burton is trying to convey. Unlike the 'pataphysical' films Alison McMahan recalls, Burton's works are deemed to be slower, inward-looking and far more personal. All the pop-cinematic allusions he gathers in his films – be it the ragged Frankenstein monster, Ed Wood's aluminium tin flying saucers or even the melting heads of wax dolls – are linked, via different modes of projection, to the childhood feelings of dejection, failure to communicate, and alienation from one's surroundings. The monstrous, the Gothic and the surreal are not, for Burton, simply effective, tried-and-tested vehicles for producing an entertaining narrative. They are far more than communication aids and adequate means of expression. Burton may be groping for words in interviews, but his visual creations, his Gothic symbols, possess remarkable depth, clarity and precision.

In interviews he also admits to having trouble creating a coherent cinematic narrative. He explains why he persistently 'sacrifices' the narrative for the sake of the visuals. Lack of delineation, definition and linguistic detailedness is Burton's way of ensuring that his films remain democratic and accessible:

> I guess it must be the way my brain works, because the first *Batman* was probably my most concentrated effort to tell a linear story, and I realise that it's like a joke. [. . .] In any of my movies the narrative is the worst thing you've ever seen, and that's constant. [. . .] Do Fellini movies have a strong narrative drive? I love movies where I make up my own idea about them. [. . .] Everybody is different, so things are going to affect people differently. So why not have your own opinions, have different levels of things you can find if you want them, however deeply you want to go. That's why I like Roman Polanski's movies, like *The Tenant*. I've felt like that, I've lived it, I know what that's like. Or *Repulsion*, I know that feeling, I understand it. [. . .] You just connect. It may not be something that anybody else connects with, but it's like I get that, I understand that feeling. I will always fight that literal impulse to lay everything directly in front of you. I just hate it.
>
> Some people are really good at narrative and some people are really good at action. I'm not that sort of person. So, if I'm going to do something, just let me do my thing and hope for the best. If you don't want me to do it, then just don't have me do it. But if I do it, don't make me conform.
>
> (Salisbury, 2006: 114)

The gaps are to be filled with what Burton calls 'the feeling', and what Tarkovsky describes as 'something amorphous, vague, with no skeleton or schema. Like a cloud' (Tarkovsky, 1989: 23). Throughout his book Tarkovsky states that he prefers freedom of expression to any theories, formulas, schemas or threadbare tricks. Like Burton, he does not normally describe his works in technical terms, attempting instead to paint 'a feeling'. Narrative causality, in Tarkovsky's view, should be replaced with 'poetic articulation': 'There are some aspects of human life that can only be faithfully represented through poetry. But this is where directors very often try to use clumsy, conventional gimmickry instead of poetic logic. I'm thinking of illusionism and extraordinary effects involved in dreams, memories and fantasies. All too often film dreams are made into a collection of old-fashioned filmic tricks, and cease to be a phenomenon of life' (2000: 30).

For Tim Burton, too, the poetry of the image comes first. This 'symbolic' approach seems to be dictated by the specifics of his creativity. By his own admission, his creative process is more intuitive than intellectual: 'I don't trust my intellect as much, because it's kind of schizy,' Burton admits, 'I feel more grounded going with a feeling' (Woods, 2002: 41). He starts with a vague image, and goes on to create a numinous symbol which often has personal significance for him, such as a dishevelled boy with scissors instead of hands, a rugged madman who calls himself a 'bio-exorcist', a menacing urban panorama, a spooky countryside landscape. The image of Edward Scissorhands, for instance, 'came subconsciously and was linked to a character who wants to touch but can't; who was both creative and destructive . . . It was very much linked to a feeling' (Salisbury, 2006: 87).

However, Burton's habit of reworking existing narratives does not indicate a lack of creativity or deficiency of imagination. It is true that he prefers to work with popular myths, but gives them a new visual interpretation. His versions of pre-existent symbols – the Joker, Batman, Willy Wonka, Topps Cards Martians, talking apes, Sweeney Todd – if they do not always outshine the original, are nevertheless instantly recognisable and visually striking. Moreover, the distinctiveness and numinosity of his symbols compensate for the inadequacy of technical and narrative elements. With Edward Scissorhands for a central character, one cannot lament the absence of a clever rhythmic pattern, inventively striking juxtapositions or intriguingly non-linear narrative. However eloquent and beautiful these tricks can be, Tim Burton simply does not need them to get his message across. When he wants to tell a story – his story – he does not refine it until it becomes a shiny, robotic work of art. He leaves it in a vaguely raw, half-unconscious (his hallmark), twilight state, devoid of the smoothness of the classic narrative film on the one hand, and the sharp precision of thought which is so typical of intellectual filmmaking on the other. There is enough power in Edward to charge the film with energy and poignancy. The creature with scissors is multi-layered and complex enough as a symbol to invite multiple, and conflicting, interpretations.

To sum up the ideas discussed on the previous pages – Burton looks as unnatural in the 'highbrow' corner as he does among the gang of 'meaningless action' directors. All the while, his style is unique and easily recognisable, with repeating visual and narrative patterns. He tends to neglect the textual aspect of film; and in doing this, he places 'the image' higher than 'the word'. Consequently, the cinematic, 'moving' narrative suffers alongside the textual aspect (storyline, dialogues, extradiegetic voices). In addition, he predominantly operates with simple, myth-like compositions. His films foreground 'bigger' symbolism at the expense of syntactic intricacy and diegetic ploys, and gravitate towards intense and vivid, but less detailed, models and blocks. This inevitably steers Burton's creative vision towards the realm of the fantastic, where such means of expression are appropriate, while almost totally neglecting realistic genres. Burton certainly feels 'at home' with a number of traditionally popular genres such as science fiction, fantasy, horror, myth and mystery, and freely uses dark and Gothic imagery.

His persistent use of simplified mythological frames does not mean, however, that he misses out on psychological complexity. The psychological depth of Burton's films is as intense as that of a Švankmajer or Lynch – but his is the archetypal insight of a good fairy tale. Moreover, the lucidity of his narratives allows the audience to access this psychological content quicker, and appreciate it more fully. Far from being plain, downmarket and populist, Burton's narratives are uncluttered, powerful and topical.

Neither does he seem to care whether his material is original, and to what degree. His interpretations, however, are undoubtedly original and – what is more important – personal. Whatever images he utilises – be it the Frankenstein monster in the form of a little dog, Dracula in the guise of drug-dependent Bela Lugosi in *Ed Wood*, or the Penguin man who, in this version, behaves like a mistreated child – the director always moulds them into a story about a misunderstood, lonely outcast; or at least links them to such a story.

People who interview Tim Burton often notice his clumsiness, his intro-version and his inability to express himself clearly and coherently. His creativity clearly visual and not linguistic, he often looks at a loss when trying to explain to journalists why and how he did a certain thing in his film. And journalists, usually being watchful and perceptive, notice his communication weaknesses immediately. One of his interviewers, David Edelstein, wrote: 'To quote him is not to get him right; you miss the air of stoned melancholy, the spastically gesticulating hands and the sentences that stop and restart and that you have to complete for him' (Fraga, 2005: 32). If Tim Burton is to be labelled an *auteur*, then he is the '*auteur* of the symbol'.

Tim Burton in context

It is interesting to compare Burton's handling of abstract imagery with the work of other directors who have also depicted the world of the unconscious in symbolic language. Symbolic cinema is not necessarily non-realistic cinema – one can make a film based on a spiritual, miraculous or super-natural idea, but use everyday images and objective representation tech-niques to express it. Or, as the French film theorist André Bazin wrote, 'realism . . . is to be defined not in terms of ends but of means' (Bazin, 1971/ II: 87).

Let us take a look at Andrey Tarkovsky. A proponent of dream-like, iconic imagery, and advocate of narrative impressionism (his films are 'poetically structured' rather than linear), Tarkovsky nevertheless con-sidered 'the real world' the only possible visual and emotional base for a film. In his view, realistic details, represented in a symbolic way, are the most suitable tools for truthful reflection of the inner world. For this purpose his level of detail is very high: 'To be faithful to life, intrinsically truthful, a work has for me to be at once an exact factual account and a true communication of feelings' (Tarkovsky, 1989: 23). Tarkovsky's symbols are not expressionistic, or grotesque, or make-believe; his underwater life is amazingly realistic, and even the death of the horse in *Andrey Rublev* – quite horrifyingly – happens in real time and is captured by the camera. Such abundance of naturalism is unusual for abstract imagery, because, at this level of archetypal depth, symbols usually become schematic and imprecise. There exists a dark, mesmerising gap between the precision of Tarkovsky's symbols, and the fathomless philosophical abstractness which they represent. Even the most blurred and metaphysical of his plotlines are built from 'real-life' bricks: a horse, a burning candle, an empty room. All this leaves an impression of paranoia and danger – the spectator cannot for a second doubt that the picture on screen is 'genuine' – but the real world portrayed is haunted, murky and uncontrollable. Tarkovsky does not draw the line between the real and the psychic life; there is no 'safe distance' between the film and the audience. His illusions, and his symbols, are extremely factual.

Burton, by contrast, steers clear of any concrete imagery. The viewer gets his distance, which allows him to participate safely in the projection/ introjection exchange. The blood in his films is 'painted' in the most unnatural hues of red which can never be mistaken for the real thing. The spectator can safely absorb the film's contents and apply them to their own life – in other words, they will 'become the main character', and fill the character with their personal qualities. At the same time, the audience can leave the enchanted world at any moment. In order to stay 'safe' and 'controllable', the on-screen universe has to be narratively schematic and visually artificial while at the same time remaining psychologically accurate. This is exactly what Burton manages to achieve in his films. He shares with Tarkovsky the desire to 'portray' a feeling, an emotion, an unconscious, dream-like state – hence the heightened attention to *mise-en-scène*. But unlike Tarkovsky, his images are far more distorted and grotesque; they are, very clearly, hyperboles – both visually and narratively. His sets are highly stylised – *Sweeney Todd*, for instance, was shot on set and not on location, because the director wanted to achieve a fairy tale London, not a real London (DVD2/'Sweeney's London'). The blades of Edward Scissorhands may look sharp and physically dangerous, but his razor blades are a figurative device, standing for inability to communicate, rather than an image-making recommendation for your average introverted–rebellious teenager.

Genre-wise, Burton's films are close to the German expressionist aesthetic, with their distortion of reality, high degree of stylisation, extensive use of chiaroscuro, emphasis on metaphor and symbol, and the pictorial composition of their stock imagery, which was achieved by 'violence to the plastics of the image by way of sets and lighting' (Bazin, 1971/I: 26). Burton's characters and *mise-en-scène* are also pictorial and plastic-expressionist, similar to those created by Friedrich Murnau (*Nosferatu*, 1922), Robert Wiene (*The Cabinet of Dr. Caligari*, 1921) and Fritz Lang (*Metropolis*, 1927). German cinematic expressionism can be analysed in terms of critical reflection of the political and social reality in Europe in the 1920s. *Caligari*, for example, was originally devised as a parable of 'unchecked authoritarianism following the cataclysm of war' (Skal, 1993: 41). In the 'negative allegorical' way typical of the Gothic mode in general, the films investigated the psychology of the crowd and the dangerous possibilities of controlling the human mind – hence the themes of authoritarianism, obsession, madness, hypnosis, trance and frenzy. The 'distorted' 'visible reality' was built of grotesque images and displayed erratic composition; at the same time, the psychological reality was reproduced as terrifyingly believable. In other words, 'the inner' distorted 'the outer', and no naturalistic means could have been employed in place of angular sets, heavy shadows and contrast lighting to render the themes of the collective shadow, conservative nationalism, political power and authoritative control. Expressionists' diminished interest in the plot (which is often erratic and directionless) can be explained by the more urgent necessity to tell the 'psychological story', to express the emotional rather than the narrative aspect of the idea.

Similarly, in Tim Burton's *oeuvre*, the psycho-visual aspect comes into conflict with the narrative structure, and especially with his films' textual plane. André Bazin argues that 'the expressionist heresy came to an end after the arrival of sound' because 'the sound image, far less flexible than the visual image, would carry montage in the direction of realism, increasingly eliminating both plastic expressionism and the symbolic relation between images' (Bazin, 1971/II: 26; 1971/I: 33). In Burton's films, out of all possible sound accompaniments, music (both extradiegetic and intradiegetic) plays a far more important part, and aids in the expression of the major idea, than would any dialogue, albeit masterfully written. Without Danny Elfman's music, which in itself is a powerful, melodramatic commentary to any moving image, neither *Edward Scissorhands* nor *Batman Returns* would have had the trademark Burtonian emotional impact on the audience. Interestingly enough, Burton began experimenting with musicals (*James and the Giant Peach*, 1996, *The Nightmare Before Christmas*, 1993) early in his career, and is now increasingly moving towards the musical genre, of which *Charlie and the Chocolate Factory* (2005) and *Sweeney Todd* (2007) are good examples. Joining the image with the musical accompaniment is a trusted method of decreasing the pressure on the linguistic and narrative planes of the film, while also an efficient way of increasing its emotional–expressive potential.

Plastic expressionism and symbolic relations between images are the defining features of Tim Burton's films. His symbols are not covered with a veil of realism – on the contrary, their structure and function are always accessible, non-elitist and interpretable. The non-realistic modes (the fantastic, the uncanny and the marvellous, to use Tzvetan Todorov's terminology), however, can be very complex too – in their own way. Juxtaposed with the reality plane (think of the cinematic and fictional *magical realism*)[5], instead of 'mythologising' and simplifying the narrative, they make it more intricate. The non-realistic plane of a magical-realist narrative sequence points at the convergences and divergences between the psychological and the real, and at the discrepancies between the inner and the outer worlds. Magical realism contains hidden niches which can be occupied by political statements, its 'magical' part serving as a safe place for political allegories. Magic can be presented in the narrative 'as a cultural corrective, requiring readers to scrutinize accepted realistic conventions of causality, materiality, motivation' (Faris and Zamora, 1995: 3).

Splitting the narrative into two planes is, by all means, a very attractive and effective stylistic device; it 'externalises' the character's psychic life, displays the dialectical intricacies of human relationships and even the transitoriness and subjectivity of commonly accepted, and seemingly 'real', discourses. While most of Burton's films, to some extent, concern the clash between the real and the psychological, he used magical realism to its maximum potential only once – in *Big Fish* (2003), which boasts a rather convoluted storyline.

By his own admission, Burton is totally at sea with narrative sequences, especially of such an elaborate kind. It is also unusual for him to employ novels as canvases for his vision. A good, and ornate, storyline is more of a Steven Spielberg thing, so it is not surprising that Spielberg was also interested in making *The Big Fish* (Le Blanc and Odell, 2005: 121). It is far more curious that Burton chose it as working material for his next film, for, although thematically the story lies within Burton's usual pool of archetypal schemata (death of the father, hero myth, a bewitching anima), stylistically it differs from the bulk of his work. The biggest observable difference is the presence of the perceivable 'reality plane' in *Big Fish*. Le Blanc and Odell note that the film, because of its 'grounding in the real world, and not the idealised pastel pseudo-1950s of *Edward Scissorhands* or the imposing futuristic megapolis of *Batman*', feels 'strangely dissociated' (2005: 124). Such narrative complexity is rather untypical for Burton and can be credited to the fact that it had pre-existed as a fully fledged magical realist novel.

Although a story about a man's final reconciliation with his father may be a good way of expressing existential angst, Burton seems to be more at home with purely grotesque structures: fairy tales (*Edward Scissorhands*,

---

5 Cinematic examples: *Being John Malkovich* (1999), *Pan's Labyrinth* (2006); literary examples: Mikhail Bulgakov's *Master and Margarita* (1928–1940), *The Magus* (1966) by John Fowles.

Charlie and the Chocolate Factory, Alice in Wonderland); comics (*Batman*); 'penny dreadfuls' cum musicals (*Sweeney Todd*); highly symbolic anti-utopias (*Planet of the Apes*); and classic Gothic hits refracted through the prism of B-cinema (the Frankenstein monster, Poe's *Raven*). One might argue that grotesque and mythological genres are schematic (which made them so popular with 'basic' formalists like Vladimir Propp, archetypal formalists like Joseph Campbell or interpretative archetypalists like Northrop Frye). For Burton, however, allegorical genres are the main, and the most effective, way of sublimating his personal material. He explains his choice (with total disregard for academic terminology):

> Because I never read, my fairy tales were probably those monster movies. To me, they're fairly similar. I mean, fairy tales are extremely violent and extremely symbolic and disturbing, probably even more so than *Frankenstein* and stuff like that, which are kind of mythic and perceived as fairy-tale-like. [. . .] Growing up, I guess, it was a reaction against a very puritanical, bureaucratic, fifties nuclear family environment – me resisting seeing things laid out, seeing things exactly as they were. That's why I've always liked the idea of fairy tales or folk tales, because they're symbolic of something else. There's a foundation to them, but there's more besides, they're open to interpretation. I always liked that, seeing things and just having your own idea about them.
>
> (Salisbury, 2006: 3)

It is interesting that Burton's choice of styles and methods is not dictated by their aesthetic qualities, but is based on an assumption which you do not often hear from an *auteur*: films can be ideologically and structurally loose, and should generally invite interpretative pluralism. This position is similar to that of another advocate of open interpretation, vague symbolism and loose structures, Andrey Tarkovsky, who held the opinion that the audience was entitled to '. . . the opportunity to live through what is happening on the screen as if it were his own life, to take over, as deeply personal as his own, the experience imprinted in time upon the screen, relating his own life to what is being shown' (Tarkovsky, 1989: 183). Unlike Tarkovsky, however, who chose a complex way of expressing the symbolic with realistic means, Burton is formally simple, schematic, plush and essentially 'pop', which allows him to attract and retain a much bigger fan base than an average circle of *auteur* connoisseurs.

Ways of analysing the symbol

It is for this reason, and taking into consideration the 'plastic' and allegorical character of Burton's films, that I have chosen Jungian analytical psychology as my principal interpretative tool. I picked it from a highly competitive pool of valid and astute methodologies because, in my view, it perfectly suits the layout and meaning of Burton's works, his creative habits, as well as his sublimation stimuli.

Tim Burton is an essentially archetypal director in the sense that he works with basic mythological motifs. The principal themes of his films, especially the father–son conflict, call for a psychoanalytic approach. As a practising psychotherapist and 'interpreter of dreams', Jung was more interested in the syntagmatic realisation of mythological structures than their history, formal properties or comparative possibilities. My choice of Jung over Freud and the post-Freudians is a matter of their different approaches to the treatment of symbols – whether in dreams or in the arts. Bearing in mind Burton's anti-linguistic (or alinguistic) tendencies, Freudian, Lacanian and post-Freudian theories are less applicable because they place the linguistic above the visual. As Steven Walker observes, 'By emphasising the image over the word, Jungian psychology differentiates itself radically from Freudian, Lacanian and other psychologies that stress the task of interpreting the *language* of the unconscious' (Walker, 2002: 3).

Don Fredericksen draws attention to another aspect of the same problem: Freud's 'semiotic' (possibility of exact interpretation) and Jung's 'symbolic' attitude (amplification, or deferred interpretation) to the creative and dream-imagery. Jung does not see the unconscious as being linguistically structured, hence his rejection of semiotics in favour of amplification. Jung writes in *Psychological Types*:

> The concept of symbol should in my view be strictly distinguished from that of sign. Symbolic and semiotic meanings are entirely different things . . . A symbol always presupposes that the chosen expression is the best possible description or formulation of a relatively unknown fact, which is nonetheless known to exist or is postulated as existing . . . Every view which interprets the symbolic expression as an analogue or an abbreviated designation for a known thing is semiotic. [. . .] The symbol is alive only so long as it is pregnant with meaning. But once its meaning has been born out of it, once that expression is found that formulated the thing sought, expected, or divined even better than the hitherto accepted symbol, then the symbol is dead, i.e., it possesses only an historical significance . . . An expression that stands for a known thing remains a mere sign and not a symbol. It is, therefore, quite impossible to create a living symbol, i.e., one that is pregnant with meaning, from known associations.
>
> (Jung, 1971: CW6: paras. 814–818)

Thus, a symbol is a relative and 'immediate' thing, rather than a permanent, ready-made set of meanings. In a symbol, the relationship between the signifier and the signified is, indeed, highly arbitrary. Drawing upon Jung's democratic position of 'anti-exactness', Don Fredericksen argues:

> We must understand that Jung's distinction between sign and symbol ultimately elaborates two distinct modes of apprehending and explaining the psyche and its products – not just two distinct psychologies but two distinct ontologies and philosophies of value.
>
> This point is succinctly illustrated by Jung and Freud's differing explanations of, and attitudes toward, incest fantasy and symbolism. Freud interpreted the incest fantasy concretely. [. . .] Freud labels the distorted or disguised expressions of the incest wish 'symbols', incorrectly so according to Jung. For the latter, Freud's 'symbols' are in fact signs, standing for the putatively known, albeit repressed, desire of the patient to have physical intimacy with a parent. Their meaning can be completely explained by Freudian analytic procedures that reduce them to their underlying cause.
>
> (Hauke and Alister, 2005: 19)

For Jung, the symbol is always bigger than the sum of the dreamer's (or the author's) biographical details, and significantly deeper than any literal or pre-existing meaning.

Even though I find the biographical material priceless, and sometimes mention it in relation to Burton's imagery, I have no intention of reducing his films to his childhood complexes. The symbolic core of his cinematic imagery – the abandoned child–monster – cannot be discussed entirely in biographical terms. Any uninterrupted analysis of Burton's films in terms of his introversion, failure to communicate or his poor relationship with his parents would be ethically incorrect and methodologically incomplete. 'The monster' is not simply an imprint of Burton's own feelings towards the outside world which he perceives as 'hostile in its normality'. Far from that, the image of the monster acquires independence and becomes an archetype – a fluid, symbolic representation of a whole range of psychological phenomena – from the child–saviour who can perform miracles, and the creative punk born in a Gothic castle, to the antidogmatic rebel with a political stance. A nonconformist director, who has to defend his ideas from the studio heads, is only one aspect of the multi-faceted symbol. Meanwhile, the audience is full of outcasts who feel unique and misunderstood, and each viewer adds his or her personal dimension to the image, thus adding to the picture's interpretative volume. Being litmus papers for the state of culture, the best films resonate in many a soul; and that is why Burton's Gothic tales of a loner's conflict with society have a very wide fan-audience. Which probably means that 'the crowd' is not so ordinary, cruel and insensitive, after all.

In his book *Sculpting in Time*, Andrey Tarkovsky discusses the use of ready-made, intellectual and decipherable imagery in filmmaking. He considers such practices bad taste. Signs that are 'fixed' by the director for the audience, images ready for consumption, are the ones that stifle the viewer's imagination rather than widen his or her range of vision. Not surprisingly, perhaps, as a long-shot director, he links such 'sign-making' to clever montage:

> 'Montage cinema' presents the audience with puzzles and riddles, makes them decipher symbols, take pleasure in allegories, appealing all the time to their intellectual experience. Each of these riddles, however, has its own exact, word for word solution; so I feel that Eisenstein prevents the audience from letting their feelings be influenced by their own reaction to what they see. When in *October* he juxtaposes a balalaika with Kerensky, his method has become his aim, in the way that Valéry meant. The construction of the image becomes an end in itself, and the author proceeds to make a total onslaught on the audience, imposing upon them his own attitude to what is happening.
>
> (Tarkovsky, 1989: 118)

Such methods, Tarkovsky argues, 'are utterly inimical', and contradict 'the very basis of the unique process whereby a film affects an audience. Directors obsessed with associative montage 'make thought into a despot: it leaves no "air", nothing of that unspoken elusiveness which is perhaps the most captivating quality of all art' (2000: 183).

Tim Burton is no Eisenstein. An anti-intellectual filmmaker, he does not make an effort to create 'signs'. He remains in the realm of the symbolic, operating with the images that are personally dear to him, which also happen to be so 'loose' that their interpretive range is endless. Edward's blade-hands, apart from Burton's own inability to communicate (which is the most obvious interpretation), also represent the double-edge (and the *edginess*) of creativity, the creator's deficiency, his inner darkness, and the inevitable tension between the creative intention and the final result.

A psychoanalytic approach – Freudian, Lacanian, Kleinian, etc. – tends to view human nature in a fixedly negative light. While Freud's theories are veiled with biological determinism, Lacan's ideas of the unconscious structured like a language display an equally fatalistic approach to the psychic life of man. Once trapped in the trans-individual symbolic order, or a variety of such orders, an individual cannot change his destiny. The Lacanian man is surrounded by endless rigid cultural signifiers, and mourns the impossibility of controlling the process of signification because the signified will always escape, and the precious moment of communication will be lost. In other words, human civilisation is yet another existentialist failure because the 'meaning' can never be 'exact'. Rather tragically, the signified cannot be pinned down. Linguistic sign is a utopian concept *per se*.

In contrast to various pro-Freudian manifestations of pre- and post-existentialist sadness, Jung never limited himself to the analysis of linguistic structures; instead, he was more interested in the visual manifestation of the symbol – in the image. As Oliver Davies puts it, 'Whereas the Lacanian unconscious is composed of potentially word-forming linguistic structures, the Jungian (collective) unconscious is made up of structures with a potential for image formation' (Baumlin *et al.*, 2004: 66–67). Images, not words, are what hold the primary importance for Jung.

Moreover, 'images', for Jung, can be further subdivided into 'personalised' (concrete realisations) and 'collective' (abstract ideas) or more concrete archetypal images and abstract archetypes (CW9/I: paras. 1–9). It is important to differentiate between the two. An archetype is an irrepresentable idea, whereas archetypal images are concrete realisations of archetypes in dreams, fantasies, myths, etc. In Jung's own words, 'the perceptible archetypal image is not identical with the inherited form [i.e. archetype], which allows an indefinite number of empirical expressions' (Jung, *Letters*, quoted in Walker, 2002: 12). For instance, 'dying-and-rising god' is an archetype, but Osiris, Dionysus and Jesus are archetypal images. Similarly, female initiation of sexual contact is an archetype, whereas stories of Beauty and the Beast, Little Red Riding Hood, and Bluebeard's castle are archetypal situations.

People may be separated from each other at the level of the personal unconscious, which *is* predetermined by cultural and familial factors. Put simply, we are different because we have been shaped by different circumstances. As a result, our linguistic signifieds (to use Lacan's terminology) or image-signifieds (to follow Jung's reasoning) do not, and cannot, match. However, human beings are united 'further down' (or is it further up?), at the collective unconscious level, which is free of the constraints of formal signification because it deals exclusively with basic, symbolic ideas.

All the while, even the concretised archetypal images unite people, and tap into their experiences, better than the heroically utopian linguistic signs, in which the signifier is forever attempting to entrap the signified, and forever fails to do so (Derrida's *différence*). In the Jungian universe, the fact that symbols cannot be precisely deciphered, or equally understood by everyone, is not tragic – it is a necessary, and important, aspect of the human condition. Symbols unite people by the very fact of their indeterminability because they contain unlimited space for interpretation and amplification. Abstract ideas, or archetypes, exist equally for everyone, and it is up to the individual to dress them up in appropriate clothes. Civilisation is not a failed project – it is an unfinished project (rather like Edward Scissorhands); it has space for dynamics and development. Jung's is a 'half-full', rather than 'half-empty', view of human nature. When 'the father of signification' is dead, it is time to go back to abstraction, to the symbol, and to re-establish dialogue with the unconscious on her terms, in her language.

At the same time, as a tool for critical interpretation, Jungian psychology certainly lacks precision. A cinema or literary critic will sooner or later notice gaps in Jungian theories which would have to be covered up using alternative methods – for instance, elements of semiotic analysis. That Tim Burton operates predominantly with basic symbols accessible to the audience via 'emotional connection' does not exclude other, stricter methodologies. Even if the unconscious is not structured like a language, this does not mean that elements of linguistic analysis do not possess the potential to illuminate its contents. It's like trying to find the nearest possible key to the mysterious door behind which lies the unknown.

True, to some extent, using semiotics and structuralism in contemporary cinematic criticism would mean looking in the direction of the failed project of modernity; it would be an exercise in rational organisation of the world. Drawing on various Enlightenment philosophies, the structuralist framework presupposed (to quote Fredric Jameson) that there is some '"pre-established harmony" between the structures of the mind (and ultimately of the brain) and the order of the outside world' (Jameson, 1975: 110). The world is a potentially 'decodable' place because the entire sign-system somehow corresponds to all of reality (1975: 110). Burton himself is not a big fan of instrumental rationality and its legacy. In several of his films, including *Beetlejuice*, *Sleepy Hollow* and *Planet of the Apes*, he disarms rationality's utopian habit of wrapping the universe into a web of rigid structures (language, scientific knowledge, etc.). Instead, he accepts the chaotic state of modern existence – because chaos is the ideal working ground for the artist. The artist re-assembles the world from pieces. Burton's own creations are the result of this world-making activity. The 'pre-established harmony', or Paradise, has been lost, but humans can regain it by being creative.

However, structuralism and semiotics, employed *sparingly*, also help to 'organise a meaning' out of chaos. Not the absolute, scientific meaning of structuralism, but the relative, imprecise, approximate, amplified meaning. In this book, structuralism and semiotics are not the principal analytical tools, but are used as secondary amplificatory instruments. They illuminate only one corner of the complex landscape that is Tim Burton's *oeuvre*.

A post-Jungian perspective is more appropriate for the analysis of Burton's Gothic mythologies than a Freudian or even a post-Freudian approach because, instead of hierarchising 'truths', such a perspective would foreground perspectivism and pluralism (Hauke and Alister, 2001: 2). Working 'upwards' from the basic 'personal' interpretation, one can involve bigger, and more general, layers of the symbol; such as (in the case of Edward's blades) the Maker's 'Janus' nature, the impossibility of absolute good and the perennial existentialist problem of 'losing' God the father. In any case, a wide-scale, 'deferred' symbol leaves space (or 'air', to use Tarkovsky's expression) for the viewer's personal projections. Luke Hockley writes that

> While remaining alert to the dangers of overstating the case, it may be that films give a symbolic expression to elements of the psyche that have been repressed. Unwittingly, we recognize on the screen images of our unconscious. The literal form of projection in the cinema turns out to mirror the process of psychological projection. Jung remarks that "projections change the world into a replica of one's unknown face" (CW 9.2: 17). So, too, we can recognize elements of unconscious lives, emotional, social, political, and so forth, on the silver screen.
>
> (Baumlin *et al.*, 2004: 78)

Similarly, Christopher Hauke and Ian Alister argue that films can 'act as a therapeutic point of reference where unconscious aspects of the self can be seen in projection' (Hauke and Alister, 2001: 11). Seen in this light, Burton's films provide their audiences with a wide projective and therapeutic potential. The person watching can place himself into the vast mythological scheme visualised on the screen precisely because of the democracy and flexibility of this scheme. Burton's 'unconfined', flexible approach is what makes him so popular. Myth, with its formal simplicity, generality and internationality, is an essentially democratic phenomenon.

Burton and the archetypes

Burton's on-screen imagery forms a complex net of archetypes, which, in their visualised form, become recognisable and 'relatable' archetypal images and situations. One of them is especially important for understanding the psychology of the Burtonian male hero – the archetype of the self.

Archetypes, as Jung saw them, are 'primordial types. Or universal images that have existed since the remotest times' (Jung, 1954: CW9/I: para. 5). Unlike complexes that inhabit the personal level of the unconscious, archetypes reside in its collective part. The archetypes, Jolande Jacobi explains,

> make up the actual content of the collective unconscious; their number is relatively limited for it corresponds to 'the number of typical and fundamental experiences' incurred by man since primordial times. Their meaning for us lies precisely in the 'primordial experience' which is based on them and which they represent and communicate. [. . .] We find them recurring in all mythologies, fairy tales, religious traditions

and mysteries. [. . .] Prometheus the stealer of fire, Heracles the dragon slayer, the countless creation myths, the fall from paradise, the mysteries of creation, the virgin birth, the treacherous betrayal of the hero, the dismembering of Osiris, and many other myths and fairy tales represent psychic processes in symbolic images. Similarly, the figures of the snake, the fish, the sphinx, the helpful animals, the Tree of the World, the Great Mother, the enchanted prince, the *puer aeternus*, the Mage, the Wise Man, Paradise, etc., stand for certain motifs and contents of the collective unconscious.

(Jacobi, 1973: 47)

In man's psychic life the archetypes are part of what Jung called 'the individuation process', or simply 'individuation'. Jolande Jacobi, a first-generation follower of Jung, defines this process as gradual self-fulfilment, self-realisation 'both in the individual and . . . in the collective sense' (Jacobi, 1973: 106). In other words, individuation is personal development which leads towards psychic wholeness – 'when both parts of the total psyche, consciousness and the unconscious, are linked together in a living relation'. The complete union of the two psychic systems is an unattainable goal, but the good news is that relative differentiation is possible (1973: 105).

In his book *Human Being Human* (2005) Christopher Hauke provides a contemporary outlook on the individuation process. He defines individuation as 'the urge found in all living things to persist in becoming themselves; in human terms this means the development of the individual personality and becoming the person you were meant to be or the person you have always had the potential of being. [. . .] It lies at the core of what I mean by *human being human*' (Hauke, 2005: 65). The important point is that the individuation process implies, to some extent, a conflict with society, because, in becoming an individual, one may start questioning collective norms and traditions. The differentiation of the personality, Christopher Hauke writes, 'is not only the differentiation of unconscious from conscious contents but the further differentiation of the personal unconscious from the collective' (2005: 65). We will come back to this point in later chapters when discussing Burton's characters' relationship with society, and their blatant refusal to comply with the collective norms.

Burton tends to create heroes who do not want to abide by any rules but their own. They feel that rules do not exist *a priori* but are always laid out by a person, or people, who currently have the power to create spoken or written legislation in a particular community or group. Burton's protagonists refuse to accept the 'official' version of the world; they constantly 'defamiliarise' the official picture, make it different, strange, 'uglily creative'. Looking at the world through magic binoculars, they can notice things other people cannot see. Burton once said about his own perception of the outside world: 'When you are a kid, you think everything is strange, and you think it is *because* you're a kid, everything is strange. Then when you get older, you realize everything really *is* strange' (Woods, 2002: 66). From the point of view of the community, the 'different' perception of the environment is a sign of madness; from the point of view of the individual, it is a chance to exercise one's independent thinking. And it sometimes happens with Burton's protagonists that their individuation becomes *individualism*, 'a sort of self-centered concern which ignores the wishes and needs of others' (Hauke, 2005: 65). Individualism in Burton's films equals (often self-inflicted) loneliness.

Following Jolande Jacobi's summary of Jung's ideas, the signposts and milestones of individuation are marked by specific archetypes: the shadow (personal and collective), animus and anima, the wise old man, the great mother, and various versions of the self (the child, the hero, etc.). The personal shadow, in Jacobi's definition, is 'a part of the individual, a split-off portion of his being which nevertheless remains attached to him "like his shadow"' (Jacobi, 1973: 109–110). In Freudian psychology the same phenomenon is labelled *doppelgänger*, while the literary term is traditionally *the double*. When undifferentiated, this function becomes '"our dark side", the inborn collective predisposition which we reject for ethical, aesthetic, or other reasons, and repress because it is in opposition to our conscious principles' (1973: 110). Put simply, the shadow is the 'dark brother', a place for projections in the human psyche, where all the dangerous, inhuman, atavistic, repressed desires accumulate. This figure is not easy to recognise and make conscious, because its activation in the psyche is bound with projections – i.e. we can only see our own negative traits when they are mirrored back to us by other people, in which case we tend to think that the traits belong to *them* and not to *us*. To use an unpleasant but functional metaphor, the shadow is civilisation's psychic garbage can which can explode if left unobserved.

The collective shadow arrives precisely when individuals have been unaware of their inner problems while being influenced *en masse* by some powerful external force – for instance, a political ideology. Because mankind is not 'just an accumulation of individuals' but possesses 'a high degree of psychological collectivity' (Jung, 1910, CW18: para. 927), all human control 'comes to an end when the individual is caught up in a mass movement' (Jung, 1936, CW10: para. 395). There are several prominent 'shadows' in Burton's films, including the Joker and Sweeney Todd. However, it is too extensive a topic to cover in the Introduction, so we will postpone full analysis until Chapter 5 ('The Maniac'), in which this archetype will be discussed in relation to the trickster.

Another archetype which stands out prominently in Burton's *oeuvre* is the self. The self is a complex psychological and metaphysical concept which was devised by Jung to illustrate man's innate propensity for psychological maturation and spiritual growth. According to Jung, the self is bigger than the ego, which is the centre only of consciousness.[6] It is at the core of the individuation process because it stands for the whole of the psyche, both consciousness and the unconscious. Jung conceived the self as a 'supraordinate personality' which regulates the psyche and is in charge of the individuation process (Jung, 1951, CW9/I: para. 306). It strives to heal the split within – inner problems – as well as the person's conflicts with the outside world. Individuation, in fact, is a gradual integration of the self's warring components, the binary opposites. The self, Jolande Jacobi writes, 'is a centre of tension between two worlds and their forces which we *know* only dimly but *feel* all the more strongly' (Jacoby, 1973: 131). In dreams and fairy tales it can manifest itself in a number of images – usually indicating its heroic struggle for psychic wholeness: religious figures such as Christ and Buddha, folklore heroes like Heracles, King Arthur and Siegfried, as well as contemporary mythological characters – for instance, Superman, Batman and Harry Potter.

Interestingly enough, Burton's 'children' never become 'adult heroes' – i.e. they never grow up, or outgrow their infantile complexes. They prefer to continue existing in proximity to the darkness of the unconscious, rather than adopt an adult, mature, conscious attitude to the world – hence the Gothic, twilight colouring of most of Burton's films. His male heroes are also quite unusual (they lack many a required 'heroic' and masculine quality), while the female characters he creates are not as scary and powerful as traditional anima figures.

For instance, a typical hero myth is characterised by the strong presence of the 'anima motif'. On his quest the hero is bound to encounter a kind female creature who offers him her knowledge and experience. Alternatively, she can happen to be a dangerous witch who cunningly devises to devour him. Confrontation with an anima figure (which will be discussed in detail in the chapter about the superhero) is an important stage of the hero's journey because it symbolises the battle for the deliverance from the mother (both real and symbolic). On a larger scale, it stands for the ever complex relationship between civilisation and Mother Nature, and for human consciousness striving to control its instincts.

Interestingly enough, the Burtonian anima is more often pliable (usually a 'Gothic angel'[7]) than dangerous, and even when she is aggressive and

---

6 By contrast, the unconscious does not have a centre and 'as a rule, the unconscious phenomena manifest themselves in fairly chaotic and unsystematic form'. If there were such a centre, Jung argues, 'we could expect almost regular signs of its existence. Cases of dual personality would then be frequent occurrences rather than rare curiosities' (Jung, 1939, CW9/I: para. 492).

7 Winona Ryder's characters – Lydia (*Beetlejuice*) and Kim (*Edward Scissorhands*); Kim Basinger's portrayal of Vicki Vale in *Batman*; Katrina Van Tassel in *Sleepy Hollow*, Sally in *The Nightmare Before Christmas*, and Mrs Lovett from *Sweeney Todd: The Demon Barber of Fleet Street*.

harmful (the Catwoman, the Witch from *Big Fish*, the female Martian from *Mars Attacks*), she does not occupy the centre stage of the conflict. One exception to this rule would be *The Corpse Bride*. Its plot is entirely based on the dual anima/angel–whore motif. Most of Burton's films, however, revolve around the issues related to social maturity and conformity. In other words, his hero quests do not usually delve into the anima problem. So far, the female heroine has only been prominent in *The Corpse Bride*, and more or less noticeable in *Big Fish* (the Witch/Jenny/Sandra), while in the rest of his films it is relegated to the background.

A much more substantial problem for Burton's weird, enchanted children is 'the crowd'. The prospect of integrating into community is perceived by them as truly horrifying. Even the most dangerous anima is a more distant threat for Edward Scissorhands, Batman and Ed Wood than the call to 'face the public'. The vital difference between the Burtonian character and 'them' is that he is in motion, he is searching, he wants 'to know' – quite in contrast to the stagnation and complacency of his environment. Unable to live near this stagnation, he distances himself from it – like Edward Scissorhands who chooses the solitary life of 'the man in the high castle' over the suburban lifestyle, or Edward Bloom (*Big Fish*) who, having outgrown his village, leaves his unambitious neighbours behind and 'goes to seek his fortune'.

In his attempt to recreate his heroes' hunger for 'knowledge', Burton often employs the motif of 'early science' – the body of knowledge that is neither a 'proper' science, nor is it art. Ideologically, it is akin to alchemy. His scientifically minded protagonists, armed with an assortment of extravagant tools, in bogus laboratories poke and probe, assemble and disassemble their monstrous victims in the hope, like their literary predecessor Victor Frankenstein, of robbing Mother Nature, and stealing 'the secret of life'. Little Victor Frankenstein (*Frankenweenie*), Dr Finkelstein (*The Nightmare Before Christmas*), Jack Skellington, the inventor of Edward Scissorhands, and Willie Wonka all manufacture hideous creatures using crude, pseudo-scientific methods. This is very much in tune with Andrey Tarkovsky's statement that art, like science 'is a means of assimilating the world, an instrument for knowing it in the course of man's journey towards what is called "absolute truth"' (Tarkovsky, 1989: 37).

Tim Burton seems to think that cinematic art, like all monsters, has to be crude. Art is something you do with your hands (well, he came from animation), and because the creator is human, and hands are not the perfect tool, the end result is bound to be imperfect. The images and materials have to look rough, and the seams, like the literal seams and scars on the bodies of Edward Scissorhands, Sally, Emily and the Joker, have to be visible. That is why, in Burton's case, the perfection of cinematic techniques is not as important as the initial impulse to create, to express a feeling, to give the audience a space where they can connect with the archetypes on their own terms, and at their own pace. As Burton's creative wingman, Rick Heinrichs, puts it, 'the budgets have gotten bigger, there's more ambition, but still, in all of Tim's films, the animated and live action, his sensibility seeps into every corner – a Burtonesque feeling prevails. His aesthetic eschews the polish and patness of what comes with cutting-edge technology because he's after an emotional connection that is much more immediate and involving' (Matthews and Smith, 2007: 280).

Crudity seems to be the necessary prerequisite for freedom of expression and perception, projection and introjection.

After all, cinema is the kind of magic that creates life out of 'lifeless matter'.

Chapter 1

The child

The child as a hero

It is essential to discuss the theory behind the child archetype before turning to Burton's films proper. I am going to examine the famed infantilism of the Burtonian protagonist in terms of his rootedness in the cultural and psychological issues of modernity, as well as in terms of his heroic clash with what he perceives as the oppressive environment.

The wonder-infant motif, which is present in so many fairy tales and myths (and which is important for our study of Burton's films), is, according to Jung, linked to the archetype of the self. The child is a future hero, and many mythological saviours are, in fact, child gods. In the individuation process, the magical infant 'paves the way for a future change of personality' and 'anticipates the figure that comes from the synthesis of conscious and unconscious elements in the personality. It is therefore a symbol which unites the opposites; a mediator, bringer of healing, that is, one who makes whole' (Jung, 1951, CW9/I: para. 278). The mythological child, as a rule, is born a prodigy who possesses miraculous abilities: he can casually kill a couple of snakes as he lays in his cot (Heracles), survive numerous assassination attempts like Dionysus, or, like Harry Potter, play a magical trick or two on the evil members of his adopted family.

The hero-child's birth is often a mystery, involving various gods and goddesses, and in most cases his actual parents are 'invisible', absent from the scene. This element of the myth is clear: a godlike infant cannot be begotten by 'normal' parents; surely his unusual abilities come from a special divine genetic pool. Nevertheless, despite such holy beginnings and all the divine blessings, the child's life is fraught with danger. He has deadly and powerful enemies: for instance, Hera, who tried to destroy the unborn Dionysus out of jealousy because he was the child of Zeus and a mortal woman, Semele; or King Herod who ordered the murder of all the babies in Bethlehem and the vicinity in the hope that baby Jesus would be among them.

According to Jung, the child motif in myths and fairy tales corresponds to a specific psychological process: the birth of the personality and its development and survival in its surroundings. It represents the 'infancy' of the individuation process, its very beginnings. When the child 'grows out' of the unconscious, he becomes a hero. The hero-ego, the conscious psyche, 'emerges' from the primordial darkness, and proceeds to fight with this darkness, while the self attempts to unite the opposites and bring them closer together (i.e. illuminate any repressed unconscious contents and make them visible to the conscious mind). Jung perceived individuation, and the emergence and development of the hero, as both an ontogenetic (individual) and a phylogenetic (communal, historical) process:

> The Hero's main feat is to overcome the monster of darkness: it is the long-hoped-for and expected triumph of consciousness over the unconscious. [. . .] The coming of consciousness was probably the most tremendous experience of primeval times, for with it a world came into being whose existence no one had suspected before. "And God said: 'Let there be light!'" is the projection of that immemorial separation of the conscious from the unconscious. [. . .] Hence the 'child' distinguishes itself by deeds which point to the conquest of the dark.
>
> (CW9/I: para. 284)

In this respect, the dual mother theme is very important because, as Jung argues, it suggests the idea of a dual birth: 'One of the mothers is real, the other is the symbolical mother; in other words, she is distinguished as being divine, supernatural, or in some way extraordinary. [. . .] He who stems from two mothers is the hero: the first birth makes him a mortal man, the second an immortal half-god' (Jung, 1912, CW5: paras. 495–496). Psychic life is often marked by this duality – even the most insignificant achievements of human spirit can be translated into 'superhuman' stories and regarded as something remarkable. This is because both the emergence of civilisation and the process of personal development are nothing short of a miracle, a heroic deed, an astonishing victory of the individual over the collective, and of rationality and culture over Mother Nature.

The motif of the prodigious child is at the centre of Burton's work. His *oeuvre* contains themes of unusual birth, dual sets of parents, abandonment, extraordinary talent expressed early, omnipotent friends and enemies, invincibility, love and hatred of the crowd, etc. Edward Scissorhands is made in a laboratory by a godlike father-figure, and subsequently adopted by a suburban American family. He is a gifted hairdresser, his ability being both the curse and the blessing, as it attracts plenty of negative and positive attention. Batman is left an orphan (an invariant of the abandonment motif), and makes himself appear 'invincible' with the help of technology (the modern miracle). The Penguin is so ugly that his parents chuck him in a sewer, where he is adopted by a sewer-dwelling population of penguins. In spite of his unsightly appearance, he is seen by the inhabitants of Gotham City as a charismatic figure; he is a dark, tyrannical leader. Willy Wonka, Burton's rather controversial[1] allegory of immaturity, is an eternal child whose emotional development was cut short because of his father's disciplinarian methods.

The abandonment motif is an important part of the child myth because, translated back into the language of personal development, it symbolises personal independence, self-reliance and self-realisation – even when they have been attained through isolation and hardship. Abandonment, Jung writes, is necessary because it kick-starts the personality's development (CW9/I: para. 285). The child is a future hero, or a future personality, and therefore has to be prepared for any prospective challenges. 'The "child",' Jung argues, 'is all that is abandoned and exposed and at the same time divinely powerful; the insignificant, dubious beginning, and the triumphant end. The "eternal child" in man is an indescribable experience, an incongruity, a handicap, and a divine prerogative; an imponderable that determines the ultimate worth or worthlessness of a personality' (CW9/I: para. 300).

For his part, the American psychologist James Hillman notes how in myths and fairy tales young heroes often face laming, crippling, bleeding, and sometimes castration. The wound, Hillman argues, 'seems to identify the puer spirit with heroic destiny' (Hillman, 1979: 101). Discussing the origins of these wounds, Hillman points at parents: 'Everyone carries a parental wound and has a wounded parent' (1979: 101). He then scrutinises examples of such parent-inflicted wounds in ancient mythology:

> Pelops is chopped up by his father, Tantalus, who served his son boiled to the gods to eat. [. . .] The boy Ulysses is wounded while he is with his grandfather, and by a "parental" boar. The soft spot in Achilles (and in Baldur) comes from the Mother. Achilles is held by the heel and dipped into the bath to make him invincible – except for where she held him. His fatal wound is precisely where his mother touched him under the guise of protecting him. One wound of Hercules occurs in a battle with a Father and Son (Hippokon and his sons). This father-son conflict wounds Hercules in the hollow of his hand; and in another tale Hercules kills his own children.
>
> (1979: 101)

In a less mythological and more theoretical key, Jung's disciple Erich Neumann (1973) discusses the child's future personality as being significantly

---

1 Many critics have pointed out that Johnny Depp's version of Roald Dahl's creation contains allusions to Michael Jackson's appearance, manners and lifestyle.

influenced by what he calls 'the primal relationship', which is the first, largely 'unconscious' step of the individuation process. In many ways, Neumann's theorising ploughs the same field as John Bowlby's concept of attachment, object relations theory, and recent findings in developmental neuroscience. The difference between Neumann and any other developmental theory lies in his inscribing subjective, concrete personal development into the general, 'objective' container – the archetypal framework.

In the course of the primal relationship, Neumann theorises, the infant feels as part of its mother, even though its body is already born (Neumann, 2002: 7–11). A normal bond presupposes a secure confidence in the mother's love (2002: 59). Because the mother is responsible for cushioning the new personality's entrance into the world of subjective experiences, repeatedly unmitigated pain, unanswered demands or unsoothed feeling of fear have the potential to turn, later in the child's life, into lifelong injuries, and to impair the person's ability to relate to other individuals, society and themselves (2002: 74–75). Mythologically speaking, the child is still part of the *uroboros*, of the unconscious, while the ego – the personality itself – has not yet been born. The 'abandonment' and 'rejection' which Jung discusses in his mythological analysis of the child archetype on the level of personal development is related to various disturbances in the initial relationship with the mother (Neumann, 2002: 72–73).

The 'magical omnipotence of the child archetype', initially observed by Jung, is explained by Neumann as pertaining to the 'cosmic character of [the baby's] still unlimited existence'. This empowering feeling, which finds expression in fairy tales and myths in the form of infantile 'heroism' and supernatural abilities, 'is not so much a feeling of omnipotence as one of cosmic all-encompassing excitedness; it is a paradisiacal state of fulfilment without oppression; neither is it centered in an ego nor has it the character of power in the sense of possession' (Neumann, 2002: 143). Put simply, the archetypal, as well as the actual, child draws its infinite power from the depths of the unconscious.

Tim Burton's version of the child archetype also involves extraordinary but Gothicised abilities, coming from the maternal unconscious. Sadness, isolation and aversion to society, Neumann theorises, are the result of a lack of love and acceptance on the part of the caregiver (2002: 87). These negative feelings become addictive for Burton's male characters because of the potential for creative productivity. They cherish and nurture the fact of being abandoned or betrayed because the moment they found themselves left alone, their creativity was born.[2] Their loneliness, therefore, is precious

---

2 Incidentally James Hillman thinks that the word 'creativity' is not a fitting accompaniment for the wound metaphor. In his view, this word 'dulls and blunts the spirit of inquiry; it covers more than it reveals, and is, in fact, a most uncreative word' (Hillman, 1979: 101).

as it is a source of anguish that feeds their dark imagination. Batman's split into two sub-personalities, for instance, occurred after the young Jack Napier murdered his parents, and Will Bloom's journalistic talent has its roots in his ever absent father's storytelling habit.

Even the most sociable of them, Edward Bloom from *Big Fish*, prefers the world of fairy tales to reality – a fact that meddles with his family life and alienates him from his immediate relatives. Bruce Wayne (Batman) chooses to live away from society, and constructs his own universe, which is Gothic, artificial, immature and full of fancy costumes and toys. The list goes on: Vincent Malloy dramatically self-isolates in his room, having rejected his mother's suggestion to become 'normal'; Willy Wonka's world is grotesquely infantile, and again, he comes to confrontation with 'the crowd'; Ed Wood exists in a kind of creative vacuum, and does not even try to relate his ideas to the tastes of the audience, or the demands of the studios; Sweeney Todd wages a brutal war against the whole of society, murdering the guilty and the innocent, and rejoices in his meaningless killing spree. The link between creativity and 'early experiences' will be discussed in more detail in Chapter 4, about the Burtonian child-genius.

Young Frankenstein

The themes of creative infantilism, introversion and the refusal to grow up permeate Burton's entire universe. As a child, he preferred to watch certain types of films – various 'monster trash', movies with Vincent Price and Ray Harryhausen animation – because he could personally relate to the 'monster mythology'. His interviews reveal (decreasingly, as he gets older) a certain amount of unspent teenage angst. He appears to identify with the cast-off, misunderstood, helpless yet weird-looking creatures who are unable to become 'like everyone else' – or at least try to be 'likeable'. Burton's perception of fictional freaks and mutants lies as far from the official, mainstream reaction to 'horrible' things as it can be; in fact, it dangerously borders on the dramatic, maximalist introversion of a troubled teenage Goth. Monsters are not the scary 'other' – on the contrary, they appear to him less alien than 'normal people':

> I've always loved monsters and monster movies. I was never terrified of them, I just loved them from as early as I can remember. My parents said I was never scared, I'd just watch anything. And that kind of stuff has stuck with me. *King Kong, Frankenstein, Godzilla, The Creature from the Black Lagoon* – they're all pretty much the same, they just have different rubber suits or make-up. But there was something about that identification. Every kid responds to some

image, some fairy-tale image, and I felt most monsters were basically
misperceived, they usually had more heartfelt souls than the human
characters around them.

(Salisbury, 2006: 2–3)

Burton's identification with on-screen outcasts and other melodramatic
characters was not accidental. As a child, he felt alien in Burbank, a small-
town type suburb of Los Angeles, the pastel-coloured parody of which
appears in *Edward Scissorhands*. He did not feel close to his parents, and
eventually moved in with his grandmother: 'My grandmother gave me the
sanctuary and she really saved me. She made sure I had food and left me
alone' (Fraga, 2005: 167).

As he explains, he was 'strangled' by suburban American culture. It was
impossible for him to become a sportsman (the dream of his father, an ex-
baseball player); neither did he want to become a musician (he played a
musical instrument). Suburban religion, meanwhile, seemed a 'bureaucratic
setup'. Drawing and watching television were some of the few available
outlets for the boy's emotions (Fraga, 2005: 166). In his characteristic
jumbled manner, Burton recalls his childhood:

> As a child I was very introverted. I like to think I didn't feel like
> anybody different. I did what any kid likes to do: go to the movies,
> play, draw. It's not unusual. What's more unusual is to keep wanting to
> do those things as you go on through life. [. . .] I never really fell out
> with people, but I didn't really retain friends. I get the feeling people
> just got this urge to want to leave me alone for some reason, I don't
> know why exactly. It was as if I was exuding some sort of aura that
> said 'Leave Me the F**k Alone'. [. . .] But punk music was good, that
> helped me, it was good for me emotionally. I didn't have a lot of
> friends, but there's enough weird movies out there so you can go a long
> time without friends and see something new every day that kind of
> speaks to you.

(Salisbury, 2006: 2)

It sounds like watching cinema was for Burton a form of sublimation, a
therapeutic interaction with the on-screen characters. Movies today, he
explains in *Burton on Burton*, have taken the place of fairy tales in that they
[I translate] became projective–introjective containers of vital archetypal
material (which is not, Burton stresses, to be perceived literally):

> It's funny because of the movies I've done, a lot of people think that
> they're very much about the way they look. People don't realise that

everything I've ever done has to mean something; even if it's not clear-cut to anybody else, I have to find some connection, and actually the more absurd the element, the more I have to feel that I understand something behind it. That's why we're all fascinated by the movies. They tap into your dreams and your subconscious. I guess it's different from generation to generation, but movies are truly a form of therapy and work on your subconscious in the way fairy tales are meant to. The Dog Woman and Lizard Man in those Indian tales, they're not meant to be taken literally.

(Salisbury, 2006: 124)

In his early interviews (Edelstein, 1990; Breskin, 1991) Tim Burton often mentions his own depression in relation to the male protagonists in his films: Beetlejuice, Batman, Edward. In interviews from the 2000s (McKenna, 2001; O'Sullivan, 2001) he tends to speak about the childhood roots of his adult problems, but admits that a troubled childhood can be a positive baggage to have: 'I wouldn't change anything, because the more pain you endure when you're young, the richer your adult life will be. [. . .] Because you're not popular, you're not out socially, so you have time to think and to be quietly angry and emotional. And if you're lucky, you'll develop a creative outlet to exorcise these feelings' (Fraga, 2005: 175). His opinion is certainly in tune with Jung's positive view of psychological complexes, and with the previously discussed heroic modality, characteristic of modernist thinking.

Burton's films are intensely private in the sense that they communicate his personal interests and are populated with his childhood idols. His love for lapdogs found reflection in *Frankenweenie* and *Mars Attacks!* (which starred Burton's own Poppy the Chihuahua); the childhood inspiration Vincent Price was invited to do a voice-over for *Vincent*, and then played the Inventor in *Edward Scissorhands*; *Mars Attacks!* and *Ed Wood* gave the opportunity to revive all sorts of old novelties – Dracula, Vampira, Bunny Breckinridge and the big-brained Martians from Topps Cards. Ed Wood's support for the aged Bela Lugosi (Martin Landau and Johnny Depp) is reminiscent of the relationship between Burton and Price. *Big Fish*, a film about the death of the father in which the son tries to finally understand and accept him, came two years after the death of Burton's own father, and the director's own attempt at reconciliation.

Displaying so much private and biographical material would make anyone vulnerable, let alone a Hollywood director whose films are watched by millions of people. 'The movie is my baby, and I'm putting it out into the cruel world,' Burton admits in a 1991 interview with David Breskin, 'It's scary, that's all. Just really scary' (Fraga, 2005: 85). Unlike Victor Frankenstein, however, Burton treats his creations responsibly, and always takes care of them.

Child's guilt and punishment

When Neumann writes that 'a central symptom of a disturbed relationship is a primary feeling of guilt', and that it is 'characteristic of the psychic disorders of the Western man', he gives a devastating diagnosis of the whole of post-Enlightenment Western society. The interdependent feelings of guilt and not-to-be-loved are 'identical with being abnormal, sick, "leprous", and above all, "condemned"' (Neumann, 2002: 86). The forlorn and rejected Burtonian hero-infant, whose failed relationship with his parents gradually metamorphoses, Frankenstein-style, into a broken-down relationship with society, or 'the crowd', as he perceives it, is a true reflection of the tragic, fragmented, infantile, individualist heroism of modernity – especially the phase which Anthony Giddens calls 'the late modern world' (Giddens, 1991: 4). Post-Enlightenment society lacks security, safety and faith in its foundations. Quite within this 'apocalyptic' paradigm, Burton's characters losing their parents metaphorically represents contemporary man's deprivation of God. 'God's death', to use Nietzsche's famous hyper-allegory, is followed by the sense of cultural and geographical uprootedness, and the feeing of psychic fragmentation.

Having received the opportunity to travel, see other countries and peoples, and enjoy the achievements of medicine, science and technology, the modern man gradually came to realise that all these lifestyle improvements and scientific accomplishments did not turn the world into a more 'logical' and protected place. But there was more to it than a simple change in human perception of the world. With urban growth, the individual was released from his 'official' duties to the community, to 'the crowd'. He could form and modify his identity. He no longer had to be 'like everyone else'. He acquired the opportunity to think independently and make 'informed decisions' which primarily benefit him, and not the social group.

Yet, ironically, the cosmopolitan man of modernity was more of a mass man than ever before because metropolitan environments made him lonely, isolated, disorientated and unsafe. A fragmented psyche without the 'centre', according to Jung, would always be looking for ways to attain wholeness. Community, and collective living, with its rigid set of rules, offers a 'meaning' and a centre to the individual. Any evil mind offering a fake or utopian substitute for inner wholeness – such as the ideologies of National Socialism and Communism – can potentially harvest millions of alienated and fragmented individuals by offering to return them to the paradisiacal state of national unity. The individual, swept off his feet by the sheer power of the movement, against his will turns back into the mass man. Eliminated in its natural form, community comes back with a vengeance – in the form of the collective shadow.

In the twentieth century, the die-hard, shadowy collectivity began to be closely associated with the dark side of technology. The much-celebrated technological progress, Giddens notes, brought with it the risk of massively destructive warfare and serious ecological issues, while 'other high-consequence risks, such as the collapse of global economic mechanisms and the rise of totalitarian superstates, are an equally unavoidable part of our contemporary experience' (1991: 4). The 'guilty', rejected heroic consciousness of modernity is constantly awaiting some cataclysmic, godly punishment.

The contemporary of late modernity, Jung alerted his fellow-citizens to the dangers of overvaluing rationality and reason at the expense of the instincts and 'nature'. He wrote in the 1930s: 'The political and social conditions, the fragmentation of religion and philosophy, the contending schools of modern art and modern psychology all have one meaning in this respect . . . we must admit that no one feels quite comfortable in the present-day world; indeed it becomes increasingly uncomfortable' (Jung, 1935, CW10: para, 290, quoted in Hauke, 2000: 35). For his part, Erich Neumann saw the outburst of 'unstable', incoherent, claustrophobic, decentred creativity in mid and high modernity as a sign of negative change in the psyche of the Western man: 'The disappearance of the certainty and security once conferred by the cultural canon shows itself primarily in a sense of isolation, of forlornness, of homelessness and alienation, which has vastly increased in the course of the last hundred years. Probably never before in the history of literature or painting have there been so many isolated individuals. The concepts of school, tradition, and unity of style seem to have vanished' (Neumann, 1974a: 111). The mythological 'abandonment' of the child archetype has now become the more global abandonment of Western humankind by God. Each artist, like the archetypal heroic child, is now isolated and fighting on his own:

> Consider, to mention only a few painters of the last sixty years, such figures as Cezanne, Van Gogh, Gauguin, Rousseau, Munch, Klee, Matisse, Chagall, Picasso – there has never been anything similar in history. Each of them is a world in himself, endeavouring alone to ward off the chaos that menaces him or to give it form, each with his own characteristic desperation. It is no accident that we hear so much today of the void and the forlornness of the individual. And the profound anxiety, the sense of insecurity, uprootedness, and world dissolution, at work in these painters also move modern composers and poets.
>
> (Neumann, 1974a: 112)

Similar processes have been happening in literature, Neumann observes, where 'the line from Goethe to Dostoevsky to Proust and Joyce is not a line of disintegration, but it does mark the increasingly conscious dissolution of style, human personality, and unified work (1974a: 114). The modernist universe, instead of coming together and forming an objective 'whole',

quickly began to fall apart. Post-Second World War existentialist philosophy (Jean-Paul Sartre, Albert Camus), with its emphasis on meaninglessness and the absurdity of existence, did not place much value on man's
ability to make the world a safer place in which to live. Its pessimism
put the final nail in the coffin of the optimistic belief in the supremacy of
human reason.

Burton's obsessive retro-habits, his compulsive return to the emblematic,
representative characters of modernity – Victor Frankenstein, Ichabod
Crane, Batman, Sweeney Todd – signal his profound interest in the problem of the 'lost God' and his possible, cataclysmic or humanitarian,
resurfacing in the human world. To demonstrate the fragmentation of the
self, Burton uses visual metonymy in almost all of his films, while the
counterbalancing visual metaphor of 'stitching up the pieces' represents a
certain fantasy of wholeness. His characters are split internally as well as
physically. Burton draws our attention to their hands, eyes, ears, arms and
legs; and then attempts, rather optimistically, to seam them together into
new dogs, women and men. The Frankenstein dog from *Frankenweenie*,
Edward Scissorhands, Catwoman and Emily the Corpse Bride are all
physically disjointed, and internally broken. Speaking about the character
of Sally in *The Nightmare before Christmas*, Burton explains his interest in
broken, detached and incomplete bodies and souls:

> I remember drawing Jack and really getting into these black holes for
> eyes and thinking that to be expressive, but not have any eyes, would
> be really incredible. Sally was a relatively new character; I was into
> stitching from the Catwoman thing, I was into that whole psycho-
> logical thing of being pieced together. Again, these are all symbols for
> the way that you feel. The feeling of not being together and of being
> loosely stitched together and constantly trying to pull yourself together,
> so to speak, is just a strong feeling to me.
>
> (Salisbury, 2006: 123)

The problem of inner fragmentation, expressed metonymically and metaphorically, brings with it the whole cumbersome question of Burton's films
as being 'modern' or 'postmodern'. Postmodernist art, reflecting the
unstable, constantly changing post-war world, is seen by some critics as a
complicated but meaningless play of images, words, worlds, literary genres
and topoi. In discussion of this contentious issue, theorists of culture have
divided into two groups, one arguing that postmodernism is a depthless and
decentred art, and the other perceiving a certain degree of meaningfulness
and even order in this style of thought. Moreover, people belonging to the
first 'cluster' may be further divided into two subgroups. Some regard
postmodernism's denial of metaphysics as positive and even parade it as a
specific virtue which results from its striving for freedom from the so-called

'grand narratives' (for example, Jean-Francois Lyotard, Richard Rorty). Others are critical of the movement's emptiness and self-delusion (these include left-wing theorists like Fredric Jameson and Terry Eagleton). Defining the peculiarities of the postmodern parody, Fredric Jameson insists that it no longer contains a proper, 'pejorative' ironic statement but has become pastiche, worn-out and useless – a true reflection of the ever changing images of consumerist society. True parody is no longer possible, because, Jameson argues, the 'normative' position from which the ironic 'judgement' was usually proclaimed no longer exists (Malpas, 2001: 25–26). The 'truthful' mirror of reality broke into myriad pieces, into an endless number of subjectivities which no longer reflect 'life as it is'. Such a shattered reality does not have a 'central reference-point', or, to speak in the language of Jungian psychology, it no longer has 'the self'; it lacks God. Underneath its brightly coloured, multi-faceted surface, instead of the underlying unifying principle, there lodges disconcerting emptiness.

Brian McHale (1992) presents us with the third option: that postmodernism is actually ontologically challenging and not at all empty and groundless. To express his thoughts concerning postmodernism's meaningfulness and philosophical value, he uses terminology invented by Dick Higgins, poet, composer and performance artist. Instead of the words 'modernism' and 'postmodernism', Higgins employs new terms, 'cognitivism' and 'postcognitivism'. The cognitive questions asked by most artists of the twentieth century till about 1958[3] are: 'How can I interpret this world of which I am part? And what am I in it?' The postcognitive *questions* which have interested most artists since then are: 'Which world is this? What is to be done in it? Which of my selves is to do it?' (McHale, 1992: 33). Thus Brian McHale draws his readers' attention to the neglected parts of postmodernism's dialectical nature – namely those in contrast with its much-advertised deconstructing, destructive and analytical roles. Postmodernism is openly ontological in its orientation, that is, it is a self-consciously world-building art, the original feature of its poetics being to expose the process of the fictional world making itself (McHale, 1992: 12). McHale uses Annie Dillard's definition, 'unlicensed metaphysics in a teacup', to define the theoretical nature of postmodernism. And as the present consists of the multiplicity of conflicting worlds, postmodernism reflects and overplays this feature, staging clashes between various 'real' and psychological, generic and stylistic, cultural and ideological landscapes. Such confrontations, in Brian McHale's view, serve to 'raise and explore ontological issues' (1992: 155). Indeed, discourse clashes tend to generate an atmosphere of intellectual vivacity, not only in fictional worlds but also in real life, with equal frequency.

3 Different theorists have proclaimed different dates as the borderline dividing modernism and postmodernism. Dick Higgins chose 1958 as the year of the beginning of what he terms as 'postcognitivism'.

At the height of the postmodern theoretical debate in the 1980s and 1990s, the principal argument laid out by the Marxist academics, such as the aforementioned Fredric Jameson and Terry Eagleton, against the much-advertised relativist perspective of postmodernist critical theory, was that contemporary lifestyle provides people with a dangerously bogus sense of liberation. Far from promoting independent decision-making, they contended, postmodern capitalism sells people a set of false choices, aimed at satisfying the crowd's age-old populist craving for instant gratification. Jameson links the emptiness of artistic pastiche to the notorious post-modern notion of 'the death of the subject', or 'the death of individualism' in the fluid postmodern capitalist society:

> . . . today, from any number of distinct perspectives, the social theorists, the psychoanalysts, even the linguists, not to speak of those of us who work in the area of culture and cultural and formal change, are all exploring the notion that that kind of individualism and personal identity is a thing of the past; that the old individual or individualist subject is "dead": and that one might even describe the concept of the unique individual and the theoretical basis of individualism as ideological. There are in fact two positions on all this, one of which is more radical than the other. The first one is content to say: yes, once upon a time, in the classic age of competitive capitalism, in the heyday of the nuclear family and the emergence of the bourgeoisie as the hegemonic social class, there was such a thing as individualism, as individual subjects. But today, in the age of corporate capitalism, of the so-called organization man, of bureaucracies in business as well as in the state, of demographic explosion – today, that older bourgeois individual subject no longer exists.
>
> Then there is a second position, the more radical of the two, what one might call the poststructuralist position. It adds: not only is the bourgeois individual subject a thing of the past, it is also a myth; it never really existed in the first place; there have never been autonomous subjects of the type. Rather, this construct is merely a philosophical and cultural mystification which sought to persuade people that they "had" individual subjects and possessed this unique personal identity.
>
> (Malpas, 2001: 25–26)

But what about the brand of individualism worn by Burton's characters? Is it contemporary and post-industrial, or is it 'vintage' and high-modern, as it wants to position itself?

On the surface of it, Tim Burton's films are essentially 'vintage', in that they often contain both visual and narrative retro-references. As previously discussed, he borrows from German Expressionism, freely employs magic realism and copies various typical elements of the horror genre. He rarely uses 'original images' (Edward Scissorhands is one exception from his 'reusing' rule – but then, the film also 'recycled' Vincent Price!), preferring to form his narratives from pre-existent characters, motifs and themes rather than invent something entirely new. In doing so, he 'slides' up and down along the entire temporal scale of modernity, picking up authors, characters, images and ideas from its young days (Washington Irving's *Sleepy Hollow*) to its final phase (James Whale, Ray Harryhausen, the *Batman* comics, Dr Seuss and numerous other literary, filmic and television influences).

Fredric Jameson attributes such retro-tendencies and retrospective styling in contemporary cinema to the postmodern inability to conceive anything new. He writes that 'in a world in which stylistic innovation is no longer possible, all that is left is to imitate dead styles, to speak through the masks and with the voices of the styles in the imaginary museum' (Malpas, 2001: 26–27). Such an extensive use of masks, Jameson argues, is 'an indictment of consumer capitalism' or 'an alarming and pathological symptom of a society that has become incapable of dealing with time and history' (Malpas, 2001: 28).

In the case of Tim Burton, I cannot agree less. His pastiche-like references and obvious allusions do not necessarily define Burton's *oeuvre* as modernist, and neither do they point out the emptily parodic and meaningless ('pataphysical', to use Alison McMahan's term) nature of his work. Rather, they signify the presence in Burton's films of the self-opposing quality of postmodernist art – its deeply hidden ontological pining; its desire to rediscover the stabilising principle, to resurrect 'God'. Speaking about the contradictory qualities of the postmodern, Christopher Hauke writes about its ability to go into the 'nostalgia' mode, which allows the possibility of revisiting the moment when 'the subject' notoriously 'died':

> It is unwise to evaluate or judge the postmodern in any moral sense precisely because postmodern culture – for all the accusations of its addiction to the image, its losses of history, the subject and a critical distance – is also expressing passionate concern for the refinding of human values, for *rebirth*: not in terms of modernity and 'what went before' (despite appearances!), but in terms as yet unknown, in language as yet unspoken. Pastiche and nostalgia are the fumblings in the dark, or, to put it another way, attempts to see through a glass darkly.
> (Hauke, 2000: 49–50)

Whereas communication breakdown in postmodernity is commonly accepted, and even perceived as an entirely ordinary and unavoidable fact of life, modernist writers (Anton Chekhov, Katherine Mansfield, Virginia Woolf), tended to regard it as a deeply tragic condition. Tim Burton is not 'pataphysical', or for that matter, 'depthless, decentred, ungrounded, self-reflexive, playful, derivative, eclectic, pluralistic' (Eagleton, 1996: vii), because he is more profound than that. His modernist references, rather just being a part of some meaningless melting pot of visual and thematic borrowings, take the film back to the era between the two World Wars, and allude to the biggest problems of modernity: the individual and the crowd, government control, science and the body, industrialisation, pollution and the dark side of the metropolis. His films do not assume that being several personalities, or being 'split right down the centre' (to quote Bruce Wayne in *Batman Returns*) equals leading a 'normal' life. The 'split' is not celebrated, or accepted; on the contrary, it is presented as tragic.

Let us go back to Erich Neumann and his unhappy 'child', who, being the victim of inadequate parenting, is loaded with guilt and complexes. Speaking about the Jungian and post-Jungian attitude to complexes, Hauke points out the essential difference between the modernist and postmodernist positions in their attitude to the condition of 'being split'. Whereas the typical postmodern approach to multiplicity and fragmentation would be the acceptance and celebration of such a diagnosis, modern consciousness concentrates on the heroic struggle with it (Hauke, 2000: 156). Contemporary superhero figures, including Superman and Batman, since their arrival into popular culture in the 1930s, have served to represent such a suffering, splintered consciousness. Burton's Bruce Wayne, for instance, does not embrace his own twofold personality, which is 'normal' by day but becomes rather eccentric at night. His answer is to fight this disturbing multi-facetedness, both within himself and in the isolating metropolitan society. He mournfully, and obsessively, goes back to a dark corner of New York to lay flowers on the spot where he lost his parents, and where his life, and his personality, were transformed forever. Metaphorically speaking, he keeps returning to the moment in time when his distressing split happened.

Burton cannot be termed a 'purely' postmodernist director because he is essentially, and deeply, individualist and pro-individualist. His protagonists battle with society for the right to keep their personality intact, to hold the pieces together. They demand the right to be different. They oppose the 'normalising', unifying tendencies in society. In doing so, they encounter a calamitous self-contradiction: although they suffer from fragmentation, they nevertheless do not want peace of mind and unity of soul. Given the choice to stay in the village of Ashton, or to seek his fortune elsewhere, Edward Bloom chooses the unsettling life of eternal traveller over the sleepy, and nameless, existence in the American village. The 'unfinished', 'sewn together' Edward Scissorhands realises towards the end of the film that, maybe, his joining the village community was a mistake. He eventually chooses 'eternal loneliness' over the joys of socialisation.

In *Jung and the Postmodern* Christopher Hauke discusses the relationship between scientific rationalism (and its political and economic derivatives) and the individual. He reminds us that as early as 1956, Jung was arguing in the same vein as current economic concerns:

> [Jung] is often critical of the contemporary tendency towards collective thinking and behaviour; the psychology of 'mass-mindedness' which overrides and eclipses the individual and individual consciousness and experience. [. . .] In Jung's view, individuals become more and more uncertain of their own judgement; thus leading to the collectivisation of individual responsibility. The real 'life carrier', the individual subject, is usurped by an 'abstract idea' – society and the state. "The State in particular is turned into a quasi-animate personality from whom everything is expected"
>
> (Hauke, 2000: 34)

Tim Burton's concerns, it appears, are similar to Jung's. In his films, he often links such 'mass-mindedness' (mostly inadvertently, it seems) to government control, the capitalist state and the suppression of self-expression. Himself a fighter with the hyper-commercialism of the Hollywood system, Burton feels empathy towards Ed Wood, a director who failed to sell his vision to the executives and the general public. Both the *Batman* films discuss, albeit in pop terms and images, the fateful connection between capitalism and politics, while Nicholson's Joker, with his deadly cosmetic advertisements, may be said to represent the stupefying effects of consumerism and advertising. *Mars Attacks!* dismantles American society into its constituents, to reveal that the lifestyle which American people regard as 'normal' is, in effect, as weird and unnatural as the green aliens' mode of being.

Being generally apolitical, Burton, nevertheless, is rather anxious about the fate of the individual today. His protagonists despise order, authority and efficiency as much as he himself mocks films like *Lethal Weapon* (Salisbury, 2006: 131). The refusal to grow up may generally be regarded as juvenile, but in the world of Tim Burton, rejection of adult values has more positive connotations. In this sense, he was the perfect choice for directing Paul Reubens's *Pee Wee's Big Adventure* (1985). Burton has a unique ability to turn what very obviously looks like demented infantilism into a form of protest against the middle-class lifestyle and its insistence on maturity and 'normality'. Maturity as 'the norm', as a socially conditioned trait, is the very enemy against which any Burtonian character is genuinely fighting. 'The dragon' in this kind of hero-myth is contemporary Western societies with their desire to 'squeeze' the baby out of every supposedly infantile individual. Andrew Samuels links this morality with the psychological ideology *du jour* – object relations theory – and argues that 'scanning part-objects for signs of movement toward whole objects suggests that the object relationships paradigm is in the grip of a maturation morality and a fantasy of wholeness, and is just as normative as Freud's strictures on love and work or about genitality' (Samuels, 1993: 274).

Referring to Samuels, Christopher Hauke widens the picture and adds that such an approach is part of the tendency within modernity and late capitalism 'to flatten out what is different, radical and challenging, and then to refashion such ideas within its own image – thus simultaneously legitimising such ideas and stripping them of power in order to maintain the status quo' (Hauke, 2000: 64). Pee Wee's intrinsic inefficiency, which on the visual plane takes the form of the Burtonian trashy-cluttered *mise-en-scène*, does not fit into the late-capitalist ideology which promotes order, professionalism, good communication and negotiation abilities, hard work and financial success. In contrast to the aforementioned middle-class values, Pee Wee does not have a job or a profession, and his negotiation skills are limited to shouting childish abuse at a rich fat kid who wants to buy his bike. He throws most of his breakfast away, and the gadgets he owns lack any observable utilitarian function. This parade of grotesquerie is not a promotion of infantilism; it is an openly tricksterish, subversive attempt to demonstrate to the professionalised, hyper-efficient society, which is equally grotesque in its utilitarianism and seriousness, that there is more to life than two children, a suburban house, and a nine-to-five job.

Refusing to grow up, rejecting any authority, clinging to his creativity-generating complexes for dear life, voluntarily fragmented but pining for wholeness, hating the unconscious but feeling overpowered by it, looking for his maternalised, idealised father, searching for the lost God inside and outside himself, cursing his lonely fate – the Burtonian postmodernist subject-individual, against all odds, stubbornly refuses to die. He does not perish after being snatched up and nearly strangled by a dreadful tree in the treacherous forest (Edward Bloom). Like a Greek hero, he triumphantly returns from the underworld (Victor in *The Corpse Bride*). He can survive the most painful type of betrayal, and come back even stronger (Willie Wonka) or angrier (Sweeney Todd). He can even cheat time, and outlive everyone else, by locking himself inside a castle and thus keeping his clean and youthful mind untainted by the outer world (Edward Scissorhands). Or, like Batman, after going through the most horrific thing – the death of his parents – he makes a decision to become a hero in order to improve the unjust world. Every time he brings the roses to the place of assassination, he relives the loss of his Paradise.

The decision to revisit the 'scene of the murder', and to lay flowers in honour of the murdered 'subject', should not be regarded as a regressive move, as some kind of unconditional return to the modernity. It is, as Christopher Hauke rightly notes, an attempt to set out a new future using the images and the language of the past – for the new language is not available yet. To heal the fracture, or at least to understand its causes, one has to go back to the moment when it took place. Burton's retro-postmodernism can thus be said to be profoundly ontological and even, in the general sense, religious.

Speaking figuratively, he is too depressed about 'the death of the father figure' (Nietzsche's 'God is dead') to celebrate the subject's release 'from itself'. His characters do not want the infinite freedom of empty choice; they want to find the answer to the ancient question: 'Why is life given to a man whose way is hidden, whom God has hedged in? For sighing comes to me instead of food; my groans pour out like water' (Job, 3: 23–24). At least, this is the kind of theological complaint which would perfectly suit all the typical Burtonian drama queens: Edward Scissorhands, Sweeney Todd, Willie Wonka, Bruce Wayne, Vincent Malloy and even the hapless villain Penguin. In their suffering, they follow in the footsteps of Victor Frankenstein, with his eternal agony, self-loathing, his unfinished 'monster in the closet', and the disastrous inability to be 'like everyone else'.

Chapter 2

The monster

Face and hands

In order to understand how Edward Scissorhands and other Burtonian monsters are made, let us look at their literary and cinematic predecessors.

Mary Shelley teaches us that monsters are not born – they are created. What in reality makes them terrible is human indifference. They will keep killing until – as they mistakenly think – they get their share of sympathy, respect and recognition. Being a fiend is a full-time attention-seeking exercise. Burton's fiends are all more or less derived from the same source – the motif that has been operating in literature (and later in cinema) for almost 200 years: the Frankenstein story. The abandoned monster theme is overtly traceable in *Vincent, Frankenweenie* and *Edward Scissorhands*, while in some of Burton's other works it is still possible to pinpoint the various elements of the bitter God–father/child–monster relationship.

This image is very dear to him personally. For Burton, 'monstrous' is synonymous with 'misunderstood'; the fiend is a metaphor for the introverted, creative outcast. True, at first sight he may seem rather clumsy, asocial or even ugly and unpleasant. However, his scary appearance is only a mask which the poor fiend is condemned to wear. Condemnation and hatred are the cross he has to carry. As a matter of fact, the original *Frankenstein* contains references to Milton's *Paradise Lost*, while James Whale controversially included a whole 'crucifixion scene' in *The Bride of Frankenstein* (1935).[1]

Always on the defensive, the monster's overreaction to external events can be perceived by others as aggression, or even a sign of derangement. But

---

1 In this scene the crowd ties the captured monster to a long pole, and the pole is then raised to reveal that Karloff's character is placed into the position of crucifixion. Another allusion to Jesus in the *Bride of Frankenstein* had to be changed because of the obvious blasphemous content: in a graveyard scene the monster trying to escape the crowd topples the figure of a bishop, and dives inside the tomb. The original version had him toppling a statue of Jesus (in the released scene Jesus on the cross remains in the background).

however terrible the fiends are on the outside, deep down they are unhappy and hurt creatures. Burton's ability to see beyond the mask, to permeate the layers of monstrous make-up that often hide a very delicate soul, has determined his trademark directorial approach, as well as his choice of material. Burton knows that the horrible outer shell, the misleading appearance, will not fool everyone; the mask is not solid – it cannot but betray the fragile creature beneath, however hard it tries to keep its sensitivity a secret. Consequently, the director seeks to identify the vulnerable points, the 'cracks' in the mask, the weaknesses beneath the official image (or persona, as it is called in Jungian psychology). In Burton's own words, the greatest thing about Batman is not his superhero status, but the childish artificiality of his claims and ambitions; the depressing naivety of his costume: 'What's great about [the costume] is it's the visual representation of the internal side of people. That's what I love. People putting on sheets or a bat costume to have some effect. It's a boldly sad statement. It's like a pathetic, last ditch attempt before death. This is it, in a way' (Fraga, 2005: 32).

As a child Burton related to the monster figures that were abundant in the B-movies of the 1930s, 1940s and 1950s: the Frankenstein demon, the Wolf-man, Godzilla, an assortment of Draculas, Vincent Price's villains, the creature from the black lagoon. The crowd torturing the outcast has represented, for Burton, the shallow, colourless suburban America, from which the only escape was the world of fantasy: 'They [characters in the films] were always taking the monster and kind of prodding him and poking him, especially the ones of the fifties. The way those movies were structured, the heroes were always these bland actors, who had no emotion. They were the suburbanites to me' (Fraga, 2005: 48).

The theme of conflict between the monster and the crowd has always been central to many a Frankenstein film. James Whale (*Frankenstein, The Bride of Frankenstein*), and Kenneth Branagh (*Mary Shelley's Frankenstein*), despite the significant difference between the storylines, utilise the same archetypal situation as a premise for their narratives: a male parent 'gives birth' to an ugly creature (no mother is mentioned), and then leaves it to its own resources. In addition, the Frankenstein industry included less meaningful spin-offs such as Rowland W. Lee's *Son of Frankenstein* (1939) and Erle C. Kenton's *Ghost of Frankenstein* (1942), as well as humorous revisions such as Mel Brooks' *Young Frankenstein* (1974). Unlike Shelley's original, film adaptations are often sprinkled with a dark sense of humour that is part of the 'mad scientist/doctor' motif.

The most famous version of the monster, undoubtedly, belongs to James Whale. Visually striking and psychologically accurate, it is not surprising that the image of the gangly fiend became such an incessant source of inspiration for Burton. Born out of Whale's fascination with Karloff's bone structure and shaped by Jack Pierce's skill, the famous uncoordinated, stitched-up face was the extension of the actor's natural features (Skal,

2001: 133–134). The bearer of the image was very proud of his new appearance: 'I was thinking this, practicing my walk, as I rounded a bend in the corridor and came face-to-face with this prop man. He was the first man to see the monster – I watched to study his reaction. He turned white, gurgled, and lunged out of sight down the corridor. Never saw him again. Poor chap, I would have liked to thank him – he was the audience that first made me feel like the monster' (2001: 133–134).

All the while, Karloff's character is less about the physicality of horror and more about the tragedy of being different (Whale's choice of subject was not accidental – being gay in the 1930s in America was not easy). Whale's monster is so childlike that, despite his unnatural appearance, he evokes empathy rather than fear. His defencelessness is expressed in the film through the medium of hands. Hands as a symbol of powerlessness are important, for instance, in the scene in which the newly built creature sees the sunlight for the first time – and clumsily raises his hands towards the ray coming from the high window in his master's scientific dungeon. When the light disappears, he looks baffled and disappointed, and slowly puts the hands down. The monster is the child, the victim, and the chained spirit.

In yet another classic scene, Karloff's character meets a little girl at the riverbank, and tries to establish some kind of human contact with her – to the best of his communication abilities. The girl shows him how to throw flowers into the river. The flowers do not sink – they stay afloat. The monster, inspired by this harmless demonstration, decides that a human child, if thrown into water, will float on the surface like a flower. His experiment is bound to end tragically, and the creature looks more and more alarmed as the girl disappears into the river. Again, his despair is communicated through chaotic hand gesticulation and agitated body language. In Whale's visual universe, the hands symbolise infantilism, imperfection, and incompleteness. The monster does not know human language, and his only means of communication is through hand gestures.

As we remember, Mary Shelley's version of the monster had to learn human language himself. As his father abandoned him immediately after realising that his invention had come out physically ugly, the 'demon' was left to his own resources, material as well as psychological. His mastering of language and gradual comprehension of the workings of the world (which Shelley based on Locke's vision of human development) was a significant achievement – especially because it was attained independently. Watching a family of poor cottagers going about their daily life, he learns their habits in the process. Shelley uses the device of defamiliarisation[2] to render the monster's vision. He is very keen on learning to speak:

2 Defamiliarisation means showing a familiar situation as if it were unusual, from an 'alien's' point of view. This term was first introduced into literary theory in 1917 by the member of the Russian Formalist circle, Viktor Shklovsky.

This was indeed a godlike science, and I ardently desired to become acquainted with it. But I was baffled in every attempt I made for this purpose. Their pronunciation was quick; and the words they uttered, not having any connection with visible objects, I was unable to discover any clue by which I could unravel the mystery of their reference. By great application, however, and after having remained during the space of several revolutions of the moon in my hovel, I discovered the names that were given to some of the most familiar objects of discourse; I learned and applied the words, *fire*, *milk*, *bread*, and *wood*. I learned also the names of the cottagers themselves. The youth and his companion had each of them several names, but the old man had only one, which was *father*. The girl was called *sister*, or *Agatha*; and the youth *Felix, brother*, or *son*. I cannot describe the delight I felt when I learned the ideas appropriated to each of these sounds, and was able to pronounce them. I distinguished several other words, without being able as yet to understand or apply them; such as *good, dearest, unhappy*.

(Shelley, 1999: 87)

With a little perseverance Shelley's monster has learned the language well enough for his soul to articulate itself in grandiloquent expressions such as 'the orb of night had greatly lessened' or 'these people possessed a method of communicating their experience and feelings to one another by articulate sounds' (1999: 86).

Whale's creature is not as lucky as his predecessor. In the first *Franken-stein* film he does not meet anyone suitable who could teach him the art of human interaction. His non-verbal communication remains alinguistic and chaotic, and he can only express his distress by flailing about, gesturing with his hands and making inarticulate sounds. At the film's finale, he is symbolically burnt inside an old mill. Only in *The Bride of Frankenstein* (1935), after being 'resurrected', does he find a kind soul, a blind hermit, who teaches him English. At last, language becomes for the monster a valid means of communication. He learns from a hermit the words 'alone . . . bad . . . friend GOOD!' (all pronounced in Karloff's specific coarse voice). Since the monster's host is blind, he cannot see what his guest really looks like, and lets him stay in the house. Nevertheless, he is able to 'see' beyond the mask and into the lonely and injured soul, which is, essentially, the soul of a mistreated and abandoned *puer* on the lookout for some care and attention.

Actually, gesticulation as a clumsy substitute for linguistic skills is a phenomenon with which Burton is closely familiar. It looks like, for him, non-verbal self-expression is one of the points of identification with the 'vulnerable monster' figure. A reviewer, Frank Rose, shares his impressions of the young Tim on the set of *Edward Scissorhands*:

The only person more dishevelled than Depp is Burton. A tall, thin
figure dressed entirely in black [. . .], with chipmunk cheeks and a
bouffant of long black hair that seems to have been created by nesting
birds, Burton looks somewhat two-dimensional, like an animated
caricature. Highly animated: his hands are in constant motion, gesturing, grabbing his hair, covering his face, at one point digging into his
flesh as if to rip it from his skull.

(Woods, 2002: 62)

Comments like this are the norm rather than the exception. Simon Garfield
calls him 'dopey and bedraggled' (Wood, 2002: 34), while David Edelstein
notes that, with his 'heavy lids and spacey eyes' Burton has 'a whiff of
stoned melancholy about him' (Fraga, 2005: 10). The best account of
Burton's demeanour, however, is given by Johnny Depp when he describes
his first meeting with Tim to audition for the role of Edward Scissorhands:

A pale, frail-looking, sad-eyed man with hair that expressed much more
than last night's pillow struggle. A comb with legs would have outrun
Jesse Owens, given one look at this guy's locks. A clump to the east,
four sprigs to the west, a swirl, and the rest of this unruliness to all
points north and south. I remember the first thing I thought was, 'Get
some sleep', I couldn't say that, of course. And then it hit me like a
two-ton sledgehammer square in the middle of my forehead. The hands
– the way he waves them around in the air almost uncontrollably,
nervously tapping on the table, stilted speech (a trait we both share),
eyes wide and glaring out of nowhere, eyes that have seen much but still
devour all. This supersensitive madman *is* Edward Scissorhands.

(Salisbury, 2006: x)

In the 'world of monsters', though, the man so aptly described by Depp
would be perceived as absolutely normal. Burton's 'otherness' is probably
the reason why he is so good at 'defamiliarising' the apparently normal
world, at seeing beyond the surface and noticing hidden meanings. Shown
from the point of view of 'the monster', the normal world, of course, looks
strange and Gothic; unpredictable and mysterious. Burton always questions
the validity of 'normalcy', of the ordinary, of established patterns of behaviour. He displaces the ordinariness of the pastel world he has never been
able to understand or accept, by planting a Gothic castle nearby, in which a
creative madman assembles a punky-looking, bedraggled, sad creature, and
leaves him alone to explore the hostile environment outside.

Creator as mother

As far as the themes of rejection, abandonment, misery and unhappiness
are concerned, Shelley's original text has no shortage of them. It abounds

with existential despair and black pessimism. These gloomy motifs, obviously, do not stand on their own; they are related to some truly grand subjects: knowledge, rationality, progress, and the responsibility and ethics of science.

Mary Shelley's first novel was a bit of an experiment – just like the creature whose unfortunate adventures it describes. The authoress grew up in a rebellious, bohemian circle where avant-garde scientists and their findings were openly discussed (Humphrey Davy and Erasmus Darwin frequented her home). Mary's father, the radical philosopher William Godwin, did not have much luck with money, and was not ashamed to accept considerable sums from his eventual son-in-law, the poet Percy Bysshe Shelley. Mary never received any formal education but had unhindered access to her father's extensive and up-to-date library. From an early age she was aware of the value of knowledge and the price of progress.

Frankenstein is not a stylistically brilliant story – actually, the ever controversial Germaine Greer called it 'an incoherent tale' with a 'tendency to proliferating parallel clauses and phrases and the occasional theatrical ejaculation', which 'has more loose ends than a grass skirt' (*Guardian*, 9 April 2007: 28). Its strongest point, however, is not its technical brilliance, but rather its ability to tie in with the overlapping socio-psychological problems which the emerging man of modernity suddenly had to face: science and ethics; the creator's responsibility for his creation; the future of religion and man's relationship with God; individual vs society; nature vs nurture, social class and social mobility, etc. The longevity of the Frankenstein creature is due to the persistence of these post-Enlightenment moral dilemmas which are more relevant than ever in the Western society of today. By all accounts, *Frankenstein* is an ugly, but truthful, mirror of the emerging industrial society. Shelley's true success lies in that she passed her social and cultural concerns down the generations of writers and artists. Inadvertently, Tim Burton works within the same philosophical paradigm as Mary Shelley – modernity, individualism and the question of the father.

Enlightened individualism and infantile irrationality are the two issues that form the moral base of *Frankenstein*. Mary read David Hume and Immanuel Kant, and discussed their ideas with Percy Shelley (Mellor, 1988: 136). Enlightenment, Immanuel Kant maintained in his famous essay *An Answer to the Question: What is Enlightenment?* (1784), was about getting rid of self-imposed intellectual infantilism and laziness in favour of cultivating one's mind, as well as being courageous enough to use one's own understanding (Schmidt, 1996: 58). An ardent believer in the power of human reason, Kant created a base for modern Western philosophy and moral theory. An enlightened individual, according to Kant, is first and foremost a *mature* individual; and maturity and rationality equal intellectual freedom:

It is . . . difficult for any individual man to work himself out of an immaturity that has become almost natural to him. He has become fond of it, and, for the present, is truly incapable of making use of his own reason, because he has never been permitted to make an attempt. Rules and formulas, these mechanical instruments of a rational use (or rather misuse) of his natural gifts, are the fetters of his everlasting immaturity. [. . .] Hence there are only a few who have managed to free themselves from immaturity through the exercise of their own minds, and yet proceed confidently.

(Schmidt, 1996: 59)

The eminent European Enlightenment philosophers, no doubt, were a good source of ideas for the young Mary Shelley, but inspiration could also be found in her immediate family. Mary's own mother, Mary Wollstonecraft (1759–1797), in her famous treatise *A Vindication of the Rights of Woman* (1792), concerned herself with the issues to which the French Revolution gave a high degree of relevancy: the supremacy of reason, the perfection of human nature, the acquisition of experience and knowledge by humans, and the relationship between the individual and society. In her view, man's pre-eminence over 'the brute creation' consists in Reason, but passions are nevertheless necessary because 'man by struggling with them might attain a degree of knowledge denied to the brutes'. Consequently, 'the perfection of our nature and capability of happiness, must be estimated by the degree of reason, virtue and knowledge, that distinguish the individual, and direct the laws that bind society: and that from the exercise of reason, knowledge and virtue naturally flow, is equally undeniable, if mankind is viewed collectively' (Wollstonecraft, 1993: 91).

Shelley's *Frankenstein* is self-contradictory; it harbours a very lively clash between Enlightenment ideas and romantic sensibility, between the maker and the monster; the father and the child, individual and family; the clash which will be passed down to future generations of post-Enlightenment thinkers. At the heart of this conflict we find the figure of the oxymoronic passionate scientist, a creative-rational individual, a kind of modern Prometheus, who represents both the Enlightenment's confrontation with 'the darkness' of ignorance, and Romantic rebellion against the establishment. He is an artistic scientist, a loner and a rebel (as Pee Wee would say) who dreams of constructing a perfect child, giving birth to an ideal creature.

Victor Frankenstein's passion for scientific progress leads him onto a dangerous spiritual journey. Like many other Romantic dissenters, Victor dares to obtain the secret of creating life, but is punished for his courage; madness descends on him and he ends up living in isolation. Shelley's choice of name for her protagonist is not surprising: 'Victor' translates from Latin as 'conqueror'. A Promethean overreacher, he plunges himself into the extremities of the Enlightenment position: his independent thinking soon mutates into total disregard for society; self-expression becomes irresponsible, creativity destructive, and family life is replaced by self-imposed, painful, ecstatic loneliness. Submerged in his great project, Frankenstein rejects the 'unthinking masses' (which happen to include his own family, his best friend Clerval, and even his beloved Elizabeth).

Eventually, Victor sacrifices his personal happiness, along with the happiness of his fiancée and his relatives, for the sake of an intellectual orgasm. At some point during his hard university life, he makes an incredible discovery: man is capable of 'bestowing animation upon lifeless matter'. Man is capable of conceiving and giving birth. Shelley describes her protagonist's intellectual exultation by piling up expressions such as rapture, delight, consummation, painful labour, which dangerously border on the semantic field of sexual reproduction:

> The astonishment which I had at first experienced on this discovery soon gave place to delight and rapture. After so much time spent in painful labour, to arrive at once at the summit of my desires, was the most gratifying consummation of my toils. But this discovery was so great and overwhelming, that all the steps by which I had been progressively led to it were obliterated, and I beheld only the result. What had been the study and desire of the wisest men since the creation of the world, was now within my grasp. Not that, like a magic scene, it all opened upon me at once: the information I had obtained was of a nature rather to direct my endeavours so soon as I should point them towards the object of my search, than to exhibit that object already accomplished.
>
> (Shelley, 1999: 42)

Having obtained the fire of secret knowledge which has been 'the study and desire of wisest men since the creation of the world', Victor enters 'a period of gestation' which will eventually lead to the birth of the terrible creature. Here he describes the process of assembling his 'son' from body parts of animals and people:

> These thoughts supported my spirits, while I pursued my undertaking with unremitting ardour. My cheek had grown pale with study, and my person had become emaciated with confinement. Sometimes, on the very brink of certainty, I failed; yet still I clung to the hope which the next day or the next hour might realise. One secret which I alone possessed was the hope to which I had dedicated myself; and the moon gazed on my midnight labours, while, with unrelaxed and breathless eagerness, I pursued nature to her hiding-places. Who shall conceive the horrors of my secret toil, as I dabbled among the unhallowed

damps of the grave, or tortured the living animal to animate the lifeless clay? My limbs now tremble, and my eyes swim with the remembrance; but then a resistless, and almost frantic impulse, urged me forward; I seemed to have lost all soul or sensation but for this one pursuit. It was indeed but a passing trance, that only made me feel with renewed acuteness so soon as, the unnatural stimulus ceasing to operate, I had returned to my old habits. I collected bones from charnel houses; and disturbed, with profane fingers, the tremendous secrets of the human frame. In a solitary chamber, or rather cell, at the top of the house, and separated from all the other apartments by a gallery and staircase, I kept my workshop of filthy creation; my eyeballs were starting from their sockets in attending to the details of my employment. The dissecting room and the slaughter-house furnished many of my materials; and often did my human nature turn with loathing from my occupation, whilst, still urged on by an eagerness which perpetually increased, I brought my work near to a conclusion.

(Shelley, 1999: 43)

Such an amazing breakthrough was only possible thanks to the vigorous cultivation of his own mind, as Kant would have put it, but Victor's individualistic rationality and fatal affair with progress soon lead to a disaster. One dreary November night, the talented student finally meets 'the accomplishment of his toils', literally, eye to eye:

His yellow skin scarcely covered the work of muscles and arteries beneath; his hair was of a lustrous black, and flowing; his teeth of a pearly whiteness; but these luxuriances only formed a more horrid contrast with his watery eyes, that seemed almost of the same colour as the dun white sockets in which they were set, his shrivelled complexion and straight black lips. [. . .]

His jaws opened, and he muttered some inarticulate sounds, while a grin wrinkled his cheeks. He might have spoken, but I did not hear; one hand was stretched out, seemingly to detain me, but I escaped, and rushed down stairs. I took refuge in the courtyard belonging to the house which I inhabited; where I remained during the rest of the night, walking up and down in the greatest agitation, listening attentively, catching and fearing each sound as if it were to announce the approach of the demoniacal corpse to which I had so miserably given life.

(Shelley, 1999: 45)

An incredulous and horrified father, Victor flees the scene of his intellectual abortion and wishes to forget about the creature. The monster, however, cannot forget its maker – *it* wants to find him, to question him about the purpose of the disastrous experiment, and to demand a companion. A monster who was born unwanted, feels unwanted forever; in Chapter 24 of the novel the creature laments his 'lost paradise' – his untainted perception of the world and its people: 'When I run over the catalogue of my sins, I cannot believe that I am the same creature whose thoughts were once filled with sublime and transcendent visions of the beauty and the majesty of goodness. But it is even so; the fallen angel becomes the terrible demon. Yet even the enemy of God and man had friends and associates in desolation; I am alone' (1999: 169).

Although Victor triumphs as an individual, having stolen the precious fire of knowledge from Zeus, he nevertheless fails as a social being, as a member of his community. He is punished by the jealous gods of nature. Echoing the Prometheus theme, Jung wrote of the blind pursuit of 'the light':

> The myth of the hero . . . is first and foremost a self-representation of the longing of the unconscious, of its unquenched and unquenchable desire for the light of consciousness. But consciousness, continually in danger of being led astray by its own light and of becoming a rootless will o' the wisp, longs for the healing power of nature, for the deep well of being and for unconscious communion with life in all its countless forms.
>
> (Jung, 1912, CW5: para. 299)

To Victor Frankenstein, a propagator of the Enlightenment, the rejected 'darkness' returned in the form of his own horrible creation. In fact, Victor is at war with the entire 'feminine' binary opposite with its connotations of irrationality, instability and loss of conscious control. For this reason there is no legitimate place for a mother in *Frankenstein*, either on the psychological level (the unconscious), or even on the level of the plot since the authoress chose to use a patriarchal version of the creation myth, the one that excludes the feminine from the process of 'bestowing life upon inanimate matter'. In the midst of his ardent scientific work, Victor even dreams of his fiancée Elizabeth, a typical 'pure angel', turning into the corpse of his dead mother. The mother figure in *Frankenstein* only lurks at the background, and is assigned a fairly negative task: to punish the protagonist for his one-sided attitude to life. Consequently, there is no redemption in Shelley's book – because, for her, monstrosity is at the heart of the human condition and is irredeemable. The two opposites are not going to make up and live happily ever after.

Creator as God

From the Frankenstein legacy, Tim Burton inherits the triangle consisting of the male creator, his creation, and the society into which this newly made individual is received. He both draws upon, and develops this legacy, wrapping it in his own signature Gothic visual style.

The power and longevity of the *Frankenstein* plot is not only due to its thematic relevance for modernity and postmodernity. It also has a much deeper, very basic archetypal layer underneath the blanket of post-Enlightenment philosophical dilemmas related to the development of capitalism in the West: industrialisation, exploitation of natural resources, rapid scientific progress, the class struggle and the supremacy of capitalist individualism and instrumental rationality. The metaphysical base of *Frankenstein* is so vast that is it rather difficult to define. It is easier to explain it with the help of a myth. In fact, the idea is roughly outlined in the Greek tale of the Titan Prometheus: man's relationship with the unconscious and with nature; man's dual character as God's creation and creator; the responsibility of the author and the pain which comes with the gift of talent. And, sat on top of this heap, is the perennial father–son problem.

The full title of Mary Shelley's book is *Frankenstein, or the Modern Prometheus*. Jung saw the Prometheus myth as a metaphor for consciousness and its pursuit of knowledge; its struggle for independence from the unconscious. Any significant victory over nature attained by civilisation is accompanied by suffering and pain:

> Genesis represents the act of becoming conscious as a taboo infringement, as though knowledge meant that a sacrosanct barrier had been impiously overstepped. I think that Genesis is right in so far as every step towards greater consciousness is a kind of Promethean guilt: through knowledge, the gods are as it were robbed of their fire, that is, something that was the property of the unconscious powers is torn out of its natural context and subordinated to the whims of the conscious mind. The man who has usurped the new knowledge suffers, however, a transformation or enlargement of consciousness, which no longer resembles that of his fellow men. He has raised himself above the human level of his age ("you shall become like God"), but in so doing has alienated himself from humanity. The pain of this loneliness is the vengeance of the gods, for never again can he return to mankind. He is, as the myth says, chained to the lonely cliffs of the Caucasus, forsaken of God and man.
>
> (Jung, 1953, CW 7: para. 243)

Victor Frankenstein, too, dares to challenge the natural order of things. He wants to 'unveil the face of Nature', pour 'a torrent of light into our dark world' and create a new species that would bless him as its creator and source. In his utopian sci-fi dreams Victor sees that 'many happy and excellent natures will owe their being' to him because 'no father could claim the gratitude of his child so completely as I should deserve theirs' (Shelley, 1999: 43).

The hapless result of the experiment, however, has a different view of the matter. He curses the scientist for giving him life, and accuses him of parental neglect, and of what we would today call a lack of 'professional scientific responsibility'. When Victor threatens to 'extinguish the spark' which he 'so negligently bestowed', the monster, rejected by all human beings with whom he has tried to have contact, replies: 'I was benevolent; my soul glowed with love and humanity: but am I not alone, miserably alone? You, my creator, abhor me; what hope can I gather from your fellow-creatures, who owe me nothing? they spurn and hate me. The desert mountains and dreary glaciers are my refuge' (Shelley, 1999: 78). The monster's protest is existentialist in the sense that, metaphorically speaking, what he actually laments is the eternal Christian problem of the wretched human condition, and the seeming inability, or unwillingness, of God to remedy the injustice, hardship and anguish that his children have to endure. The monster's becoming the 'fallen angel', the twilight creature, is only a reflection of Victor's own behaviour; his own misery and his own darkness. The creator, as it happens, can be the perfect father if he chooses to – or he can be careless and unreliable, in which case his children will have to fend for themselves.

Jung often wrote of this dual perception of God by various cultures and religions. He was particularly interested in the image of Yahweh in the Old Testament. In *Answer to Job* (1952, CW 11) he argues, quite in line with Mary Shelley's 'monster logic', that the man of modernity has difficulty coming to terms with what he calls 'the divine darkness'. Jung held the view that God, in all his incarnations, be it the powerful demiurge in the sky as some religions see him, or the assemblage of unconscious mental processes in the human psyche, is plagued by the same old archetypal war of opposites as man. This is part of Jung's fractal-shaped idea of individuation – the endless rows of eternally irresolvable problems that are passed from 'parents' to 'children'. According to Jung, God, who comprises both good and evil and is greatly afflicted by this duality, wants to resolve his own 'internal' conflict with the help of man. The following phrase from *Answer to Job* perfectly sums up the philosophy of the monster-maker conflict which is present in most Burton's films: 'We can, of course, hope for the undeserved grace of God, who hears our prayers. But God, who does not hear our prayers, wants to become man, and for that purpose he has chosen, through the Holy Ghost, the creaturely man filled with darkness – the natural man who is tainted with original sin and who learnt the divine arts and sciences from the fallen angels' (Jung, 1952, CW11: para. 746). This shifts the responsibility for the eventual resolution of the conflict from God to man, who has inherited his divine Father's weaknesses and imperfections. In the Bible, Jung notes, this metaphysical responsibility takes the form of the redemptive Christ metaphor:

Since the Apocalypse we now know again that God is not only to be loved, but also to be feared. He fills us with evil as well as with good, otherwise he would not need to be feared; and because he wants to become man, the uniting of his antinomy must take place in man. This involves man in a new responsibility. He can no longer wriggle out of it on the plea of his littleness and nothingness, for the dark God has slipped the atom bomb and chemical weapons into his hands and given him power to empty out the apocalyptic vials of wrath on his fellow creatures. Since he has been granted an almost godlike power, he can no longer remain blind and unconscious. He must know something of God's nature and of metaphysical processes if he is to understand himself and thereby achieve gnosis of the Divine.

(Jung, 1952, CW11: para. 747)

As an epigraph, Shelley used a line from Milton's *Paradise Lost*: 'Did I request thee, Maker, from my clay/ To mould me man? Did I solicit thee/ From darkness to promote me?' (Milton, 2003: 743–745). Just as the monster and Victor never come to an understanding, their relationship turning into eternal struggle and spiteful hatred, the relationship between man and his Creator is equally troublesome and complex. In an existentialist vicious circle, Victor fails as a parent because God, too, fails to make his creation perfect.

The basic myth itself, the story of the male god, the nonconformist, and the crowd, is quite flexible. Its only stable point is that the spotlight is always on the rebel – it revolves around his 'descent' from the divine heights, his gift to the people, and his subsequent physical and spiritual sufferings. Beyond this point, however, the secondary emphasis may vary: the protagonist may be on the side of the male god, or he may be inclined towards the group of ungrateful humans, and even attempt to shield them from the divine wrath. Alternatively, he may start cursing both parties, God and the human race: the father for bringing him into this horrible world, and the crowd for being so insensitive and cruel. Prometheus, for instance, is on the side of the people. He challenges Zeus, and is prepared to endure the agonising punishment sent to him for his act of misbehaviour. The Christian tradition, too, makes the 'bringer of light' sacrifice himself for the sake of mankind. Mary Shelley's version examines the rebel's difficulties in dealing with both the creator and the crowd. It is their communal effort which ensures the monster's final downfall. The paternal figure (both as Christian God and Victor the maker) is neglectful and egoistic, while the crowd is prejudiced and murderous. The only way out left for the outcast is to start destroying them one by one (incidentally, this is also the narrative scheme that was adapted in *Sweeney Todd*).

In Burton's films, the rebel is simultaneously the artist and the child. His usual interpretation of the myth is to put the artistic individual closer to the 'father' rather than to the 'crowd'. The reason for this is that God is creative and ordinary people are not. In other words, God, too, is an artist. Here Burton works within the ancient myth of the divine origin of creativity: the 'human artist', metonymically speaking, is a representative of God on Earth, and is therefore tragically torn between the desire for celestial perfection and the restricting nature of his own humanity. The necessity to live among other humans, and accept their norms of existence, is one such impediment for a man of talent. As Flaubert once wrote in a letter to his friend, the Russian writer Ivan Turgenev, 'I have always tried to live in an ivory tower, but a tide of shit is beating at its walls, threatening to undermine it' (Steegmuller, 1982: 200).

The Burtonian protagonist, at once Victor Frankenstein and his monstrous shadow, is usually depicted as being the victim of this metaphysical conflict. He loathes both his surroundings and his 'human form', which is not flexible enough to accommodate all his projects and dreams. He sees himself as 'extraordinary', almost divine, endowed with supernatural powers. He owns something which the crowd does not have – God's gift.

The Frankenstein puer

Vincent (1982) and Frankenweenie (1984)

Burton's early Frankenstein experiments establish a simple structure which, in his later works, will be artfully concealed underneath cinematic flesh and blood. Formally, one can isolate the following syntagmatic skeleton in the meta-fabula which Burton often follows in his work:

1   A boy with extraordinary powers
a   . . . can reanimate people and animals
b   . . . and/or creates worlds

2   Who is also human
a   . . . and destructive
b   . . . and/or has strange behaviour and/or ugly appearance

3   With no parents
a   . . . they abandoned him
b   . . . and/or they died
c   . . . and/or he renounced them for being insensitive to his needs

4   Who sometimes meets face-to-face with the monster(s)
a   . . . that he himself created
b   . . . and/or that are helpless, ugly and unhappy
c   . . . and/or who are part of him and whom he understands

The short animation film *Vincent* (1982), featuring the voice of Vincent Price (as narrator), follows this pattern. It already contains all Burton's hallmark ideas and motifs. The protagonist is Vincent Malloy who looks like an ordinary boy. On the surface of it, he is a nice and polite seven-year-old. Deep down, however, he imagines himself to be just like the famous Gothic villain of old Hollywood – Vincent Price.

Although the boy does not mind living with his sister, he would rather share a home with bats and spiders. His 'tormented' mind harbours an assortment of tortures, including mummifying his overweight aunt in hot wax, and making a zombie out of his pet dog. Society does not exist for him. And anyway, he prefers to be on his own, in the darkness of his room, talking to himself (cf. Dr Finkelstein in *The Nightmare Before Christmas* cloning himself, and giving the beloved copy half his brain).

Vincent's principal hobbies are monster-making and reading Poe's poems. His sensitive imagination weaves every single signal coming from the outside world into a dark tale, and turns the ordinary into the extraordinary. A flower bed becomes the grave of his bride who had been buried alive. When his mother sends him to his room, the boy imagines that he is 'banished to the tower of doom' where he is going to spend 'years of isolation'.

Predictably, Vincent's suburban mother is very concerned. Instead of a normal boy who enjoys playing games outdoors with other children, she has a little monster thinking that 'he is almost dead' and burying his 'bride' in inappropriate places. Finally, the angry mother orders him to get outside 'and have some real fun'. Faced with such a gross failure to grasp the essence of his inner world, the only thing Vincent can do now is lie on the floor in the dark, quoting his favourite author:

and my soul from out that shadow
that lies floating on the floor
shall be lifted –
Nevermore . . .
(Poe, 1991: 26)

Already Vincent has all the traits of a typical Burtonian protagonist: he is introverted, a daydreamer, darkly creative, with a number of a quirky at best, or suspicious at worst, hobbies. He has a very original personality which stands in contrast with the bland 'ordinariness' of those around him. He likes to be alone, locked inside the darkness of his own mind. He is dissatisfied with his parents. His proximity to the world of the unconscious, and the warped talent, which he cannot as of yet control, make him feel suicidal. And most importantly, Vincent makes no attempt to 'understand' the common people out there. Vincent is suffering from the traditional form of teenage maximalism in the sense that he is uncompromising: he wants complete and immediate acceptance, or nothing at all.

The film's dubious finale raised a few eyebrows at Disney: so, did the boy *really* die? Burton defended his choice of ending, saying that it does not matter whether he is really dead or alive (Salisbury, 2000: 17). In a sense, 'the people at Disney' played the role of Vincent's mother, and wanted things in the film to go back to 'reality'. But Vincent could not go back to reality. It does not work like this with rebellious artists, whose gift of creating magical stories is founded on the inability to tell the difference between life and fiction. The grotesquely melodramatic finale symbolises Vincent's metaphorical death for the outside world. Since it is not possible for the artist to exist in the community full of 'normal people', he can only be alive in his own imaginary universe.

Unusually, for the Frankenstein framework, which traditionally presents the monster in 'exteriorised' form, Vincent is both the scientist *and* the monster. He is simultaneously the artist and his shadow, and the finale in which the inner darkness swallows the carrier from the inside is typical for *doppelgänger* narratives[3]. It comes as no surprise that Victor's surname eventually became confused with the name of the (initially nameless) creature because, in the last instance, they are one and the same.

Burton's next infantile experimenter, little Victor (Barrett Oliver) from the black-and-white short *Frankenweenie* (1984), is already physically 'detached' from his monster, a little dog called Sparky, but is very attached to him emotionally. When Sparky gets hit by a car, he hopes to bring the dog back to life using electrical impulses. He builds an exact copy of Frankenstein's lightning lab, complete with the moving operating table. A number of complex machinations and a lightning strike bring Sparky back to life. The revitalised dog, however, is not very popular with the locals. The conflict between the terrified neighbours and Sparky ends up in the archetypal Whalean windmill tragedy: Victor and Sparky find themselves inside a miniature mill, which is accidentally set on fire by the locals. Sparky drags Victor out but is himself crushed by burning pieces of wood. Having realised their fatal mistake, the locals use their cars to 'recharge' the dog. Sparky comes back to life and everyone is happy. The film's plotline quite openly follows Whale's *Frankenstein* and *The Bride of Frankenstein*. There is even 'the bride of Frankenstein' in the shape of a poodle with a hairstyle similar to that of Elsa Lanchester in Whale's sequel.

The screenplay was written by Lenny Ripp from Burton's story (Salisbury, 2000: 31). It was Burton's third directorial work, after *Vincent* and *Hansel and Gretel*, a live-action short film featuring only Japanese actors. *Frankenweenie was* made in 1984, but, having received a PG rating instead of a G, was shelved until 1991 when it was finally released on video. The problem was that the film about a reanimated dog was deemed too dark for the Disney audience.

---

3 Oscar Wilde's Dorian Gray (*The Picture of Dorian Gray*) and Robert Louis Stevenson's Mr Hyde (*The Strange Case of Dr Jekyll and Mr Hyde*) are good examples of 'pure' literary doubles.

Frankenweenie may look naïve and primitive, both visually and narratively, but it already contains all the trademark Burtonian themes: the monster, the mob, the genius, the absurd death and the miraculous rejuvenation. What it still lacks is the depth of the archetype and truly independent, original vision.

The Frankenstein teenager

Edward Scissorhands (1990)

The trademark Burtonian insight into the 'dark child' problem became truly visible for the first time in *Edward Scissorhands* (1990). This film can be perceived as Burton's flagship work, as far as creative identification with the main character is concerned. Burton, who had been for a while trying to express the 'cursed genius' theme, finally found a frame into which it would fit perfectly: a story about a punky-looking teenager whose unusual talent brings him recognition, as well as misery and heartbreak.

Fabula-wise, *Edward Scissorhands* is another *Frankenstein* variation – but without any direct references to the Whalean aesthetic. True, Burton's film contains none of the special markings of Whale's *modus operandi*: gone is the laboratory with its pseudo-scientific equipment and a moving 'stretcher'; the burning windmill; and the spring-haired 'bride'. The same archetypal situation is now translated into a different language – a Goth/ punk fairy tale played out against the empty, artificial, pastel world of American suburbia. Burton's version of the outcast, however, inherits all the perennial dilemmas, troubles and doubts of a Frankenstein monster: the missing father/creator problem with its existentialist bitterness; the unusual, 'unfinished' appearance; the cursed uniqueness; and the hatred of the crowd. The punk monster is assembled by its elderly maker in a Gothic castle, which is an entirely viable substitute for the mad scientist's lab. Burton explains the origin of the image of the boy with scissors instead of hands in terms of his childhood experiences of living in American suburbia:

> The idea actually came from a drawing I did a long time ago. It was just an image that I liked. It came subconsciously linked to a character who wants to touch but can't, who was both creative and destructive – those sort of contradictions can create a kind of ambivalence. It was very much linked to a feeling. The manifestation of the image made itself apparent and probably came to the surface when I was a teenager, because it is a very teenage thing. It had to do with relationships. I just felt I couldn't communicate.

(Salisbury, 2006: 87)

The autistic character of Edward, who is 'estranged' from his surroundings, reflects his creator's original vision of the world. Burton, too, seems to perceive everything through the lens of defamiliarisation, refusing to accept the 'normality' of things: 'I used to look at my house and say, "Why is this hanging on the wall? This weird blob of wood that's been shellacked and has a clock on it?" (Woods, 2002: 66).

At the same time, it would be all too easy to explain the character and appearance of Edward as a metaphor for Burton's introversion. Edward, who is unable to touch without hurting or transforming, can be taken as a visual metaphor for any genuinely talented artist – he is lonely, edgy, helpless, suffers from communication problems, and has a distorted sense of reality. The only trait that is not universal is his lack of ability to express himself verbally – but this must have indeed come from Burton. Edward Scissorhands epitomises the very essence of the Burtonian hero; he is the Burtonian protagonist unfiltered.

Edward, a pale, bedraggled young creature with an impossible hairstyle consisting of unruly black curls, lives in a Gothic-looking castle (take any old *Dracula* or *Frankenstein*), which the inhabitants of the pastel town fail to notice (translation: the apparently 'normal' suburbia is never free of freaks, but for most of the residents they do not exist). One day a well-meaning, motherly Avon lady stumbles upon this strange home, and goes in out of curiosity (and in the hope of finding new customers for her cosmetics). She takes pity on Edward, takes him to the village, and introduces him to her family and suburban community. The curious, bored villagers are ready to tolerate Edward provided that his idiosyncrasies and deviations are under their control. They are happy to use 'the fruits' of his unusual personality, but are not prepared to accept its less safe side. It is, however, impossible for Edward to pretend to be what he is not. The truce between him and society gets broken when he refuses to accept 'the rules of the game', or to follow the agreed-upon patterns of behaviour which are 'the norm' in this particular group of people. In the end, he chooses loneliness and exile over all the benefits which being a member of society brings. Having done his share of compromising, Edward decides that 'having human hands' is simply not for him.

Form-wise, the film is rather eclectic and peculiar, containing references to punk culture (by his own admission, 'alternative' punk music helped Burton to survive in the bleak suburbia of his childhood), Hollywood Gothic (the traditional props such as Dracula's castle), as well as elements of The German expressionist cinematic tradition (Friedrich Murnau, Fritz Lang). The stylistic eclecticism is not accidental; its different aspects help to express the 'asocial artist' allegory. Edward's punk appearance symbolises rebellion and alienation, while the expressionist angular shadows emphasise Edward's existence 'on the edge' and provide a stark contrast to the vacantly luminous world of suburbia. Burton admits being influenced by the expressionist style, saying that it was its 'strength and simplicity' that he really loved. This, 'and the fairy-tale element' – which, by the way, in its turn comes from the 'terrific' [sic] German folktale tradition (Woods, 2002: 61).

'The edge' is a prominent extended metaphor. It evokes numerous cultural and linguistic moments associated with living 'outside the norm': knives, shadows, punks, edgy teenagers, geeks and the sharp corners of creativity. Art, Burton is trying to tell his audience, is a two-edged weapon. While Edward makes the villagers happy by practising his hairdressing skills on their heads, their dogs and their trees, he nevertheless remains himself. He does not become more 'civilised' or socially acceptable. Edward's genuinely clumsy self is only received well while he does what he is told. Within the framework of the 'artist-society' metaphor this narrative line means that bourgeois culture is willing to consume the products of the artist's creativity, and even absorb his rebellion because it, too, is suitable for consumption, but does not like the actual sharpness of his demeanour. In many ways Johnny Depp was the perfect choice for the role because, independent-thinking actor as he is, he has had to make profit-orientated choices in order to survive in his industry. According to Burton, Depp's own 'edge' is quite noticeable in the film:

> When you look at him, he is one of those people – and there are not many of them – who make you believe in past lives all of a sudden. It sounds kind of New Age, but you look at him and you think his soul has been around throughout the centuries. There is a lot of himself in that movie, because he is somebody who is at odds with himself and not at all how he's perceived to be in the entertainment industry. He has a very strong, tormented, passionate internal life that is very much at odds with the way he looks.
>
> (Woods, 2002: 59)

Edward can be seen as a very grotesque, but nonetheless truthful, reflection of such a conflict of interests between the artist's perception of himself, and the outer image that the audience ideally wishes to consume. Once the artist is accepted into the game, the edge must be discarded. Edward is unable to do that – not because he does not want to betray his internal principles, but simply because he can't escape his naïve and introverted view of the world. When, in the empty hairdressing salon a woman jumps on top of him, he is horrified. He has no idea what it is that she actually wants.

Such a complex man, Burton implies, must be the result of a very special upbringing. And indeed, he is. His father is no ordinary parent – he is a magician, an inventor of mad devices and fascinating, but useless, contraptions. In line with the conservative myth of creation, which excludes women from the process, Edward was made out of various bits and pieces by the Inventor, a good-natured and generous version of the Gothic 'mad scientist'. Edward is brought up in an isolated environment, and his father's kindly teaching and instruction is the only communication he receives. Interestingly enough, for the role of the father Burton chose his own childhood hero Vincent Price. The Inventor, a beautiful old sage, dies of a heart attack before completing his creation, leaving him with skeletal, scissor-like hands (uncannily, this was also Vincent Price's last role. He died of lung cancer in 1993).

Like *Frankenweenie*, *Edward Scissorhands* is at odds with Shelley and Whale about the polarity of the inventor figure. Whereas Victor Frankenstein (or Henry Frankenstein, in Whale's version) is a bad parent, Edward's father is a good god. He does not 'exit' in an unnatural way – by running away and thus relinquishing his parental duties, for example. The only indicators of the Inventor's 'evil' side are his place of residence (the Gothic castle) and quirky hobbies (for instance, monster-making). Overall, however, Burton wants to keep 'god's' personality wholesome and intact; the divinity must be generally good, while the 'evil' has to be displaced elsewhere in the world. This is also how Vincent Price himself saw his role: '. . . I have always thought that *Frankenstein* was really one of the great, puritanical Gothic novels. It's this great moral tale: "Don't fool around with God's work". This film, too, has that. This creature, Edward Scissorhands, has been created by the old man out of love. And love can be frustrating, when it's not complete' (Woods, 2002: 61).

In the scene of the Inventor's death, Price's character gives Edward a pair of new hands for Christmas, and for the next few moments all the attention of the audience is on the boy as he is touching and admiring the gift. Suddenly, the sharp blades that Edward has for hands pierce the soft material of the gift and cut the rubber limbs into pieces. The Inventor, who was holding them and handing them over to Edward, loses consciousness and collapses. The Frankenstein archetype presupposes that the creative force, which originally gave life to the protagonist, should eventually disappear, leaving him to survive in the open plains of society. The natural death of the paternal figure is a clever theological trick which allowed the film's authors to shift the injustice that befalls the male protagonist from 'the father' to the community.

Jung writes regarding the split between the 'good' and the 'evil' side of God: '. . . the Christian definition of God as the *summum bonum* excludes the Evil one right from the start, despite the fact that in the Old Testament he was still one of the "sons of God". Hence the devil remained outside of the Trinity as the "ape of God" and in opposition to it. [. . .] the real devil first appears as the adversary of Christ, and with him we gaze for the first time into the luminous realm of divinity on the one hand and into the abyss of hell on the other' (Jung, CW 11, paras: 243–285). Having been dislodged from the Inventor's portrait, 'the evil' mostly ends up in 'the crowd'. In this sense, the theology of *Edward Scissorhands* is closer to the Christian doctrine of the Trinity plus the devil than to the dualism of the Gnostic systems. In other words, God (Vincent Price's character) and his 'son' (Edward) remain positive characters save for the Gothic background, while the community members display all kind of negative traits and behaviours.

Collectively, they represent the seven deadly sins, and are a brilliant example of Burton's traditionally simplistic, plastic fairy-tale moralising. The oversexed Joyce (played by Kathy Baker) represents the sin of lust while Edward's arch-rival Jim is greedy and proud. The neighbours, with their vials of ambrosia salad, plates of hors d'oeuvre, barbecued meats, coleslaw, cookies and jugs of fresh lemonade are the picture of gluttony and sloth. At the same time, they are not entirely 'bad'. They can be kind (the Boggs family certainly are), welcoming (they give a party in Edward's honour), helpful (the neighbours do their best to help him get integrated into his new community) and emphatic ('Don't let anyone call you a handicap,' an ex-soldier tells Edward at the party). In other words, the neighbours are simply human.

Interestingly enough, 'Christmas', in the film's narrative, is the defining temporal point. It marks the most significant events in Edward's life: the gift of hands and subsequent death of the Inventor, and the final conflict with the villagers (and the killing of Jim). Within the framework of *Edward Scissorhands*, Christmas symbolises death and conflict, and not, as is the tradition, birth and peace. Or, rather, it symbolises the birth of the new man; a new personality, plagued by pain and suffering.

In fact, Christmas is one of Burton's most loved and used narrative backgrounds. It will come back in *Batman Returns* and *The Nightmare Before Christmas*. *Batman Returns* portrays the holy holiday as a time not of familial unity, but of abandonment, ugliness and rage; this time of year is especially hateful for the orphaned monster, the Penguin. In *The Nightmare Before Christmas*, all the monsters and social rejects are relegated to their own 'town of Halloween' where they can cultivate and enjoy their 'alternative culture'. Burton explains how he has always perceived American holidays as sets of visually striking rituals, summoned to bestow onto the bland suburbia an impression of busyness and life (Salisbury, 2000: 124). Put simply, they are summoned to give a sense of rootedness, meaning-fulness, organisation and unity to a bunch of ordinary humans.

Burton, however, is keen to emphasise the dark side of community. According to Burton's theology, it is society itself that harbours the 'devil', and then projects its fears and anxieties onto those who are 'different'. In the film's theological structure, Edward represents a kind of Gothic Jesus who is sent to redeem the sins of the crowd, but is eventually betrayed by everyone whom he considered to be his friend. 'The devil' actually appears 'in person' in the film – in one scene towards the finale when the hyper-religious woman aptly named Esmeralda gets a 'present' from the 'anti-christ' Edward Scissorhands. Esmeralda is playing her religious hymns when she hears a strange rasping sound outside. She comes to the window and opens the curtains only to find a topiary, in the shape of a glowing Satan's head, staring at her. 'The stinking hell', of which Esmeralda is so terrified, can be found right here, in the midst of this small town. The town is hell personified because its atmosphere is stifling for anyone who dares to be different.

Back to the 'hands' metonymy

'Hands' in the film symbolise both creative flame and imperfection, and in this sense it is a very dialectical image. A profound symbol, it stands at the crossroads of metonymy and metaphor. In a way, Edward *is* hands, and little more, because his entire life is shaped and determined by his disability.

Visually, hands appear as a series of rhythmic synecdochies – similar to *Batman*'s obsession with faces and smiles. Images of hands are abundant in *Edward Scissorhands*. Hands, Burton implies, come in all colours, shapes and sizes. The seductress Joyce, a sort of lonely Circe of the suburbs, has long manicured nails which are painted pale orange. There are several close-ups of her hands in which they look just as dangerous and Gothic as Edward's scissors. Esmeralda the religious one rubs her hands together in a clumsy, uncanny manner when she is angry, or makes weird gestures when she is lost for words. There are plastic hands given to Edward by the Inventor as a Christmas present, topiaries in the shape of hands, a small metallic 'hand' bookmark hanging from a row of books in the Inventor's study, Vincent Price's kindly hands and Kim's bleeding hand when she is accidentally cut by Edward. In some shots it is the hands, and not the whole person or a person's face, that are the first to appear. When Edward enters the seemingly empty house while everyone has gone to search for him, Kim enters the room and greets him by touching his shoulder. Her hand appears first in the frame, followed by the rest of her body.

Speaking about the image of the wounded puer in mythology, James Hillman (1977) establishes a direct link between the symbol of maimed hands and the puer's creative imagination. The hands, he writes, 'may be clever and manipulative, but there is difficulty at hanging-in or hanging-on to the *matter at hand* so that it can be resolved. Knots are sliced open with a brilliant stroke, rather than carefully sorted out strand by strand' (Hillman, 1987: 104). This is certainly true of Edward. Psychologically, Edward represents a 'wounded' artistic personality whose detachment from real life means that he cannot perform basic everyday tasks without other people's help. He cuts threads, slices meat and chops cabbage for Peg but cannot hold a pea at the tip of his blade-finger. He is not capable of careful consideration and small steps; everything he does is loud and sloppy – and crudely brilliant. His sloppiness, however, is self-harming. It is as if his blades are turned inside – he persistently cuts himself and his face is covered in scars and scratches.

The unbearable pain, Hillman argues, generates the fantasy of being repaired:

> The inabilities of the hands are sometimes repaired in dreams by surgical operations. A slug-like worm is pulled out of the metacarpus of a woman who feels herself slow at grasping ideas. A surgeon operates painstakingly, seemingly for hours, at the base of a young man's right fingers, as if the careful slowness is the operation itself, giving a base to the patient's deft but fluttery finger that drop everything too soon. A young potter's hand is cut open down to the bone. He is horrified and fascinated by the sight. The dreamer can now see that his hand which forms is itself formed by deep, hard, ancient structures and that the shapes he makes have a preformed interior pattern. The dream has released an archetypal sense of what he is doing.
>
> (1987: 104)

Edward's surgical operation, as we know, did not happen due to the doctor's untimely departure. Unfinished, he cannot hold the gift bestowed on him; or, as Hillman puts it, 'the talent placed in my hands does not necessarily become mine. To seize the talent may realise it, but it also may make the talent vanish' (1987: 105). With the executive (spiritual) function of the hands wounded, the imaginative function cannot control itself, and eventually fails to attain the desired perfection: 'The man whose life-style follows the puer and lives from the spirit shows wounded hands when he cannot handle gifts or manage that spirit which comes and goes of its own accord. His handicap reminds him of his limits, keeping him to the fingers of fantasy rather than the fist of control' (Hillman, 1987: 105).

The Bible, too, links the symbol of hands with the idea of perfect creation. The phrase 'made without hands' consistently reappears throughout the New Testament, and means 'made by God'. For instance, Mark 14:58 says: 'We heard him say, I will destroy this temple that is made with hands, and within three days I will build another made without hands' (King James version). In Corinthians 5:1, we encounter: 'For we know that if our earthly house of this tabernacle were dissolved, we have a building of God, an house not made with hands, eternal in the heavens' (King James version). Colossians 2:11 mentions a circumcision performed without hands, meaning that the operation was performed by the divine power (King James version).

Edward, who is born neither with fleshy hands, nor with the divine prerogative which would allow him to make things without physically touching them, occupies a clumsy, and painful, in-between position. The real tragedy of any artist is the desire for, but inability to, reach perfection. In fact, the whole film is crammed with imperfection. Edward's tree-sculpting and hairdressing style is wonderfully grotesque rather than polished (like Burton's cinematic style). Everything in the pastel suburbia is flawed or faulty: each neighbour is imperfect in his or her own way, Edward himself is 'unfinished', and even the Inventor is not an ideal person because, by having a heart attack, he undermines his status as an omnipotent, magnificent god. He 'betrays' his creation, if only in the most exceptional of circumstances. Although he does not abandon his child on purpose, like Victor Frankenstein, the end result is rather similar: the abandoned 'monster' who is unprepared to meet the world face to face becomes bitter, disillusioned, and eventually becomes a figure of hate in his community. The only character who is close to perfection is Peg Boggs but, by Burton's own admission (he says it in his audio commentary to the film), she is the 'suburban angel' of his own invention. Whereas all the other neighbours are more or less drawn from the real people he used to know, Peg's psychological layout is entirely fictional. In other words, she is less real than the unbelievable Edward himself.

The idea of 'imperfect humanity' permeates the film's narrative structure: 'the villagers' in *Edward Scissorhands* are as human and unhappy as Edward himself, their hand movements as erratic, lives as directionless, and dreams as unrealised. However, while the suburbanites are little concerned about the blandness of their lifestyle and are not planning to change their lives, Edward is not prepared to join them in their ever boring everyday activities. To that I can only add Hillman's remark that the puer, in a rather tricksterish way, does not want perfection and is characterised by 'an unfulfilled failing combined with a longing for the wider shores of further comprehension' (1987: 100).

Within the film's world, hands are more eloquent than a human face, with its limitless expressive possibilities, can ever be. In fact, Edward's face is so rigid and mask-like that it certainly cannot express the complex emotional tumult that goes on inside him. His hands, however, mirror his externally invisible emotions; the blades tremble, they move, they bristle, they create, they pierce and kill. Edward's blades, like Boris Karloff's large working-class hands, have to compensate for the 'monster's' autistic inability to read and express emotions. Such abundant use of visual synecdoche, which foregrounds a particular part of the human body, draws attention to the semiosis of *action* and *making*, but drains power from 'the mouth' – language, speech, socialisation, extroversion.

The hands take centre stage not only because language fails this particular 'monster'. Human language, according to Burton, *does not exist* as a reliable, unified means of expression. In this, he sides with a whole line of debasers of the rational approach to linguistics and human expression, from

Ferdinand de Saussure (the duplicity of the sign) and Claude Lévi-Strauss (the cultural origins of the signifier) to Jacque Derrida's *difference*. Edward, like his inventor Tim Burton, understands that 'humanness is socio-culturally variable' (Berger and Luckmann, 1967: 48). He can transcend the artificial surface of 'everyday life' with the help of his unusual abilities, his emotions hyperbolically projected onto various dark images: the castle, a symbol of Flaubertian creative puritanism and artistic loneliness; the blades, an emblem of the danger and beauty of talent; and the hands, symbolising fallibility, humanity, and via the 'communication' metonymy, unitedness with one's community, the desire to join in, to be a part of society. To quote from Hillman again, 'damage to the hand discloses the fate of one who is purely and only puer: life as broken gesture, unachieved, a fragment that points beyond itself. At the same time, this damage offers the very possi- bility for moving from this fate into a human world where handicaps give soul' (1987: 109). Edward, as we remember, prefers to keep his blades sharp and his tragedy alive.

Edward Scissorhands foregrounds one of the central issues of modernity: should the individual choose isolated independence over the stifling atmosphere of communal paradise? In the first instance, the hands are damaged (Edward piercing his rubber prosthesis) because the inventor is dead. As a result, the blades (speaking metonymically) 'cannot hold, grasp the tools, comprehend the problems, seize the issues. Then, puer conscious- ness complains that it cannot "manage"' (Hillman, 1987: 104). But, as 'human existence is wounded from beginning to end' (1987: 111), who is more to blame for the individual's wretched condition: the disappeared God, or the brooding, easily swayed crowd?

'At last, my arm is complete again'

Batman Returns (1992) and *Sweeney Todd* (2007)

When God's place is vacant, there is always danger that some unscrupulous individual will want to take his place and 'wield the mace'. While Edward is simply disappointed and disillusioned with life and society, Burton's two other characters – the Penguin and Benjamin Barker/Sweeney Todd – are desperately, tragically angry. So angry, in fact, that murdering people in batches seems to them the only possible way to act.

Batman Returns (1992) and *Sweeney Todd: The Demon Barber of Fleet Street* (2007) are 'dark' and pessimistic even by Tim Burton's standards. The *Batman* sequel received some bad press because, as often happens to Burton, the critics and public once again confused his fairy tale-like cinematic style with an innocent outlook. McDonald's, which had a promotional link to the film, announced it would not encourage people to see it (Woods, 2002: 80). Although it made a good profit, the general mood was that the movie did not live up to the audience's expectations – or rather, went beyond them as far as the Gothic atmosphere is concerned. Interestingly enough, *Sweeney Todd* was a highly successful film, both in terms of critical response and financial gain. Perhaps, this time Burton delivered the exact product the public expected, so there was no way for the 'wrong' people to watch it accidentally.

Despite being so different in disposition, appearance and background, there is one character trait that unites the Penguin and Benjamin Barker – their existentialist emptiness, a kind of 'no-return, no-regret' attitude towards the outside world. On the 'wounded monster' scale they undoubtedly score maximum points. Again, the 'theme of absent God' is central to their misery, and determines their gloomy outlook on life in general. Both the Penguin and Sweeney want to know why life has been unfair to them. Having found no benevolent God in the sky, they altogether arrive at the decision to start destroying society because, ultimately, the masses are breeding grounds for the collective evil.

In a way, Benjamin Barker/Sweeney Todd takes up where Edward Scissorhands left off 30 years ago, and his weapon, his blade, is a valid extension of Edward's scissors. We leave the punk boy at the moment of his final and deliberate withdrawal into the ivory tower of his dreams. This escapist move into an idealised, infantile world is dictated by his bitter disillusionment with 'the way life is'. Benjamin Barker (as he was known before the birth of his terrible *doppelgänger*) enters an entirely new phase: his disappointment becomes a fully fledged rage, and instead of disengaging himself from reality altogether, he starts to turn it into a nightmare.

Barker was unfairly treated, and his life was ruined when the corrupt judge Turpin took a fancy to his beautiful wife. Having lost his wife and daughter to the wily judge, and wasted the best years of his life in a penal colony, he is, as he confesses to his young friend aptly named Anthony Hope, 'a man with no hope in his heart'. His change of name marks the transition from the human being to a murderous, God-wrestling rebel. He seems to think that, by donning the mask of the monster, he will perfectly mirror the horrors of his society.

Edward's knives and scissors are a natural extension of his body, and his hurting other people is not deliberate until the very end of the film, when he stabs Jim. Conversely, Sweeney Todd holds his professional instrument firmly but his hand is, nevertheless, human. He is a 'bloody artist'. Following the film's allegorical logic, art becomes crude and brutal not because it can't act otherwise, but because it is the artist's decision to transform it into a bloody, senseless affair. An artist can claim that his creations are simply true reflections of the nightmarish, unfair or grubby outside world. Isn't this what contemporary installation artists such as Tracy Emin and Damien Hirst are also trying to convey to their audience?

The Penguin is yet another outgrowth of the disillusioned boy with scissors. As Ken Hanke notes, '*Batman Returns* is far more closely related to *Edward Scissorhands* than to its source film' (Woods, 2002: 94). The man who looks and feels like a freak, and deliberately emphasises his ugliness, is an amazingly precise allegory of an anxious adult who did not receive much love from his parents. Scissors metamorphose into flippers, real talent becomes a devilish Hitleresque charisma (or rather, the dark infantile charisma of Hoffman's little Zaches[4]), and the protagonist becomes the antagonist. The poor boy's romantic loneliness boils down to rage – crowd-gathering, and crowd-infecting rage.

Of all Burton's antagonists, the Penguin is the most poignant, and most hurt. Burton made a good choice in making the villain less mysterious and 'distant' than Nicholson's Joker, and paying plenty of attention to the relevant retrospective events, as well as to the narrative moments dealing with Oswald's identity problem: birth and parental rejection, abandonment in the sewer, visit to the parents' grave, genealogical search, the bizarre underworld full of penguins, clowns and carousel umbrellas. The Penguin is a more aggressively regressive Edward, an Edward who 'wants his toy back', an Edward who will butcher the world for the sins committed by his parents. The little plastic bird that was attached to the Penguin's crib when he was ditched into the sewer grows into a giant plastic duck which he uses as a riding vehicle. Oswald Cobblepot's make-up, his mask, his toys are all allegorical, hyperbolical, grotesque, hysterical offshoots of his childhood complexes. 'You are just jealous because I'm a real freak, and you have to wear a mask,' he says to Batman.

A number of Christian parallels help to inscribe Oswald's story into Burton's usual Frankenstein scheme: the story takes place at Christmas; Oswald orders the destruction of all first-born male children in Gotham city; the baby is abandoned in a basket, which is a reference to the legend of Moses, etc. The Penguin's fight with Gotham City is, in fact, his battle with the (absent) creator. Coincidentally, it is also Batman's battle with God – and with himself. The three of them, Oswald Cobblepot, Bruce Wayne and the celestial parent (or the personal parents) turn Gotham city into a kind of 'nightmare before Christmas'.

Behind their mask, Burton's Frankensteinesque monsters are both vulnerable and bitterly resentful. When their attempt to tune in with 'common people' fails, they resort to violence and bloodshed. Themselves angry children, they go out and start murdering adults. They crave popularity and human contact, but are unable to establish it. Their desire to be loved takes truly monstrous proportions. The freaks are doomed, and Burton's message is that the main reason for their unhappiness is the parents' imperfection.

---

4 E.T.A Hoffmann, *Little Zaches called Zinnober*, 1819.

Or, as the original Monster put it, 'All men hate the wretched; how, then, must I be hated, who am miserable beyond all living things! Yet you, my creator, detest and spurn me, thy creature, to whom thou art bound by ties only dissoluble by the annihilation of one of us' (Shelley, 1999: 77–78).

Chapter 3

The superhero

Why should a man dressed up in a leather costume with a built-in six-pack, and wearing a black mask with bat ears, be implicitly considered as brave, sexy and magnificent? Behind the superficially grandiose narrative of this contemporary streak of American mythology lies the ironic truth: a guy in a tight-fitting leotard (black, red or any other colour), which shows off his male bulge, not only looks funny – he looks hilariously gross. And, in a way, also tragic – because anyone choosing this kind of attire, *and* taking it seriously, is clearly out of his mind.

Well, this kind of synthetic, pretentious, self-erasing hyperbole is very much to Tim Burton's liking. Of course, he is under no delusion and can see the image's internal contradiction, and the irony, very well. In fact, the 'sad geek', 'billy no-mates' tinge of contemporary superheroes is what attracts him most to them. For Burton, it is all about the tension, the incongruence, between an inner feeling and the outer reality: 'What's great about [the costume] is it's the visual representation of the internal side of people. That's what I love. People putting on sheets or a bat costume to have some effect. It's a boldly sad statement. It's like a pathetic, last ditch attempt before death. This is it, in a way' (Fraga, 2005: 32).

Tim Burton's heroes, to use David Edelstein's precise definition, are 'poignantly absurd' (Fraga, 2005: 32). The hero myth is the natural extension of the child archetype, and is therefore likely to include various regressive elements such as fear of growing up, fear of relationships, enthusiasm for fancy costumes, and aversion to socialising. And while the task of a classic hero myth (Gilgamesh, Jason, Beowulf) is to show how to overcome all these issues, and become a valuable member of one's community, Burton's mythology is aimed at preserving the hero in his infantile state for as long as possible. Following Burton's logic, adult masculinity is a sham, while regression, on the contrary, is precious.

What for Joseph Campbell was the hero-myth, Carl Gustav Jung preferred to call 'the individuation process'. He regarded individuation as 'coming to selfhood' or 'self-realisation', as the process of becoming 'an individual' (CW7: para. 266). Fairy tales have the potential to clarify personal psychology, providing it with a shape and a sense of direction. An ordinary decision, such as leaving your parents' house and finding your own place, or getting married, when projected onto a myth, can be transformed into a heroic fit of extraordinary proportions. Once this happens, everything metamorphoses grotesquely. A middle-aged mother becomes a dragon, a neighbour turns into a guardian angel, failure to fit into a community amounts to the sufferings of Christ, and a visit to a prostitute transforms into a descent into hell. Personal events get encoded into symbolic units. In his essay 'On The Relation of Analytical Psychology to Poetic Art' Jung wrote about the magical appeal of art and projective capacities:

> In each of these images there is a little piece of human psychology and human fate, a remnant of the joys and sorrows that have been repeated countless times in our ancestral history, and on the average follow ever the same course. [. . .]
>
> The moment when this mythological situation reappears is always characterised by a peculiar emotional intensity; it is as though chords in us were struck that had never sounded before, or as though forces whose existence we never suspected were unloosed. What makes us struggle for adaptation so laboriously is the fact that we have constantly to be dealing with individual and atypical situations. So it is not surprising that when an archetypal situation occurs we suddenly feel an extraordinary sense of release, as though transported, or caught up by an overwhelming power. At such moments we are no longer individuals but the race; the voice of all mankind resounds in us. The individual cannot use his powers to the full unless he is aided by one of those collective representations we call ideals, which releases all the hidden forces of instinct that are inaccessible to his conscious will.
>
> (Jung, CW15: paras. 127–130

Hero myth has traditionally been one of the biggest projection-magnets. Contemporary epic mythology – such as *Superman*, *Batman*, *The Lord of the Rings*, *Star Wars* or *Harry Potter* helps readers and viewers (predominantly male) inscribe their scattered personal experiences into a meaningful, well-organised framework. They create an alternative space where one can store one's fantasies, desires and aspirations; realign one's values, ideas and views. The viewer's personal development acquires a handy set of signposts which suddenly make his or her own everyday experiences look and feel important and worthwhile.

Burton's superheroes are loosely structured and therefore have a good projection capacity. They are fallible, human and endearingly grotesque. Almost anyone can imagine himself to be a Burton superhero.

I will now discuss them one by one – in order of increasing maturity.

Infant superheroes and infantile superheroes

The World of Stainboy (2000) and Pee Wee's Big Adventure (1985)

Burton's body of work contains a number of films with embarrassingly puerile protagonists: Stainboy (*The World of Stainboy*), the demented but likeable Pee Wee from *Pee Wee's Big Adventure*, the eternally young Edward Bloom senior from *Big Fish*. These three do not even have to wear a costume, or lead a double life. The costume *is* their reality, and they are unaware of, or unwilling to accept, any other.

The little flash animation called *The World of Stainboy* (2000) is a brilliant example of a Burtonian 'regressive superhero'. A 'superman' boy who has the fault of leaving stains everywhere he goes, he works for the Burbank police department. He is a frail-looking creature with large sorrowful eyes. His special superhero adornments include a large 'S' on his chest, the compulsory cloak, and three strands of hair on his head. By the way, Stainboy's Burbank looks exactly like the dead-end suburbia in *Edward Scissorhands* – pastel, geometric and lifeless.

The protagonist's boss is a moronic sergeant named Glen Dale. Stainboy has to eliminate a whole range of monsters: Roy the toxic boy, Bowling Ball Head, the Robot Boy, the Staring Girl and the dangerous Match Girl. Each of them has his or her own 'darkness', or 'difference', which is perceived as corrupted and evil by the people of Burbank: the toxic boy eats all sorts of poison and vomits, the Robot Boy wastes electricity, while the Staring Girl's dangerous activity lies in her habit of staring at things for hours. In the end, all the monsters are successfully destroyed by the Burbank superhero. His 'killing styles', however, are far from being macho (the wounded puer can only be 'complainingly heroic', Hillman (1977: 111) argues, because his fate is beyond macho). In one case, the Stainboy produces a growing stain, which creeps up the wall and ceiling like a shadow and causes a heavy grape chandelier to fall right onto the Staring Girl's head. On another occasion, his stain ignites the Match Girl, and the vomiting Toxic Boy expires, vampire-busting style, on application of a pine tree-shaped air freshener to his forehead.

The stain, which follows Stainboy like a shadow, is the metaphor for the dark, evil side which is an integral part of every mythological superhero. It is the equivalent of Victor's monster. Stainboy, like all of Burton's characters, is an outcast – the unhappy owner of a dark side which he has to resist every minute of his life. Speaking psychologically, the shadow lives inside the protagonist, and then projects itself onto people and objects in the outer world. Being the owner of such a big internal 'stain', Stainboy belongs to the world of the miserable fiends rather than the bland shallow world of Burbank which he is supposed to protect against the forces of evil. His method of dealing with the monsters consists of projecting his own darkness onto theirs, which always proves to be successful. Like the archetypal wounded hero, he is both the carrier and the conqueror of the diabolic. In fighting the miserable fiends, he, in fact, is trying to destroy himself – or the bad, unacceptable part of the self. *Stainboy* follows the rudimentary hero myth schema.

Pee Wee Herman, the brainchild of the American comedian Paul Reubens, is a relatively more complex character. He is also a most wonderful example of infantile escapism. Burton was 26 when he was offered the chance to work on the offspring of the TV show 'Pee Wee's Playhouse': 'I remember seeing Paul's show and loving it because it really tapped into the permanent adolescence thing, and I completely connected with that. It was good for me too, because at that point in my life I really wasn't the best communicator, and it would have been a nightmare if we hadn't been so in synch' (Salisbury, 2006: 43).

The film was released in the summer of 1985 and, devastatingly for the budding director, received negative critical response. Burton reminisces that the reviews were 'not just on the fence bad, but *bad* bad' (Salisbury, 2006: 50). Despite this disconcerting experience, however, in the end he was left feeling positive because the film made money – which is not surprising because it is genuinely entertaining. Although it is, for the most part, Paul Reubens's project (Matthews and Smith, 2007: 53), it is also an unmistakably Burtonian work – in its endearing sloppiness, its concentration on the magic-visual, yet rather clumsy, effects, and its emphasis on the emotional story, rather than technical brilliance.

The camerawork, as Matthews and Smith (2007) rightfully point out, is deliberately simplistic, unobtrusive, 'defamiliarised' so as to perfectly reflect Pee Wee's uncluttered vision. It is, as Nigel Floyd puts it, a 'Pee-Wee-centered view of the world' (Matthews and Smith, 2007: 47). An oxymoronic 'grown-up child', he lives in a house full of gadgets and toys. His breakfast is assembled on a production line, which is set in motion by a burning candle, the final section of which is a life-sized doll of Abraham Lincoln. The Lincoln figure is holding a frying pan, and rather meaninglessly throws pancakes flying to the ceiling.

In fact, most of what Pee Wee does, as well as what he owns, is meaningless. He is chronically, and stubbornly, inefficient. His morning would not make much sense to an adult whose life revolves around responsibility, self-restriction and control of others: Pee Wee wakes up, spends a few minutes playing with his favourite toys (which include rabbit slippers and a cloth carrot), then descends into the kitchen down a pole, which sticks out from a hole in the bedroom floor. Most of the time in the bathroom is spent on bandaging his nose in sticky tape, and pulling faces. In the kitchen Pee Wee piles food onto his plate, only to eat a few cereal flakes crowning the pile.

Pee Wee's ambitions and dreams of grandeur also remain firmly within his puerile world. He links success to his precious bike; in fact the bike, for him, *is* success. With the help of this two-wheel talisman he dreams of winning the *Tour de France*. The winning, phallic power is displaced from the owner onto the object, leaving Pee Wee safely asexual and naïve, with the bike being the projective container of sexuality, manliness and power. The bicycle is Pee Wee's 'dream of masculinity'; his fantasy of becoming a hero. As such, it is precious.

The heroic bike, of course, is not for sale. Pee Wee refuses to enter what could be termed as 'the capitalist exchange process' with his neighbour Francis who, like his father, believes that 'everything is negotiable'. Pee Wee declines the fat boy's suggestively generous offer because his beloved object could not be sold 'for all the money in the world. Not for a hundred *million*, trillion, *billion* dollars!'. In doing this, he places the mythopoetic qualities of the object higher than the possibility of good financial gain. Again, this shows his stubborn inefficiency – at least, that is how it might look like from a middle-class adult's point of view.

The audience is never shown what Pee Wee's financial situation is, or where he gets the money for his useless 'gadget shop' purchases. The exclusion of such a practical and realist moment from the film's narrative rings psychologically true: its principal framework is a child's world, in which money appears 'as if by magic'. Like most young children, Pee Wee does not care where the money comes from.

Another area that is beyond his interest is women. When a friendly girl, Dottie, from the bike shop invites him to a drive-in cinema, Pee Wee replies with an air of self-importance: 'You don't wanna get mixed up with a guy like me. I'm a loner, Dottie. A rebel'. He does not need a woman because he has his bike (insert your own lewd joke here). The anima, at Pee Wee's level of psychological development, has not yet become a valid issue.

Suddenly, the peace in the manchild's idealistic world is broken, and he receives 'a call for adventure' (Campbell, 2008: 41). His precious bike gets stolen by the similarly demented Francis Buxton – the richest kid in the neighbourhood. Pee Wee goes on a cross-country quest to retrieve his treasure. And, after many adventures and encounters, he not only wins it back, but even has a Hollywood film made about his journey. The film ends on a self-referential note, with Pee Wee watching his on-screen ego (a James Bond-esque guy in Pee Wee's trademark suit and red bow tie) triumphing over half a dozen ninjas, and in this way impressing a glamorous 1970s-style female in a shiny blue tight-fitting suit.

The odyssey (or road movie, as this genre is properly termed[1]) is a perfect narrative canvas on which to delineate Pee Wee's maturation process. He

---

1 Notable examples of this genre include such drastically diverse cinematic specimens as *Easy Rider* (1969), *Rain Man* (1988), *Fear and Loathing in Las Vegas* (1998) and *Dumb and Dumber* (1994).

travels all across America before he can find 'himself' (and he does, literally, in the form of the handsome 'Hollywood Pee Wee'). The genre of the American road movie is traditionally characterised by a recognisable quest structure, complete with all the accompanying hero-myth elements: the treasure, the call to adventure, challenging encounters with various anima figures, meeting with the shadow, supernatural aid, etc. In *Pee Wee*, very much in line with Campbell's quest schemata, the 'actual' America is remapped as a dangerous and wonderful fairy-tale country which stretches for miles into an untamed vastness. It is the kind of magical place (akin to Alice's Wonderland) where 'anything can happen' – for there are no rules and restrictions for heroes who dare to challenge the boundaries. Its inhabitants, shown through the warped prism of Pee Wee's perception, are ghosts (Large Marge), princesses imprisoned by giants (the waitress Simone and her boyfriend), and bands of devilish ghouls (the biker community). To use Joseph Campbell's expression, the call always leads the hero into 'a place of strangely fluid and polymorphous beings, unimaginable torments, super-human deeds, and impossible delight' (Campbell, 2008: 48). Or, at least, this is how they would look to a traveller who wishes to go through the grinding mill of the quest, to experience metaphorical death and resurrection, and become a changed person. At the end of the film, the 'loner' phrase boomer-angs back to Pee Wee from his on-screen double, which means that Pee Wee is beginning, metaphorically speaking, to recognise himself in the mirror.

The final, drive-in cinema scene, clearly demonstrates the change in Pee Wee's level of maturity. A four-year-old Pee Wee is transformed into an eight-year-old. First, he is no longer scared of Dottie; after all, he finally goes with her to the cinema. Second, he attains partial socialisation. The crowd of weirdos and social outcasts attending the premiere at the drive-in – the waitress Simone with her French boyfriend, Mickey the convict, the BMX kids, the tramps – symbolise Pee Wee's partial integration into society (or at least, into its 'abnormal' section). Still, this is a far cry from the protagonist's initial position of being preoccupied exclusively with his own persona, and its idealised projection (the bike). The bike is 'alchemic-ally transmuted' into a spiritual achievement, as 'the spirit' is released from 'matter' (Jung, CW12: para. 405).

Thirdly – and importantly – Pee Wee's trip leads him to a 'grown-up' inclusion into the economy. Pee Wee was right to protect and pursue his dream because, in the end, the bike is revealed to be true gold. In the self-referential ironic finale, Pee Wee gets an introduction into the powerful Hollywood world, in which money and creativity are supposed to peace-fully coexist. The dream, the journey, and the achievement find a fantas-tically rich bidder, and are sold at a much higher price than Francis Buxton and his father could have ever offered. Pee Wee's infantile 'magic economy' enters the fantastic economy of Hollywood, where giant people possessing enormous influence manipulate colossal sums of capital.

'I am a loner, Vicki. A rebel'

Batman (1989)

Batman was Burton's first big-budget film. By the time Burton started working on the project, it had already been in preparation at Warner Bros for ten years: 'I'd just met Sam Hamm [the screenwriter] on weekends to discuss the early writing stages. We knocked it into good shape when I directed *Beetlejuice*, but as a 'go' project it was only greenlighted by Warner Bros when the opening figures for *Beetlejuice* surprised everybody – including myself!' (Fraga, 2005: 17). And while Tim Burton himself has never been a comic-book fan because of their layout (he could never tell which box he was supposed to read), Bob Kane's original creation moved him because of the character's split personality – one of Burton's favourite themes: 'It's a character I could relate to. Having those two sides, a light side and a dark one, and not being able to resolve them – that's a feeling that's not uncommon. [. . .] I mean, this whole split personality thing is so much a part of every person that it's just amazing to me that more people don't consciously understand it' (Salisbury, 2000: 72).

Burton's directorial success was precisely due to his acute understanding of the character's psychology, of what it means to be an outsider with a 'hidden life'. His Batman is not about physical strength, masculinity or animal sex appeal, for 'Why would this big, macho, Arnold Schwarze-negger-type person dress up as a bat for God's sake?' (Salisbury, 2000: 72). The casting of Michael Keaton as Batman outraged some comic-book fans. Burton, however, has always insisted that Michael Keaton was the perfect choice for the role. In Keaton's Batman one can see the psychological seams, the pretentiousness, the fakeness, the theatricality, the imperfection. He is very clearly human, and not superhuman. As the director explained in his analysis of the character: 'He's trying to create an image for himself, he's trying to become something that he's not. Therefore, every decision that we made was based on that. What's he trying to achieve? [. . .] You're trying to scare criminals, you're putting on a show, you're trying to scare and intimidate people. The idea was to humanize the character' (Salisbury, 2000: 76–78). Like Edward, Batman is a suffering 'in-between'; neither human nor superhuman.

Burton's rendition of the classic character emphasises Batman's inner fragility, mental and physical isolation, and inability to establish a meaningful contact with the very people he wishes to protect. Burton wanted the audience to understand that Batman's pointy ears are both laughable and heroic. They are a sign of weakness – but heroes, too, have the right to be weak. To quote James Hillman again, 'It might be well to relate complaining to woundedness, rather than to a search for mothering and a childish inability to take the hardship of life and "be a man". Complaint then may be regarded as part of woundedness, a first realisation of imperfection. [. . .] The invulnerable spirit becomes human just by feeling miserable' (Hillman, 1987: 111).

One can recognise in the plot of *Batman* all the central *Frankenstein* themes (and Shelley's *Frankenstein*, as we remember, signalled the birth of modern man): 'death of the father figure', urban isolation, the dangers of science and industrialisation, individualism and its shadow, etc. Bruce Wayne's battlefield is the urban space and its obligatory companions: political corruption, street crime, the power of mass media, pollution, wasteful lifestyle and overcrowding. Gotham City is the modern, and modernist, metropolis, in which isolated, fragmented and de-centered individuals catch mass psychic diseases. The city is infected, and it passes the infection on to its inhabitants. Urban diseases are connected in the film by perceivable narrative threads: criminality is linked to chemical pollution; consumerism and abundance to art and media; mass gatherings are associated with mass murder.

In his attempts to depict the crumbling core of postmodernity, Burton does the usual cyberpunk trick, and goes back to the beginning of the twentieth century, the time of the explosion of modernism in the arts in Europe and the US. *Batman*'s Gotham City has been compared to the sets of the similarly retro high-tech *Blade Runner* (directed by Ridley Scott) and Terry Gilliam's *Brazil*, as well as the father of sci-fi cities, Fritz Lang's *Metropolis* (Fraga, 2005: 23). As usual, Burton is always honest about his visual influences:

> So few great cities have been built. *Metropolis* and *Blade Runner* seem to be on the accepted spectrum. We [Burton and the production designer Anton Furst] tried to do something different although people tend to lump things in categories. We conceptualized Gotham City as the reverse of New York in its early days. Zoning and construction was thought of in terms of letting light in. So we decided to take that in the opposite direction and darken everything by building up vertically and cramming architecture together. Gotham City is basically New York caricatured with a mix of style squashed together – an island of big, tall cartoon buildings textured with extreme designs.
>
> (Fraga, 2005: 23)

What Burton and Furst built was, in fact, a shadow of New York – the reverse, problematic side of the modern metropolis. In this their creative aims are not that different from those of Lang and his expressionist colleagues. Sandwiched between the two terrible wars, the impressionist masters of chiaroscuro Robert Wiene (*The Cabinet of Dr. Caligari*), Fritz Lang (*Dr Mabuse, der Spieler; Metropolis*), Paul Wegener (*The Golem*) and Friedrich Murnau (*Nosferatu*), instead of showing the bright technological future, chose to portray the darkness descending onto urbanised humankind. Closed urban spaces endorse isolation, and promote claustro-phobia and fear of external control. A typical expressionist antagonist (Dr Mabuse, Nosferatu, Dr Caligari, Rotwang) is a maniac (inscrutable and unfocused) who takes, or seeks to take, control of the minds of unthinking citizens. Actually, *Caligari* was originally devised by writers Carl Mayer and Hans Janowitz as an allegory of political authoritarianism during the First Wold War: 'Caligari stood for the state, while Cesare represented the sleepwalking masses that had been sent by the millions to kill and to be killed' (Skal, 2001: 41). German expressionist films reflect the biggest problem of modernity – the amalgamation of personal shadows into one collective evil.

It is not surprising, then, that Tim Burton, who has always been suspicious of crowds and collectivity, borrows from the Germans both thematically and stylistically. The Gothic cathedral in *Batman* refers to modernism's indebtedness to Gothic architecture, and symbolises the sublimated, collective guilt of the city's inhabitants. The dark angularity and verticality of Gotham's architecture delineates spaces in which people are so cut off from each other, emotionally as well as physically, that their dark sides begin to merge. When this happens, they stop being individuals, and become a crowd.

In Burton's hands, the individuation of Batman the hero has at its core the problem of finding and retaining identity in the face of growing societal pressure on the one hand, and the unceasing necessity to control his instincts on the other. Christopher Hauke argues that in modern times, the tension between culture and the individual lies at the core of the hero myth:

> Individuation is about the dual struggle of the subject with, on the one hand, the 'inner world' of the unconscious, and all its infantile, personal and collective aspects, and, on the other hand, the struggle with the 'outer world' of collective society. In modern times, this latter struggle concerns the fate of the individual under the State and its levelling effects [. . .] post-modern concerns now focus on the effects of the global economy, mass media representation, and the homog-enisation of styles and values – governed by those of North America and Europe – which comprise equal, and to some extent, more hidden threats to the potential for subjects to become individual men and women.
>
> (Hauke, 2000: 169)

Bruce Wayne even loses his parents to the dark and gluttonous city-machine (cf. the capitalist M-Machine in Lang's *Metropolis*). It is only logical that Batman the urban warrior is born the minute his father is murdered by Jack Napier in a street attack. Although Jack does not kill the child, he nevertheless 'presents' Bruce with his signature phrase 'which he asks all of his prey': 'You ever dance with the devil in the pale moonlight?' The phrase becomes the burning scar which turns Bruce Wayne the ordinary person into Batman. Napier gives him a gift of painful duality, which Batman duly returns when he pushes his enemy into a vat of chemical liquid.

The 'professional shadow' Jack Nicholson created was the kind of *doppelgänger* whose powerful voice ordinary Americans hear every day – the voice of mass advertising. Within the framework of *Batman*, mass production is as an effective, but *deadly*, means of control. Advertising is one of the several collective scares which predominate in contemporary Hollywood anti-utopias, and it firmly rests among other mass-infecting urban horrors such as plastic surgery, alienation from one's body, Big Brother-style corporate control, moral vacuum and absence of truth, meaninglessness of work and leisure, etc. All of them are reflected, for instance, in Wachowski's *Matrix* series, which outlines, in urban retro-tech symbolism, the contemporary hero's struggle with the tenets of late-capitalist lifestyle, and his quest for meaning in the consuming, and consumed, world.

Plastic surgery in cinematic anti-utopias seems to possess a very special significance: it is the symbol of the ultimate betrayal of (physical and spiritual) wholeness and the sign of the final disintegration of the self (*Brazil* (1985); David Fincher's *Fight Club*, 1999). Similarly, Burton's *Batman* links plastic surgery to the Baudrillard-esque erosion of the subject, while its shadow mutates into a green mask which proceeds to replace the original facial features.

The Joker is at the core of the disintegration/surgery axis of the film: his face is destroyed by chemical waste, and he gets a new one with the help of an underground plastic surgeon. He destroys his girlfriend's iconic face (she is played by the model Jerry Hall), and then murders her altogether. He produces poisoned cosmetics, which kill two models and cause 'mysterious deaths at a beauty parlour in Gotham', and promotes it in a series of bizarre advertisements: 'New, improved Joker products with a new secret ingredient: Smilex. That luscious tan, those ruby lips, and hair colour so natural, only your undertaker knows for sure. I know what you're saying: where can I get these fine new items? That's the gag. Chances are, you bought them already!' In fact, he embodies the metonymic nature of the beauty industry, which places a lot of emphasis on the perfection of different parts of the body, but pays no attention to inner wholeness. The Joker is extremely metonymic – the smile, the face, the hands. Playing the role of an artist, he sees human beings as artistic installations, as kinds of temporary constructs, which can be created, dismantled, changed or destroyed; their parts removed or replaced. He is a mad, but creative, scientist. Like Whale's Doctor Pretorius, he wants to make monsters for the fun of it.

It is against this hegemony of metonymy in the fluid, destabilised world that Batman the hero fights. Timeless yet inescapably rooted in his own era, he challenges the fragmented and fragmenting shadow (cf. Agent Smith in the *Matrix* films) in his pursuit of being an *in-dividual* – someone who resists the metonymic division of his body and soul. While Bruce Wayne fights to keep the integrity of his personality, Batman wrestles with the external, impersonal force which makes smiling idiots out of the ordinary citizens of Gotham City.

'Touching evil brings with it the grave peril of succumbing to it', Jung wrote in *Memories, Dreams, Reflections* (Jung, 1995: 361). Psychologically speaking, Batman and the Joker are the same ('I made you, you made me first', Bruce Wayne says to his arch-enemy). Burton's remark about the 'laughability' of bat ears is, in fact, a comment on the tragic comedy of dealing with one's shadow on a day-to-day basis. When the shadow plays tricks on its 'carrier', it becomes a trickster, a clown, a performer, a man with a mask. The bat ears in this case are a sign of inner darkness, which is seeping onto the surface from inside the psyche; but it also signals that a performer is born, and is ready to entertain the audience with his stupid antics and his pretentious, idiotic costume. Conceptually, the antagonist and the protagonist complement each other: Batman is dark on the outside, whereas the Joker wears a mishmash of the maddest colours. At the same time, the Joker is internally dark, and Bruce Wayne inwardly mad. His behaviour, if not openly lunatic, is clearly odd – or at least, that is what Vicki Vale and her colleague Alexander Knox notice about him.

Vicki's profession makes her a very suitable girlfriend for a contemporary epic hero: an investigative photographer, her task is to piece together fragments of reality and make sense of them. In a way, she has her own pursuit for wholeness, in taking a series of pictures of an event, and then restoring 'the truth' behind them. As Christopher Hauke argues, in his comparative study of Jungian psychology and postmodernist theories, 'the photographic image dominates in the determination of reality for the contemporary urban psyche. So much so that images which start out as representations of reality end up as representations without any "reality" "behind" them at all' (Hauke, 2000: 46).

Vicki's method of overcoming fragmentation, alienation and extreme subjectivity is less militant than that of her potential boyfriend. She does not fight a *doppelgänger* or *doppelgängers*; instead, she stalks, she watches, she collects. Intent to learn more about the mysterious Bruce Wayne, Vicki follows him to the spot where his parents were murdered many years ago, and takes pictures of him leaving two red roses on the ground. She waits for him to leave, picks up the roses and looks at them, trying to understand what the man's gesture might mean. At home, she examines the photographs, and makes a phone call to a colleague to find out what is so special about the alley at Pearl and Philips Streets. Armed with the information that a street robbery had taken place there, which involved Bruce Wayne and his parents, she can now observe a more complete (but not *completely* complete) picture simply because she possesses a few more pieces of the puzzle. Although the 'true' picture does not exist (as it was replaced by the Baudrillardian *simulacrum*, an 'imitation of reality'), Vicki goes on a quest for it. Her determination to catch the elusive 'truth' is probably more important for her than the end result itself. For her, a wholesome goal in the meaningless world, even without the hope of ever reaching it, seems to be the only source and guarantor of inner stability.

Like Pee Wee, Bruce Wayne never grows up to be able to sustain a serious relationship. Apparently, Bruce Wayne and Vicki have two completely different quests, even though they seem to have a similar objective: to heal the split in the psyche. As Bruce explains to Catwoman in *Batman Returns*, his relationship with Vicki 'did not work' because she had difficulties reconciling his two personalities. His union with Selina Kyle does not happen, either, even though they 'are the same, split right down the centre'. In fact, Batman cannot work in tandem with any of them. Their languages are entirely different, like their masks. The 'communication breakdown' streak is entirely supported by Burton's apparent belief that 'language fails' the speaker, making it difficult for people to have any stable interpersonal connection.

The cat and her quest

Batman Returns (1992)

Jung described the process of individuation as consisting of several stages. These stages he believed appeared in a fixed order: meeting with the shadow, followed by the encounter with the contrasexual element (animus and anima), then by the archetypes of 'spirit' and 'matter' (wise old man and magna mater, or wise old woman). Only then does the individual arrive at the entrance of the uniting archetype of the self (Jacoby, 1973: 107–136).

Whether the process of personal development entails any precise order is, of course, a contentious issue which begs to be discussed and argued over. However, this order is certainly true for Burton's male heroes, for many of them (Pee Wee, Bruce Wayne, Edward Scissorhands) cannot start or sustain a relationship without first tending to the problem of the *doppelgänger/* shadow (Francis Buxton, the Joker, the Penguin, the blond Jim (*Edward Scissorhands*)).

The situation with the female superhero – Selina Kyle, aka the Catwoman (played by Michelle Pfeiffer), is entirely different. While Bruce Wayne fights off his multiplying, many-faced doubles, who are the carriers of his personal, as well as the city's, collective evil, the superwoman only sees them in an exclusively personal, and feminine, light. Selina, too, leads a confusing double life: men hurt her during the day, but when nightfall comes around, she becomes a female avenger, a demonic cat who demands satisfaction for all the wounds that careless and selfish males have inflicted on her.

Selina's dual character is a textbook Jungian *anima* (when analysed from a male point of view), who has problems with her numerous *animuses* (when regarded from the female standpoint). Jung (and, subsequently, his immediate disciples) believed the *anima* to be a two-sided image, possessing a light and a dark aspect: the 'angel' and the 'whore'.

For Jung, human beings are characterised by psychological androgyny, and every person carries in his psyche a cluster of qualities and attitudes that are more typical for people of the opposite sex. The anima is thus not simply a convenient psychological, anthropological or literary concept, but is, according to Jung, biologically predetermined. He argued that 'either sex is inhabited by the opposite sex up to a point, for, biologically speaking, it is simply the greater number of masculine genes that tip up the scales in favour of masculinity' (CW9/I: para. 58). In this way, the man carries in his psyche the anima, an ideal feminine image, while the woman has 'the animus', or even a handful of them, in her personal unconscious. Although the animus/anima is a psychological phenomenon, it has a tendency to project itself onto real men and women. The anima and the animus present a great deal of opportunity for projections and introjections, and therefore are often a cause of internal and external conflicts. Jolande Jacobi writes:

> The variety of forms in which the soul-image may appear is well-nigh inexhaustible. It is seldom unequivocal, almost always complex and ambiguous; the traits belonging to it must be typical of one or the other sex, but otherwise may embody all sorts of contradictions. The anima can equally well take the form of a sweet young maiden, a goddess, a witch, an angel, a whore, a devoted companion, an amazon, etc. Highly characteristic anima figures, for example, are Kundry in the Parsifal legend, or Andromeda in the myth of Perseus; typical anima figures in literature are Helen of Troy in the Homeric legend, Beatrice in the *Divine Comedy*, Don Quixote's Dulcinea, etc. The animus can also assume a variety of forms. Typical animus figures might be Dionysus, the Pied Piper, the Flying Dutchman, and on a lower, more primitive plane a famous star or boxing champion, or in particularly troubled times like ours [Jacobi is writing these lines in 1939], an outstanding political or military leader.
>
> (Jacobi, 1973: 116)

The positive, idealised aspect of the *anima* seemingly lacks the erotic element and can take the shape of various angelic figures – like the Virgin Mary or Dante's Beatrice, for example. The negative anima, as described by Marie-Louise von Franz, may look like 'a beautiful creature who has weapons hidden in her body or a secret poison with which she kills her lovers during their first night together'. In this guise 'the anima is as cold and reckless as certain uncanny aspects of nature itself, and in Europe is often expressed to this day by the belief in witches' (Jung and von Franz, 1964: 190).

The character of Catwoman is supposed to represent the duality of Batman's *anima*, and his inability to resolve the cluster of problems with his inner feminine. Von Franz explains that the only way to deal with the *anima* and its projections, is to recognise it as an inner power: 'The secret aim of the unconscious in bringing about such an entanglement is to force a man to develop and to bring his *own* being to maturity by integrating more of his unconscious personality and bringing it into real life' (1964: 191). Maturity, however, is the worst thing that can happen to Bruce Wayne – that would truly be the end of his career as a hero. This does not mean that he does not try. At the splendid climax of *Batman Returns* (the scene in which the Catwoman burns Max Schreck with a kiss and a power cable), Bruce does his best to prove to Selina that it is time for both of them to grow up: '. . . don't you see, we're the same, we're the same, split right down the centre.'

His appeal for maturity famously falls on deaf ears. Selina the meek secretary ('executive assistant') is not prepared to shed her brilliant, and dangerous, alter ego, because every man is a potential aggressor and she has to be vigilant. She trusts no one, not even a fellow superhero, who can understand her drama-queenly passion for dressing up in a weird, shiny, too-tight, clingy, potentially pornographic costume. If we dissolve the allegory, all we get is the psychologically believable situation when two people are not ready for a relationship. That is why it does not exactly come off in either of the film's narrative planes: the 'real life', or in the eroticised, sado-maso-fantasy-world in which a sexual act is more about torture, and less about love.

The fact that Selina is surrounded by many hostile men seems to be in line with Jung's theory about the multiple character of the *animus* arche-type. He believed that the woman was characterised by an inclination towards a polygamous trait in her soul-image, and, consequently, the female psyche was inhabited by various inner males, both 'good' and 'bad', who invariably offered their bearer a variety of contradictory opinions. This motley chorus of '*animuses*', according to Jacobi, would often take the form of 'uncritically accepted opinions, prejudices, principles, which make women argue and bicker' (Jacobi, 1973: 121). Although the last statement should be regarded as a manifestation of Jung's own sexism (partially explainable by the historical context in which he lived and worked), it satisfactorily explains Catwoman's pleiad of aggressive 'animuses' – Max Schreck, the Penguin, Batman, all of whom wear a mask but none of whom, with or without his costume on, is suitable for cohabitation.

According to the movie's plot, Selina Kyle lives alone because, being shy and intelligent, she cannot find an appropriate partner. As the film progresses, it becomes clear that, in fact, she lives with a number of 'internal' people; her male and female sub-personalities. While she herself is split into two – the 'Angel' and the 'Whore' – her perception of men (Jungian *animus*) is so fragmented that she fights hard to keep the picture together. And the picture is indeed very complex: none of her numerous men match any of her two women. Selina's fall from the skyscraper (when Max attempts to murder her), and subsequent magical rehabilitation, is a good metaphor for her splintered psyche. A female equivalent of Edward Scissorhands – this is also noted by Ken Hanke (Woods, 2002: 94) – she is broken and rebuilt, killed and resurrected, to become a contemporary warrior. She is one of those 'more proactive' Burton characters (Batman, Sweeney Todd) that pick up Edward's unfinished quest.

Her quest for wholeness takes place 'in the darkness' of the metropolis. Unfortunately, the ultimate symbolic 'union' of the opposites – that of a man and a woman – does not take place because in the world of multiple identities, communication barriers, excessive information and fluid realities such a union is not easy to achieve.

Diving into the depths of oneself

Big Fish (2003)

In the introduction to his philosophico-biographical book, *Catching the Big Fish* (2006), David Lynch poetically meditates:

> Ideas are like fish.
>
> If you want to catch little fish, you can stay in the shallow water. But if you want to catch the big fish, you've got to go deeper.
>
> Deep down, the fish are more powerful and more pure. They're huge and abstract. And they're very beautiful.
>
> I look for a certain kind of fish that is very important to me, one that can translate to cinema. But there are all kinds of fish swimming down there. There are fish for business, fish for sports. There are fish for everything.
>
> Everything, anything that is a thing, comes up from the deepest level. Modern physics calls this level the Unified Field. The more your consciousness – your awareness – is expanded, the deeper you go toward this source, and the bigger the fish you can catch.
>
> (Lynch, 2006: 1)

The 'fish' anaphora (and simile!) is gently amplified by Lynch to outline how creative ideas emerge, grow, merge, transform, disappear and reappear

– but also how the film industry harvests and cooks them, for the viewers to enjoy. And of course, the fish caught in shallow waters are not going to be as 'huge and abstract' as the ones that live in the depths.

Back in 2003 Tim Burton caught the kind of fish for which he did not usually go. Compared to *Edward Scissorhands* or the *Batman* series, *Big Fish* untypically lacks a pervasive Gothic flavour. However, the resulting film can be regarded, both stylistically and thematically, an unmistakably Burtonian creation since it invariably discusses double identity, the death of a father figure, refusal to fit into the community, and the hero's quest for professional realisation and spiritual wholeness.

Big Fish has three narrators and focalisers, and therefore boasts a complex narrative structure, in which three planes are closely interwoven: 'actuality', associated with grown-up Will and old Edward; then Will's flashbacks; and finally, Edward's mythologised recollections of his life. Such narrative intricacy is unusual for Burton, and can be primarily attributed to the novelist Daniel Wallace and screenwriter John August. The three subjective planes offer three views of Edward's life – but none of them gives us the 'true' version of events. Edward Bloom's life can only be amplified with the help of the fish symbol – the many-faced metaphor of aspiration, perseverance, longing and entrepreneurship.

Edward is a failed father but a good storyteller; he is creative but amazingly self-centered. Reality is too bland for him, so he prefers to describe his experiences metaphorically. His son Will stops talking to his father after an incident at Will's wedding when Edward turned the limelight onto himself by telling the guests the story of 'catching' his beautiful wife. Afterwards, Will feels that such shameless attention-seeking and showing off was not appropriate, and that his father could have refrained from talking about himself for once in his life – on the day which is actually about his son, and not him. In the story of 'catching Sarah Templeton', the enraged Will explains to Edward, the son is only the footnote, and in actuality has never been of much interest to his father. Even on the day of his birth Edward was away, selling novelty products.

When Edward is dying, his estranged son comes all the way from Paris to Alabama. Will had never trusted his father because he could never identify the boundary between fantasy and reality in his father's tales. Edward would tell his son incredible stories which formed his hero quest: growing up in a small town; meeting a local witch; stumbling upon a ghost community aptly named Spectre; working in a circus; fighting off a werewolf; winning a princess's heart by gathering all of the daffodils from five states; being sent to Korea as an American soldier; being declared dead; coming back to become a travelling salesman; receiving a cheque for $10,000 from his friend, an ex-poet from the town of Spectre, whom he had timely advised to get a job on Wall Street, etc. In order to discover his mysterious parent's true identity, Will becomes an investigator of his father's individuation: for instance, he meets his father's 'other woman', Jenny (played by Helena Bonham Carter). As the film progresses, the fog around Will gradually disperses, and real people become visible in the picture through the top level of paint. Armed with the numerous fragments of 'fantastic' and 'factual' information, Will makes an attempt to assemble them together and paint a more or less comprehensive portrait of his unusual father.

Edward Bloom, in the words of the circus owner (Danny DeVito), 'may not have much but what he's got, he's a got a lot of'. He has got a lot of heart and courage. As a boy, Edward Bloom was romantic, lively and full of ideas; he felt that the town of Ashton was not big enough for him. Quite understandably, he did not want to be attached to his small community with its routine lifestyle, and decided to go out there and seek new thrills in the vast, exciting world. He was, as he put it, trying to cure his 'giganti-ficationism'. Edward describes the hopes he has in an allegorical hyperbole: 'If goldfish are kept in a small bowl, they will remain small. With more space, the fish can double, triple or quadruple its size.'

In his aspiration to seek new experiences at the cost of a more stable lifestyle, Bloom is no different from many other Burtonian characters – Pee Wee, Bruce Wayne, Edward Scissorhands – whose narratives also fit into the framework of modernity's inevitable metropolitanism. Small com-munities may be cosy and peaceful but, as a rule, they do not offer much support for large-scale ambition, aspiration and talent. A man of modern-ity, Edward undervalues community and seeks self-realisation 'in larger ponds'.

Modernist literature (and, indeed, other art forms) thrived on the theme of the common man lost in the maze of the metropolis, alien to himself and others, unable to make a decision, doing small, insignificant things. *Big Fish* (both the film and the book) contains an important retro-modernist refer-ence – James Joyce's *Ulysses*, with its 'small and insignificant' Leopold Bloom who is compared to the legendary Odysseus, and elevated by the writer to the status of a hero of mythical proportions. As the book mirrored the splintered psyche of a modern urban man, and reflected the endless combinatorial possibilities of objects in the technologically enhanced world, Jung considered it 'schizophrenic' – but also admitted that it was no more schizophrenic and deliberately incoherent than any art of late modernity. He wrote that the book was:

> "cubistic" in the deepest sense because it resolves the picture of reality into an immensely complex painting whose dominant note is the melancholy of abstract objectivity. [. . .] The clinical picture of schizo-phrenia is a mere analogy in that the schizophrenic apparently has the same tendency to treat reality as if it were strange to him, or, con-versely, to estrange himself from reality. With the schizophrenic the

tendency usually has no recognisable purpose but is a symptom inevitably arising from the disintegration of the personality into fragmentary personalities (the autonomous complexes). In the modern artist it is not produced by any disease in the individual but is a collective manifestation of our time. The artist does not follow an individual impulse, but rather a current of collective unconscious of the modern psyche.

(CW15: para. 174)

The aptly named Ed Bloom, a small man fighting against fate for the right to become 'a bigger fish', is also a hero of almost epic stature. A creative person, a local Homer, a tale-teller, he 'estranges' himself from his community, and escapes the ordered normality of rural life in favour of new experiences. He does not want a ready-made wholeness, like that of the town of Spectre, the inhabitants of which hang up their boots because they have no ambition and do not want to go anywhere. To Edward, Spectre feels 'so strange yet so familiar' because it is a defamiliarised copy of Ashton; it is the paragon of a small, sleepy American settlement. Edward gathers his will and courage to defeat the poisonous lure of a happy, contented lifestyle, and runs away in the middle of a big village celebration. He does not want to be happy; he would rather feel pain, be challenged and become a broken hero.

And really, to pull together fragments of the world – which began to fall apart because it became so impossibly enormous – looks like a truly fabulous achievement. As the primary extended metaphor, the 'big fish' also covers Edward's identity and his quest for wholeness – not the kind of contented, easy wholeness which is given to the inhabitants of Ashton and Spectre *a priori*, but the 'good catch' available only to those who dare to go out and seek it; the treasure which the hero has to earn in the process of personal development.

Whereas Will cannot separate his father's lies from the truth, Edward himself does not want to draw a clear line between the inner perception of individuation and outer events. He prefers to tell his stories in the style of magic realism. For him, life is a beautiful, challenging quest; he translates everyday occurrences and common people into supernatural events and magical creatures. In his world, a girl-next-door turns into a fairy-tale princess, a stringent but lonely boss is transformed into a werewolf, and his own desire to get away from Ashton, and be recognised in the bigger world, metamorphoses into a tale of gigantism.

Edward leads a double life, and, as a result, everything in his world has a 'negative' reflection. For instance, an angelic wife has a 'bewitching' counterpart who lives in Spectre, and possibly harbours plans to steal Ed from his family. When Will comes to meet Jenny as part of his archaeological project to 'unearth' his father's secret life, she explains to him that, indeed, Edward always had a 'fairy tale' life 'on the side', but he never took it

seriously: 'I was make-believe and . . . his other life, you, you were real.' At
his father's funeral, Will finally gets to see all the friends and acquaintances
Edward mentioned in his unbelievable stories: Karl the Giant, Amos the
werewolf, the poet Norther Winslow, the Korean twins. Edward, it appears,
embellished 'actuality' with lies for the sake of psychological accuracy.

'To be "normal",' Jung wrote, is the ideal aim for the unsuccessful
[. . .] But for those people of more than average ability, people who never
found it difficult to gain success and to accomplish their share of the
world's work, for them the moral compulsion to be nothing but normal
signifies the bed of Procrustes – deadly and insupportable boredom, a hell
of sterility and hopelessness' (CW16: para. 161). Edward complains to his
son that 'dying is the worst thing that has ever happened to him' because,
after a life of activity, he became pretty much immobile. His tragedy is that,
being a man of more than average ability, his talents are raw and
unpolished. Despite his heroic stance and fighter spirit, Edward Bloom
eventually loses the battle against the 'cruel fate' – both on the professional
and the personal front. Trying to catch two fish at once, Edward eventually
loses both.

His striving for a new, fuller life takes him very far geographically – but
not socially. He ends up working as a travelling salesman, which means that
he is never at home, and anyway, being an attentive family man, by his own
admission, 'would be too confining'. He admits to Will that he never did
any of the 'diapers and the burping and the midnight feedings' but he heard
that it is terrible. Will, the Telemachus who grew up with his father being
constantly absent from home, is not impressed.

Will's seemingly irresolvable bitterness towards his problematic father,
pitted against his father's frantic quest for self-realisation and freedom, is a
classic, archetypal situation which has been played out in many myths and
fairy tales. In fact, Edward's translation of the individuation process into
the myth of Odysseus helps Will to understand himself, and locate his own
position in his father's life. When the son embarks on his detective venture,
he does not realise that he is about to begin a process of self-discovery –
and the discovery of his roots.

Even though Edward Bloom does not achieve his dreams personally, he
nevertheless leaves his legacy, and passes on his talent and motivation to his
son. Despite his enormous ambition, he still 'does not have a lot' underneath the courageous and bright surface. Very crudely and biologically
speaking, although Ed fails as an individual, he manages to transfer advan-
tageous traits to the next generation. Will, reluctant as he is to accept his
father's gift, has to admit that he is part of an evolution, and his journalistic
talent, in fact, is an improved version of Edward's muddled, fanciful
storytelling.

The big fish is a complex, dreamy image which, as its vehicle suggests, is
so powerful, clever and slimy that catching its exact meaning would be

impossible. As the cover metaphor and the central symbol, the fish is only perceivable in the film's narrative through the process which Jung called *amplification* – a 'process by which the dream content is broadened and enriched with the help of analogous images' (Jacobi, 1973: 84). Amplification is thus a 'directed association process which circles round the dream nucleus and so helps the analyst to put his finger on it' (Jacobi, 1973: 85).

The fish metaphor which permeates all the film's layers and sub-layers, upon a closer look falls into a myriad of fractions, each reflecting a small aspect of Edward and Will's lives. On one level, the fish of Ed's dreams is the fish of Christianity – the symbol of Jesus, suffering and self-sacrifice. 'A fisher of men', he caught such a great number of small fish that his net broke – but he never found his whale (Mark, 1:17; Luke 5: 6). There are, however, numerous other mythological and literary associations. A punished mariner, he is forced to wander the seas to atone for original sin; an Odysseus, he leaves his wife and son in search of new impressions and greater challenges. Similar to Victor Frankenstein and his ungrateful monster, Edward is struggling to explain to his son why he was constantly absent from the picture of family life. Like Joyce's Leopold Bloom, Ed is a common man who wants to break out of his dreary existence by introducing a fantasy plane into the 'reality canvas' of his everyday life, and by translating ordinary occurrences into grand-mythological individuation thresholds.

The fish of the title may symbolise a woman, an idea, a life, a career – in short, an achievement. Ed's biggest achievement, however, is his son, because he goes on to become the person his father has always wanted to be – a writer. Edward Bloom did not realise that the biggest fish of all was at home, inside his own family, and not in faraway lands, among strange people.

Never lose your head over a woman

Sleepy Hollow (1999)

Washington Irving describes the protagonist of his tale *The Legend of Sleepy Hollow* (1820) as a local bearer of the torch of knowledge in a small lethargic settlement:

> The schoolmaster is generally a man of some importance in the female circle of a rural neighbourhood; being considered a kind of idle, gentlemanlike personage, of vastly superior taste and accomplishments to the rough country swains, and, indeed, inferior in learning only to the parson. [. . .]
> From his half-itinerant life, also, he was a kind of travelling gazette, carrying the whole budget of local gossip from house to house, so that

his appearance was always greeted with satisfaction. He was, moreover, esteemed by the women as a man of great erudition, for he had read several books quite through, and was a perfect master of Cotton Mather's "History of New England Witchcraft," in which, by the way, he most firmly and potently believed.

He was, in fact, an odd mixture of small shrewdness and simple credulity. His appetite for the marvellous, and his powers of digesting it, were equally extraordinary; and both had been increased by his residence in this spell-bound region. No tale was too gross or monstrous for his capacious swallow. It was often his delight, after his school was dismissed in the afternoon, to stretch himself on the rich bed of clover bordering the little brook that whimpered by his schoolhouse, and there con over old Mather's direful tales, until the gathering dusk of evening made the printed page a mere mist before his eyes.

(Irving, 2008: 7–8)

Although he is a suitably enlightened individual, Irving's Ichabod, nevertheless, may be occasionally startled by a shrub looking like a sheeted spectre, or become scared of the sound of his own steps 'on the frosty crust beneath his feet' (Irving, 2008: 9). But the biggest scare of all is the legendary Galloping Hessian, the ghost of a trooper who had lost his head in the American Revolutionary War.

A specialist in witches, Ichabod ends up being utterly bewitched by the beautiful Katrina Van Tassel, the daughter of a wealthy farmer, Baltus Van Tassel. One night, coming back from his beloved's house, he is pursued by the terrible Horseman, and mysteriously disappears from town. Katrina marries a rival suitor, Brom Bones, who might have been the true cause of Ichabod's mysterious disappearance.

Irving's tale deals with the themes and motifs typical of international Romanticism, with its anti-Enlightenment, anti-industrialist stance. *The Legend of Sleepy Hollow* denigrates the confidence of rationality in the face of 'terrors of the night, phantoms of the mind that walk in darkness', juxtaposes the values of the city and the countryside, and laughs at the unhealthy, pseudo-intellectual, sexually frustrated city dweller.

Burton and his screenwriters entirely changed the modality of the tale: gone is Irving's Romantic sarcasm disparaging the puffed-up confidence of instrumental rationality. Burton transforms a farcical teacher into a suffering scientific hero, who, armed with Enlightenment ideas, is always ready to fight off the darkness in people's minds. Touching upon the same subjects as Irving, Burton makes *Sleepy Hollow* more transparent and the binary oppositions more visible and contrasting. Ichabod Crane is now a New York police detective who, being a great believer in scientific progress, wants to apply the newest forensic techniques and use the latest instruments in the criminal investigation process.

Sleepy Hollow has a profoundly dreamy feel to it – which is highly appropriate for a film about the murky depths of the unconscious. This visual depth was created using a number of clever techniques. Burton used forced perspective to give the film a graphic quality 'reminiscent of those Hammers' (Salisbury, 2006: 173). The colours are muted so that there is a 'binding together of the sets and locations': 'It is not sepia, it's not mono-chromatic, it's just a colour filter with a slightly muted quality' (2006: 176). He manipulates colour in order to remove the 'naturalness' of the world he is depicting. The internationally acclaimed cinematographer Emmanuel Lubezki, who worked with Burton on *Sleepy Hollow*, remembers how Burton wanted the film to possess a high degree of artificiality: 'Tim wanted the blood to be much brighter, almost artificial. So we tested various levels of colour, finding that a bright orange read right after the film was processed. This 'fantasy blood' looked very strange on the set, but worked on the screen' (www.cameraguild.com). The result is deeply expressionistic, hazy, subjective and unrealistic, which, Burton says, was the exact outcome he wanted (2006: 175).

What the makers of the film did, in fact, was to create an entirely new tale, using Irving's story as a base, but turning it into a tale of detection – which is, essentially, Poe's genre ('The Murders in the Rue Morgue', 'The Purloined Letter'). The detective story is firmly rooted in the issues of modernity, and, broadly speaking, explores the possibility of the existence of universal truth. Michael Holquist described the link between detective story as a genre on the one hand, and the predominant credo of modernity on the other: 'For just as the form of the detective story has its source in the comforting certainty that an acute "eye", private or otherwise, can solve the crime with resounding finality by inferring causal relationships between clues which point to it' (Holquist, 1971: 150, quoted in Bertens, 1997: 197). At the same time, Ichabod's detective quest is as personal as it is 'in the name of science'. As Luke Hockley writes, from the analytical psychology perspective, 'the detective is . . . on a personal search: the elements of the story operate as symbols and represent the quest for self-awareness' (Baumlin *et al.*, 2004: 78).

Ichabod's view of knowledge is comfortably optimistic and grounded in the 'well-made positivistic universe', in which facts are always accurate (Holquist, 1971: 150, quoted in Bertens, 1997: 197). He believes in the civilising influence of the city, and the rest is incurable medievalism: 'We have murders in New York without benefit of ghouls and goblins', he explains to the village authorities. For him, all homicides can be traced back to specific criminals and their intentions.

Upon his arrival at the village, the disgusted Ichabod discovers a whole range of ignorant people and uncivilised behaviours (from public sex to primitive beliefs to religious dogmatism). The village authorities prefer to stick to the Bible as their only true weapon against the terrible Horseman, and seem to be unwilling to look for a scientific explanation of the phenomenon. When he was alive, the Dutch trooper had the reputation of being invincible and ferocious in battle, and used to chop up the enemy with characteristic Viking brutality. Now his ghost wanders in the woods and murders passers-by, cutting off their heads and posting them to back to hell. Equipped with his innovative devices (which look, controversially and suspiciously, like instruments of torture), Ichabod is determined to leave no stone unturned in this grave mystery.

However, by the end of the film Ichabod Crane's expectations are debased in such a way that he can no longer subscribe to his detection theory. He discovers that the 'criminal' does not exist objectively, and the law was actually broken by 'the unconscious'. It cannot be 'caught' or 'brought to trial', even if one summons all the capacities of human reason to accomplish such a heroic feat. The hero, if not defeated, will at best be left in a state of confusion and powerlessness. Any victory against the unconscious is always relative and partial because, as Jung argued, 'rationalism and superstition are complementary . . . the more rationalistic we are in our conscious minds, the more alive becomes the spectral world of the unconscious' (CW18: para. 759).

In fact, Burton's *Sleepy Hollow* is to Washington Irving's short story what *Edward Scissorhands* is to Mary Shelley's *Frankenstein*. Walker and Burton's Ichabod embodies the controversy that has surrounded the development of science in modernity: although he is prepared to dispel the cloudy enigmas of nature with the ray of rationality, he himself does not admit that the brutality and crudity of his methods match the savagery of nature. To emphasise the dialectical nature of his beliefs, he is given a set of features suitable for a 'Messiah of Modernity': stigmata, a religiously fanatical father, a metropolitan background, radical mistrust of the unconscious, and the desire to examine and explain everything.

Ichabod's parental background is very relevant to his progressive tendencies and the pursuit of truth. The detective's father, who had always 'hid behind the mask of righteousness', murders his wife (played by Burton's then-girlfriend Lisa Marie) inside a Nuremberg iron maiden, a medieval torture cabinet with spikes on the inside.[2] When the elder Crane suspects her of witchcraft, he locks her inside the iron coffin, with his son witnessing the terrible deed. Ichabod is persistently haunted by nightmares about the murder (narratively presented in the film as flashbacks).

Like his father, Ichabod is a patriarchal fighter with the 'feminine', the unconscious darkness, even though his methods are now far more progressive. A man of early modernity, he is an improvement on his father;

---

2 The 'iron maiden' moment, by Burton's own admission, was a tribute to Barbara Steele's witch character in Mario Bava's *Black Sunday* (1960).

his profession, behaviour and mentality promote what Christopher Hauke describes as 'the movement from the medieval world order to Enlightenment values' (Hauke, 2000: 32). This fundamental shift is characterised by 'the progressive crossing out of God and an accelerating emphasis on instrumental rationality: that is, reasoning aimed not at metaphysical speculation ('How many angels can you get to dance on the end of a pin?' 'Why was Christ not born as a pea?'), but reasoning aimed at the unmasking and control of nature for human purposes and, inevitably, for financial reward' (2000: 32). Ichabod Crane 'crosses out' his father, not noticing the continuity between himself and his parent, and thinking that he is actually starting an entirely new era.

Both the 'outdated' form of universal rationality, religion, and its new incarnation, science, are patriarchal, rationalising forces, aimed at subduing and suppressing the instinctual, animalistic side of human nature – and indeed, nature in general. Ichabod's sharp instruments penetrate human bodies, desecrating the divine temple of nature. In becoming a scientist, Ichabod negates his parents, and the values for which they symbolically stand: ruthless fundamentalist righteousness and treacherously pliant femininity.

The idea of 'penetration' permeates all levels of the film; it is present both narratively and visually. In a way, it is an expansion of the 'hands as blades' metaphor of *Edward Scissorhands*. In *Sleepy Hollow*, the act of penetration takes a variety of forms, depending on the type of masculinity that performs it. The Hessian mercenary, who represents outdated medievality, is a ruthless and brainless animal who chops people up just because he derives sadistic pleasure from the process. The elder Crane embodies sterile remorselessness of religion as he uses sharp objects to torture his 'unclean' wife. Ichabod's penetration has a higher purpose: it is all in the name of science. Like Victor Frankenstein, he cuts people open in order to gain 'an astonishing power' and learn about the 'bounds of life and death' (Shelley, 1999: 42–43). Throughout the film, Burton keeps foregrounding and metonymising Ichabod's technological inventions because they are extensions of his hands. Once again, using a slightly different set of images, but executing them in comparable expressionistic and impressionistic fashion, Burton brings together the ideas of sharp individualism, intense isolation, detachment from community, urbanism, cutting-edge science and the dangers of rationality.

Ichabod seems to believe that the human brain is as cold and objective an instrument as his knives. However, contrary to his inner resoluteness, on the outside he looks very shy and innocent. Burton admits that Ichabod Crane is not your typical action hero: '. . . even though we changed the Ichabod character from the original story, there was a certain spirit of this sort of prissy, wimpy guy. He lives in his head but then he's forced to open up and become physical, not because he wants to, but because he has to' (Salisbury, 2006: 177). All these years of thinking and analysing drained him of masculinity, and he lost touch with his 'animal' side. His uncontrollable 'femininity' can also be interpreted as a sign of dependence on the mother, and rebellion against the father. This fragile representative of the intelligentsia stands in complete contrast to both his arch-enemies: the Horseman and the brash, Viking-like Brom Van Brunt (Casper Van Dien).

We are back to Hillman's 'complaining' hero who is bleeding and whose body is 'broken through' (Hillman, 1987: 111). The effeminising of Ichabod's character rings true if we take into consideration that he, with the stigmata scars on his palms, and his painful attempts to reconcile the opposites both inside and outside himself, is another Burtonian Christ figure. Hillman argues that bleeding (and bleeding hands!) expresses the outpouring dynamics of the puer: 'We see it as an inflation and enthusiasm. The vitality of the puer spreads and stains like the red tincture of the alchemist's *lapis*. His bleeding is a *multiplicatio*, the infectious giving out of essence for the sake of transforming the world around. The archetypal structure of the puer insists on gushing forth, hyperactive, charismatic, sacrificial' (1987: 111). Ichabod's superhuman power – or at least, this is how he perceives his scientific abilities, 'emanates through the open wound and through being wounded' (cf. Batman's 'split right down the centre', 1987: 111).

Ichabod's energy is generated by an inner conflict. Having imbibed the conflict from his parents' hateful relationship, he will continue exploring it throughout his adult life, either in everyday life or in his persistent nightmares. One can see why the contemporary audience can embrace such an 'intensely human' character which provides endless possibilities for introjection.

The 'wimpy' hero with 'too much head', and the character with no head at all, indeed, constitute a classic archetypal pair. Ichabod's instrumental rationality goes head to head with the Horseman, representing the protagonist's fear of the unconscious, his fear of 'losing control' – primarily over himself. In this, the film directly echoes the Romantic idea of the invincibility and mystery of nature (along with all other exemplifications of the 'female' binary opposition) in the face of scientific progress.

'The unconscious' takes various shapes in the film, and is firmly tied to the notion of unmanageable instinctiveness. The mad Hessian, the dead mother, the attractive and playful daughter of Baltus Van Tassel all persistently disturb Ichabod Crane's peaceful sleep. To add insult to injury, Katrina's stepmother happens to be the biggest witch of all, controlling the Horseman and occasionally sending him on murderous errands. Following a fight with Lady Van Tassel near the tree of the dead, Ichabod manages to retrieve the missing head, and hands it back to the Hessian. Ever a detective, he is pleased to see all the pieces of the puzzle come together when the Horseman, after regaining his head, grabs Lady Van Tassel and carries her to hell with him.

Sleepy Hollow sends ideologically confusing messages because it starts with (modernist) epistemology, then plays the classic postmodernist trick of demolishing the seemingly stable system of objective knowledge, and in the end presents the viewer with the alchemical *coniunctio oppositorum* (the term Jung used), or the famous 'marriage of heaven and hell' (to use William Blake's expression). Yes, Ichabod wins, but he also does not because his 'belief in the susceptibility of Nature to rational explanation' has melted (Holquist, 1971: 150, quoted in Bertens, 1997: 197). His attempt to trap the Horseman into the 'iron cage of instrumental rationality' has failed (Hauke, 2000: 37). Instead, he reached a certain compromise, a 'settlement by concession'. 'Lack of head', metaphorically speaking, equals 'lack of meaning', lack of precision, lack of direction, while Ichabod is involved in the favourite pastime of modernity – 'meaning-making activity', a twofold process of metonymising and de-metonymising, cutting and pasting; a kind of scientific montage. He collects pieces of knowledge, hoping that, in the end, he will get a unified picture. Christopher Hauke writes: 'Since the Enlightenment, meaning has been formed out of Nature's chaotic secrets by the genius of human scientific rationality. By selecting phenomena and then combining selected observations into rules, science believes it has 'understood the meaning' – but this position has resulted all too often in the discovery of an infinite regression of further 'puzzles of Nature' (Hauke, 2000: 27). Ichabod, the detective working with metonymised bodies, is himself metonymised by his instruments, reduced to being the mere '"objective" private eye of the scientific observer (to use Christopher Hauke's expression), while his bleeding hands betray a much more fragile personality – one that draws its power from the maternal depths of the unconscious.

The evil pair now gone, the angelic couple can leave the haunted place and settle in the emerging metropolis in time for the new century. Here, the film's symbolism explicitly states that the outdated medievality has lost to the new age of rationality and reason. By replacing the head and pacifying the monster, Ichabod the hero subjugates the 'headless' unconscious, with its lust, hypnotic control and meaningless violence.

At a more personal level, Ichabod finally comes to terms with his problematic parents, and the disturbing emotional legacy they left to him. The ruthless father and the bizarre mother have at last been exorcised.

Time to grow up

Corpse Bride (2005)

Remember little Vincent whose beautiful wife has been 'buried alive' in the flower bed? In *Corpse Bride* the romantic necromaniac returns in the shape of Victor Van Dort who, instead of getting married to a real woman, mistakenly attaches himself to the melancholic corpse bride – Emily. When he fails to recite his wedding vows at the wedding rehearsal, he wanders into a forest and practices the vows there, using a warped dry tree as a dummy 'bride'. After putting a gold ring on the tree's 'finger', the horrified groom watches it turn into a blue-faced woman in full bridal attire. Victor, whose name calls to mind Vincent and Victor Frankenstein (Victoria's father even 'mistakenly' calls his future son-in-law 'Vincent'), feels trapped and out of control. The part of the vows that terrified him most, 'With this candle I will light your way in darkness', begins to materialise all too soon. Whereas Vincent just fantasises about being in love with a dead woman, and hears 'his wife call from beyond the grave', Victor's fantasy actually comes alive.

Burton's second full-lengh stop-motion animation film (the genre in which Burton's career originated) was co-directed with Mike Johnson (Page, 2007: 228). It is abundant in references to the Gothic genre; in fact, narratively, it *belongs* to the Gothic genre. Here we observe all the traditional paraphernalia of the Gothic revival/Gothicised Romanticism: castles, ruins, vicious aristocrats, scary priests, undead maidens and evil mothers. Burton roughly establishes the time-scale of the film as 'Victorian' (Salisbury, 2006: 256), but ideologically and thematically it goes back to the roots of European literary Gothic.

Gothic fiction originated in the decade between 1780 and 1790; the years of major political and social changes in Europe are traditionally considered to be the peak of classic Gothic fiction. The so-called 'Gothic Revival' of the 1790s brought such writers as Ann Radcliffe (*The Mysteries of Udolpho*, 1794, *The Italian*, 1797), Matthew Gregory Lewis (*The Monk*, 1796), William Godwin (*Caleb Williams*, 1794) and William Beckford (*Vathek*, 1786). Gothic novels of this period usually contain a recognisable socio-ideological code, that of the emerging middle class attempting to revise its historical position in relation to the aristocracy. It is only logical that at the time of the French bourgeois revolution, aristocrats should be presented in literature as ultimately evil, barbaric and amoral. David Punter theorises that,

> . . . Gothic was a mode of writing in which middle-class audiences and writers attempt to come to grips with their changing relations to a myth of aristocracy, and simultaneously try to invent myths to justify their own dominance. The kinds of fear in which Gothic deals are, from one aspect, general psychological forces: fear of isolation, claustrophobia, paranoia. But they are consistently presented as connected with a world of feudal class relations in which baron, priest and monk are seen as principal agents of evil, thus displacing evil from the everyday. Most of the major Gothic works are fables of persecution, in which heroes and heroines with largely middle-class values, not always underwritten by

the authors, are haunted and pursued by these agents, but on the whole emerge, presumably to the relief of the reader, untainted by the crude social violence which they represent.

(Aers *et al.*, 1981: 116)

The Romantic years of the nineteenth century produced a number of prominent British novelists whose works incorporate Gothic elements: Mary Shelley (*Frankenstein*, 1818), Charles Maturin (*Melmoth the Wanderer*, 1820), James Hogg (*The Private Memoirs and Confessions of a Justified Sinner*, 1824). By the 1840s–50s the American line of the late Romantic Gothic tradition was emerging. Often it echoed European anxieties and used similar Gothic archetypal images, its best representatives being Washington Irving ('The Legend of Sleepy Hollow', 1819–20 and 'Rip Van Winkle', 1819–20), Edgar Allan Poe (*Tales of the Grotesque and Arabesque*, 1839–40, poems including *The Raven* and *Lenore*), and Nathaniel Hawthorne (*Twice-Told Tales*, 1837, *The Scarlet Letter*, 1850).

It is unlikely that the film's creators deliberately introduced a serious social context into *Corpse Bride*. Nevertheless, the social context is present in the film as a formal tribute to the Revivalist/Romantic period of the genre. Victor, with his *nouveau-riche* background, intends to marry into the aptly named aristocratic Everglot family. Their only redeemable feature is their daughter Victoria, otherwise they are suitably Gothic in the worst sense of the term: greedy, tyrannical, with a dozen skeletons in their closet. The dim Everglot household is no more cheerful (in fact, far less cheerful!) than the underworld in which the poor Victor ends up after saying his vows to the wrong woman. Scenes depicting 'the land of the living' are deliberately drained of colour, while 'the underworld', far from being cold, is friendly and bright.

A friend of the family, the scheming Lord Barkis (a classic example of a 'talking name'), is a stereotypical Gothic villain. The Revivalists liked their patriarchal aristocrats to have a dual nature: outwardly civil but inwardly amoral and oversexed. The demonic seducer Barkis Bittern is a match for Walpole's Manfred or Radcliffe's Montoni, or indeed, much further down the line, Bram Stoker's Dracula.

Edgar Allan Poe is another obvious influence. Burton confesses to have always liked the heavy emotional charge of Poe's poetry and prose (filtered though Roger Corman's B-movies) because they disclosed the dark side of deceptively peaceful reality:

Growing up in suburbia, in an atmosphere that was perceived as nice and normal (but which I had other feelings about), those movies were a way to certain feelings, and I related them to the place I was growing up in. I think that's why I responded so much to Edgar Allan Poe. I remember when I was younger, I had these two windows in my room, nice windows that looked out on to the lawn, and for some reason my parents walled them up and gave me this little slit window that I had to climb up on a desk to see out of. So I likened it to that Poe's story where the person was walled in and buried alive ['The Cask of Amontillado'].

(Salisbury, 2006: 4)

Apparently, Burton imbibed various aspects of Poe's multi-faceted *oeuvre*; not only genre elements, such as the tale of detection, but also narrative ingredients – ravens, bats, live immurement and undead spouses. Poe had a very peculiar taste in female characters – he liked them romantically dead, which allowed him to lament poetically their early departure from this life. The motif of the untimely death of a beautiful maiden is diffused through Poe's writings: it is present in the story 'The Tomb of Ligeia', and the poems *Annabel Lee, Lenore, To the One in Paradise* and *Ulalume*.

There was something deeply wrong with Poe's 'brides'. One of them, the heroine of the 'Bridal Ballad', regards her (loveless but potentially prosperous) marriage as a form of entombment, the ring as a symbol of enslavement, and the entire idea of matrimony as claustrophobic, funereal and generally doomed:

Bridal Ballad

The ring is on my hand,
And the wreath is on my brow;
Satin and jewels grand
And many a rood of land
Are all at my command,
And I am happy now!

He has loved me long and well,
And, when he breathed his vow,
I felt my bosom swell,
For – the words were his who fell
And the voice seemed his who fell
In the battle down the dell,
And who is happy now!

But he spoke to re-assure me,
And he kissed my pallid brow –
But a reverie came o'er me,
And to the church-yard bore me,
And I sighed to him before me,
'Oh, I am happy now!'

And thus they said I plighted
An irrevocable vow –
And my friends are all delighted
This love I have requited –
And my mind is much benighted
That I am happy now!

[. . .]

I have spoken – I have spoken –
They have registered the vow –
And though my faith be broken,
And though my heart be broken,
Behold the golden token
That proves me happy now!

Would God I could awaken!
For I dream I know not how!
And my soul is sorely shaken,
Lest an evil step be taken –
And the dead who is forsaken
May not be happy now.

(Poe, 2008: 787)

In the 'underworld' where the Corpse Bride takes her new husband, 'the dead' are very happy indeed. Upon hearing the news of Emily's wedding, they sing, drink and dance merrily. As a cinematographer, Burton tends to think allegorically, not realistically, and therefore, more often than not (with the exception of *Ed Wood*, perhaps), his films are in great need of deciphering. In the case of *Corpse Bride*, the most obvious parallel would be the archetypal journey to the underworld for the purpose of spiritual enlightenment. The film's plot evokes numerous allusions to classical mythology, including, for instance, the myth of Ariadne – the famous ditched bride who helped her lover Theseus to defeat the Minotaur. Ariadne gave the hero a ball of string, provided him with the necessary instructions, and escorted him to the Labyrinth. The grateful Theseus was (honestly!) going to take her home with him – if it was not for Dionysus (in one version of the story). The god told Theseus to leave the bride on the island of Naxos because he, Dionysus, was going to marry Ariadne himself (Robert Graves, in Leeming, 1998: 114).

Like Theseus, Victor, a hero on the quest for maturity, is 'terrified of marriage', and is therefore taken by his anima on a journey into the world of the unconscious – where he can explore his fears and weigh his options. 'The land of the dead' is a suitable subject for foregrounding one of

Burton's favourite tricks: visual metonymy – as well as its thematic co-partner, fragmentation of personality. With the 'underworld', especially expressed by means of stop-motion animation, Tim Burton could show an abundance of metonymic imagery without resorting to close-ups and extreme close-ups of hands and faces. In *Corpse Bride* parts and fragments reign: skeletons[3] keep breaking, scattering, losing bones and reassembling – even after being kicked apart; Victor's favourite dog (long-departed), given to him as a wedding present in a box, rebuilds itself from fragments; corpses lose eyes, legs and arms; they split apart. Emily the blue-faced bride has an eye which keeps popping out, and her bridal frock is disintegrating (cf. Sally from *Nightmare Before Christmas* whose arm is intermittently being ripped off and sewn back onto the body).

Eyes in the soup and bones on the floor are not exactly cheerful images, but in *Corpse Bride* such a macabre kind of metonymy (technically, synecdoche) looks extremely well-placed. In the 'alternative' land fragmentation is the norm rather than an exception. It is 'OK' not to be superficially 'wholesome', or to put up a public show of success. Once the 'official' surface is gone, there is nothing left but the naked frame. Masks, personas, outward pretences and formalities are no longer important, and will not help their bearers to flourish in the 'dead' society. The skeletons' transparency is therefore a sign of their frankness and ingenuity – as juxtaposed to the orotund manners of Lord Barkis Bittern or the Everglot couple. The contrast between the ghosts' transparency (literal) and sincerity, and the aristocrats' artificiality, can, at a stretch, even be regarded as a social critique.

As often happens to Burton's male characters, Victor is stuck in-between the two worlds, the 'real' and the 'fantastic', and has to go through *purgatorio*, whereby his values towards the world are revised and reassessed. When we apply the classic Jungian analytical framework, we get the following picture: Emily, 'the other woman', is Victor's *anima* who harbours his preconceptions about marital life, and reflects his doubts about relationships. Victor does not know whether he wants to live with Victoria 'till death them part'. After getting in touch with his inner 'woman', alongside other archetypes (such as the skeletal Elder Gutknect – the wise old man figure), he is finally able to make an 'informed decision'. *Anima*, to follow Marie-Louise von Franz's account, is 'a dream that lures men away from reality' (Jung and von Franz, 1964: 190). Victor realises that permanently fleeing from reality into the dreamland is not how an adult male is supposed to behave. In the end, Victor chooses the 'real' woman over the ghost from his psyche because

---

3 Burton's interest in 'live skeletons' goes back to Ray Harryhausen's extraordinary stop-motion animation in *Jason and the Argonauts* (1963). Burton, Depp and Helena Bonham Carter even called on Harryhausen at his home in London, and then the big man himself visited the set of *Corpse Bride* (Page, 2007: 228).

he finally grows up, and is therefore prepared to take responsibility for another human being. The ghost, meanwhile, dissolves into a thousand petals, and gives over her bridal bouquet of blue flowers to Victoria. This act marks the connection between Victor's anima and the girl whom he chooses to be his bride. The hero's fantasy gets integrated into reality.

Although the film's plot revolves around the indecisive hero, and he is 'appointed' the principal focaliser, the heroines' psychological dilemmas are also highlighted. Both Victoria and Emily have at least one annoying 'voice in their head' who is not to be trusted. Interestingly enough, their animuses' polarities complement the female roles they are supposed to play in the hero's life. Emily's *animus* is a mouthy and innocuous bore, who is cease-lessly plying her with a mishmash of advice, premonitions, suspicions and flatteries. He is a maggot, a thoughtworm, who, by way of realised meta-phor, lives in her head. The maggot is a 'serial *animus*': he introduces himself to a guest at the wedding party with the words: 'You don't know me, but I used to live in your dead mother.'

Victoria, as an 'angel', is entitled to an entirely different *animus* – the shady Lord Barkis. Barkis Bittern is a serial womaniser and a Bluebeard (the original Bluebeard was also an aristocrat), who lures unsuspecting ladies into his net, and brutally murders them. In the schematic narrative of *Corpse Bride* he functions as a 'materialised' representative of pervasive, forceful male sexuality, and abrupt initiation into sexual relations. Lord Barkis, as revealed in the last portion of the film, was also the mystery seducer who robbed and killed Emily. Von Franz argues that, as a soul-image, Bluebeard has no redeeming qualities and 'embodies the death-like, ferocious aspects of the *animus* in his most diabolical form [. . .] He draws woman away from life and murders life for her. He has to do with ghost lands and the land of death. Indeed, he may appear as the personification of death' (von Franz, 1973: 125). It is only logical, then, that, after drinking the poisoned wine, Barkis ends up in the underworld where he belongs.

Metaphorically speaking, Lord Bittern represents Victoria's reservations about marriage, and 'sexual obligations' that inevitably come with it. When partners have doubts about the union, the union cannot happen, hence the allegorical depiction of the bride and groom being stolen by 'the other man' and 'the other woman'. Intimidated by Victoria's seasoned *animus* at the rehearsal, Victor withdraws into himself, and cannot be reunited with his beloved until he faces up to his (Emily) as well as Victoria's (Barkis) doubts and fears. Afraid that the conjugal life might turn out to be a nightmare, both the bride and the groom seem to regard the marriage ceremony as a death sentence.

And their symbolic 'deaths' very nearly happen as Victor makes the decision to drink the poison in order to be 'lawfully' married to Emily, and Victoria ties the knot with the lethal Barkis (who is scheming to eventually get rid of her). Marriage marks the death of their old life, and the beginning of a new one, that of mutuality and togetherness. To follow the mythology of *Corpse Bride*, a wedding is a ceremony of renewal; symbolic 'death and resurrection'. It involves the decision to give up your phantom 'other half' for a real person – or, to use Poe's wording from 'The Bridal Ballad', to 'forsake' the ghost and 'be happy now'. Put simply, to get married, both Victoria and Victor have to grow up.

In the end, the heroes manage to overcome their panic, and emerge *victorious* from their encounter with the figures from 'the underworld'. Both the soul-images self-obliterate, very much in the manner of the Headless Horseman: they voluntarily go back to the unconscious where they belong.

'A grown-up hero' who does not tell his woman that he is 'a loner' and 'a rebel', was clearly a new species for Tim Burton; an improvement on the production line models consisting of Pee Wee, Edward Scissorhands, Bruce Wayne, Ed Wood and Edward Bloom. The very fact that Burton picked the *anima*, and not the shadow, as a central conflict for his new work, was surprisingly refreshing.

Chapter 4

The genius

To be a director you can't have any fear

(Tim Burton, quoted in Salisbury, 2006: 49)

As this chapter will mainly deal with the origins of talent in Burton's 'monsters', let us temporarily return to the eternally problematic trio of God, artist and the crowd.

Jung, very much in disagreement with the Christian tradition, regarded God as having a dual nature, as the bearer of both 'good' and 'evil' (CW11: paras. 243–285). God allows human misery to exist because he wants to become man; it is through us, human beings, and their pain, that he can *know himself* and thus achieve *gnosis of the Divine* (CW11: paras. 736–747). Man's suffering can be 'actual' (such as hardship) or spiritual, for 'neurosis is always a substitute for legitimate suffering' (CW11: para. 129). God and Man are united in the suffering Christ, 'a totality of life' (CW11: para. 712).

Andrey Tarkovsky presents us with a similar view of the human–divine relationship and the reasons behind its tormenting complexity: 'And with man's help the Creator comes to know himself. This progress has been given the name of evolution, and it is accompanied by the agonising process of self-knowledge' (Tarkovsky, 1989: 36–37). This process of self-development, of finding yourself and your place in the world, which Jung calls individuation, is perceived by Tarkovsky in a vein that is astonishingly analogous to that of Jung:

> In a very real sense every individual experiences this process himself as he comes to know life, himself, his aims. Of course each person uses the sum of knowledge accumulated by humanity, but all the same the experience of ethical, moral self-knowledge is the only aim in life for each person, and, subjectively, it is experienced each time as something new. Again and again man correlates himself with the world, racked with longing to acquire, and become one with, the ideal which lies outside him, which he apprehends as some kind of intuitively sensed

first principle. The unattainability of that becoming one, the inadequacy of his own 'I', is the perpetual source of man's dissatisfaction
and pain.

(Tarkovsky, 1989: 37)

The artist, a Christ-figure, filters the world through his own being, and thus
connects man to the divine universe. Art gives people the precious
opportunity to reflect on their life via the symbols provided by the artist;
to experience the shocking recognition of one's image in the mirror of
imagination. In this sense, cinema is especially effective because it allows
visual–emotional involvement with the events happening on the screen; it
is, in fact, a form of projective–introjective exchange. In the words of Ira
Koningsberg, 'the introjection of the film images triggers an internal process by which we invest these images with our own psychic and emotional
overlays and then project them back out, along with our own involvement
onto their imprints on the screen – a process that continues, back and
forth, as we watch the film' (Koningsberg, 1996: 886, quoted in Izod, 2006:
16). The viewer establishes an interaction with his unconscious. This contact is potentially therapeutic because he gains access to problems deeply
hidden in the psyche. A film can provide the key for that 'sealed tobacco
tin', as Paul D, the character from Toni Morrison's *Beloved*, called the
painful memories locked in his heart.

Any admittance into the archetypal field, Erich Neumann writes in *The
Child: Structure and Dynamics of the Nascent Personality*, is characterised by
an *abaissement du niveau mental*, a diminution of consciousness, 'an
intensification of the phenomenon that may be described as *participation
mystique*, in which the boundaries between subject and object available to
consciousness are blurred and the unitary reality takes the place of the
normal reality posited by our consciousness' (Neumann, 2002: 48). The
exposure to unitary reality has its roots in the child's experience of the primal
relationship (with its mother), but can continue into adult life, for instance,
in the form of creative or religious moments. *Abaissement du niveau mental* is
vital for the creative process, 'quite apart from the fact that nearly all the
peoples of history have attempted to induce such experiences ritually with
the help of intoxicants' (2002: 49). The psychological mechanism behind this
process is a shift in the ego-self axis: 'the ego is taken back into the Self and
normal ego-centered consciousness is suspended' (2002: 49).

Similarly, Tarkovsky links art (or 'poetry' as he calls it) to childlike states
and religious experience. For him, an artist is a child and a prophet at once.
Making art, as well as responding to art, is akin to engaging in a sacred
ritual, and requires a degree of faith on the part of the audience (Tarkovsky,
1989: 37).

In Tarkovsky's version of individuation, art induces the process of
'knowing' and takes it to its emotional pinnacle – catharsis (1989: 36).

Controversially, it traumatises, alongside providing hope, because 'touched by a masterpiece, a person begins to hear in himself that same call of truth which prompted the artist to his creative act' (2000: 43). In other words, a work of art is a pathway to God; and the artist builds a bridge between 'the crowd' and the divine image. Spectators watching a film are, figuratively speaking, experiencing a collective *participation mystique*. For their sake, the artist (or, in this case, the director) 'has plunged into the healing and redeeming depths of the collective psyche, where man is not lost in the isolation of consciousness and its errors and sufferings, but where all men are caught in a common rhythm which allows the individual to communicate his feelings and strivings to mankind as a whole' (Jung, CW15: para. 161). While the makers of the film have a more direct access to the archetypes, they can catch the 'big fish' in the deep waters of the unconscious, and then invite everyone to take part in the ritual feast.

In the father's shadow

Burton's messianic creators are far from being angels. They do everything to look and remain different, and sometimes even adopt a disdainful attitude towards the 'common people'. The youngest example of such a 'dark and misunderstood poet' is Vincent Malloy, whose vision runs parallel to everyday life experiences, and who constantly dramatises simple things to the point that they become supernatural experiences. The boy shuns sunlight in favour of the darkness of his imagination. The result is comparable to the myth-making ventures of his more mature successors: Bruce Wayne, Edward Bloom, Ed Wood. Vincent has the reverse 'Midas touch': everything he touches, which used to be bright and cheerful, turns Gothic and terrifying: a lapdog transforms into a zombie; a kindly aunt is mummified in wax; a common flower bed becomes the grave of the boy's 'wife'; and the nursery becomes a chamber of horrors. Vincent borrows heavily from his favourite Gothic movies, and uses them as 'casings' for his own fantasies. His imagination works within a pre-existent cultural framework.

Little Victor, the protagonist of *Frankenweenie*, chooses the same route: inspired by 'professional' horror films, he shoots his own super-8 movies such as 'monsters from long ago' (Burton, by his own admission, used to make them too (Salisbury, 2006: 5)). It finds realisation in the classic mixture of science and art – the process of 'bestowing animation upon lifeless matter'. Only, in his case the word *animation* has several meanings: creating a motion picture, as well bringing his favourite dog back to life. The dog, and all the Frankenstein laboratory paraphernalia, work as metaphors for Victor's aspiration to make movies. Victor is the director who makes images come back to life on screen; he preserves and maintains them; he is a magician. A small version of the creator, Victor already possesses his own worlds, in which he has to handle life and death, and perform miracles. His talent, however, has an edge.

So, where does the dark side of Vincent and Victor's creativity come from? To use James Hillman's expression, in search of the 'wounder', we should look in the direction of the parents. The 'big Creator', to paraphrase Jung, can be morally ambiguous and even openly cruel. The child's darkness, therefore, can be traced down to his father's duality. The father bestows the gifts of imperfection and creativity onto his offspring, thus producing the next generation of troubled world-makers. Burton's *oeuvre* contains several extended examples of such parent–child relationships: Edward Scissorhands and the Inventor, Ed Bloom and his son, Ed Wood and Bela Lugosi, Ichabod Crane and his heartless father, Willy Wonka and the sadistic male parent.

For Jung, the 'child' means something evolving towards independence. This it cannot do without detaching itself from its origins: abandonment is therefore a necessary condition, not just a concomitant symptom (Jung, 1951, CW9/1: para. 287). Erich Neumann built on Jung's ideas about the archetype of the divine infant. He discusses 'the wound' in terms of parental inadequacy and incompetence (the parents being not only 'personal' but also metaphysical and mythological).

Neumann postulates the existence of the pre-ego period (which comprises intrauterine development and the first year of life), in which the child and the mother, psychologically, and even physically, are still one organism. The infant is dependent on its mother for warmth, food and comfort, her body being its only psychic reality. It lives in the previously mentioned 'unitary reality', in which 'inside' and 'outside' are experienced as identical (Neumann, 2002: 11). This pre-ego phase is distinguished by the unity of I and thou, subject and object, self and the world, and is known to myth as paradisiacal (Neumann, 2002: 14). Since 'the object' (or 'thou' as Neumann terms it) does not yet exist for the child, there is no tension between automorphous self-development and thou-relation. Therefore, there is no conflict between the individual and his or her environment. 'Experience of this phase,' Neumann theorises, 'which sets its imprint on all future development and is of particular importance for the psychology of creative individuals, is a source of lasting nostalgia, which can have a progressive as well as regressive effect on the adult' (Neumann, 2002: 15).

This initial connection with the mother is extremely important for the subsequent psychological development of the individual as it influences the ability to relate and communicate. It can be positive as well as negative. The positive primal relationship leads to the formation of the *positive–integral ego*, 'an ego that is able to assimilate and integrate even the negative or unpleasant qualities of the outer and inner worlds, such as deprivations, pain, etc.' (2002: 58). The child with the *positive–integral ego* can easily deal with the split between automorphism and cultural adaptation, and is able to endure inhibitions, imposed on them by the group into which they are born.

A negative constellation of the primal relationship occurs wherever the infant, speaking figuratively, 'loses' its mother; or, to be more precise, loses the emotional connection with her. It can happen due to the parent's inadequacy, death or separation – or may even be dependent on other factors outside the mother's personal conduct (2002: 73). Such a loss of emotional connection leads to the dissipation of the baby's faith in the foundation of its existence. 'The mother', for Neumann, is by no means just a physical female who gives birth and subsequently looks after the child, but rather the symbolic mother, the ultimate secure foundation of the infant's life: 'The mother of the primal relationship is the "good Great Mother". [. . .] In this sense, she is anonymous and transpersonal, in other words archetypal, as the one part of a specifically human constellation which operates between her and the child' (2002: 21).

Neumann describes the state of the distressed ego: 'The negativized ego is deprived of its foundations. Thus its despair is perfectly understandable. Its anxiety and fundamental insecurity in the world are the expression of an isolation which shakes the foundations of automorphous development, and shatters the ego's roots in the Self [in Jungian psychology, the centre of the psyche], i.e. its own encompassing nature' (2002: 81). The mother, Neumann writes, is also the child's first model for the experience of its own Self (2002: 60). Since the self represents psychic wholeness and the unity of the opposites, the ego that happens to be alienated from it experiences fragmentation and disorientation.

A fragmented psyche is no good if one aspires to become a useful member of society. Eventually, the infant has to go out of the primary 'all in one' state, and start adjusting itself to the objects of the external world. It has to develop relationships with 'the thou of society', as well as learn about prohibitions and boundaries. That is when the tension between subject and object, automorphism ('the unique tendency of every individual to realise his potentialities') and cultural adaptation occurs. Such a conflict is normal, and signals the child's entrance into the 'conscious' world; the local, culturally determined reality. But, since people tend to model their relationship with the world of objects on their primary experiences, a leftover disturbance during the initial mother–child phase may make the person less capable, or even incapable, of societal integration. In this case, the tension between ego and thou may become especially dangerous (2002: 68–69). In other words, where there is lack of adaptation, there is also lack of desire to communicate with the outside world.

In Burton's films, mothers are scarce – but there are plenty of father figures. In fact, in Burton's films it is the father, and not the female parent, who 'gives birth', looks after the child, and then disappears. Such a 'swap', Erich Neumann explains, is mythologically viable. In fact, it frequently occurs in some world religions with a patriarchal base; for instance, in Christianity and Hasidism. The constellation of the primal relationship in these religions is transferred to God, and the role of the mother is taken over by the father (Neumann, 2002: 61–62). In this case, any negativity on the part of the 'child' which comes with a dissatisfactory primal relationship, will be shifted onto the father figure (on the personal level) or to God (on the metaphysical plane).

Many of Burton's protagonists are deeply dissatisfied with their personal fathers; and all of them are very unhappy with the highest father of all – the Creator. The protagonists' mothers, at best, play secondary roles or serve as a context. At worst, they are altogether not mentioned. In *Vincent*, for instance, the mother represents the 'normalising', patriarchal voice of society; in *Edward Scissorhands* (Peg) and *Big Fish* (Sandra) she is given the role of a guardian angel, a kind of feminine stability to balance out the unsteadiness of the father figure; in *Sleepy Hollow* she is victimised. Whether or not such a neglect of femininity by Burton is indicative of a sexist attitude, is open to debate. Far from being sexist, it could simply be down to the question of Burton's creative and conceptual influences. Meta-narratively, he tends to follow the scheme of the Frankenstein myth, in which the feminine (Victor's own mother, his fiancée Elizabeth) is 'angelised' and relegated to the background while her functions – gestation and birth – are performed by a man who 'plays god'. Anyway, in Burton's films, such patriarchisation and usurpation of traditional feminine roles does not change the protagonist's destiny. His problem is not the parent's sex, but in the fact that he was abandoned by the parent. The father could have been good and attentive, but instead he chose to play 'the terrible mother'.

Actually, the father figure – whether he is a generous, wise god like the Inventor in *Edward Scissorhands* (1990), the budding, yet irresponsible creator like the little boy Oliver from *Frankenweenie* (1984), the family-neglecting adventurer in pursuit of his selfish needs from *Big Fish* (2003), Willie Wonka's father, who is ruthless to his child because he wants him to be the best, or the Penguin's unsympathetic parent – is always the cause of his son's unhappiness and misery. Sometimes the father is too young (and careless); sometimes too old (and feeble); often far too strict – but he is invariably flawed in some way. The result is that he is unable to properly look after the human being he has created. The absence of love and the trauma of betrayal inevitably transform into the conflict of the light and dark forces in Burton's characters. Talents, according to Burton, are born out of pain, confusion, maladaptation and deficiency – that is why the gift of imagination is often melancholy. Just as Jung saw psychological complexes as vital for the individual because without them psychic activity would come to a fatal standstill (Jacobi, 1973: 38), Burton sees conflict as crucial to the artist's creativity.

In Burton's films, the paternal shadow takes many forms. The father's disappearance and death, his cruelty and strictness, his neglect, or even his immaturity can all be seen as having a negative influence on the offspring. Negative childhood experiences are a crucial factor in the emergence of a disturbed talent. As a result, the younger generation of Burton's geniuses – the boy with scissors, the boy dressed as a bat, the boy inventing weird instruments, the boy devising new sweets – inherit the dual boon of negativity and creativity. Locked in their unhappy childhood experiences, 'unfinished', they remain forever immature. To use Neumann's theory of the ego negativised through abandonment and neglect, once reduced to their own emotional resources, such children acquire 'forced and violent self-assertion', behind which there is always 'anxiety, forsakenness, and a lack of trust embracing the entire sphere of what is normally contained in the primal relationship, namely, the child's relation to the thou, the world, the Self, and the unconscious' (Neumann, 2002: 81).

Introverted, maladapted, self-absorbed yet sensitive, the Burtonian 'child' fits Neumann's illustration rather well. He is born with a conflict, and out of a conflict. His incentive to move, to act, to go ahead emerge only out of a negative situation, a profound discontent with the parents, himself and/or the world. He persistently places himself and his interests above 'the thou of society', which, on the one hand, allows him to pursue his own path and realise his talent, but on the other, puts a barrier between himself and 'the people'. Edward's and Benjamin Barker's hairdressing, Willie Wonka's sweet-making and Bruce Wayne's undercover policing are supposed to benefit the community. However, instead of a mutually beneficial coexistence, there arises a conflict whereby the crowd threatens to eliminate the stubborn, proud and overall 'different' artist.

Jung, who had always been interested in the genesis and attributes of the artistic temperament, regarded creative people's proverbial maladaptation as a positive phenomenon. In his view, such self-assertion and 'asociality' is necessary for the advancement of the artist's talent and aspirations: 'The artist's relative lack of adaptation turns out to his advantage; it enables him to follow his yearnings far from the beaten path, and to discover what it is that would meet the unconscious needs of his age. Thus, just as the one-sidedness of the individual's conscious attitude is corrected by reactions from the unconscious, so art represents a process of self-regulation in the life of nations and epochs' (CW15: para. 131). To that Neumann adds his explanation of the artist's loneliness and his consistent inability to form stable relationships: He writes in *Art and the Creative Unconscious*:

> In the creative man we find a preponderance of the archetypal in keeping with his creative nature [. . .]
> The consequences of this accentuation of the archetype in the creative man, who by his very nature is dependent on his receptivity

toward the creative unconscious, manifest themselves partly in deviations from the development of the so-called normal man; here we need not deal with the somewhat similar condition of the neurotic. In the life of the creative man the emphasis always lies on the transpersonal factors; i.e., in his experience the archetypal factor is so predominant that in extreme cases he becomes almost incapable of personal relations. But even where he retains his capacity for human contact and human relations, it is always at the price of an essential conflict that he assimilates the archetypal projections and does justice to the human limitations of his counterpart. And this is why so many artists, even among the most gifted, have such intense anima relations with the 'distant loved one', epistolary relations, relations to the unknown, the dead, etc.

(Neumann, 1974a: 18)

The Burtonian 'child's' self-assertion and self-centeredness, indeed, are positive forces which allow him to progress, and go beyond not just the crowd's abilities and aspirations, but also beyond his father's achievements. He chooses to become the inventor of new worlds both *in spite of* and *because* of his father. The child continues yet modifies the father's occupation and interests. Will Bloom, for instance, is a journalist, while Edward has never moved beyond amateur storytelling. The son's profession can be explained both as a negation and on acceptance of his father's hobby. Edward's stories are *selfish* and *untrue*, while Will's profession is about collecting *facts* about *other people*. The son's love for facts was probably born out of the wish for a 'genuine' father instead of an attention-seeking clown, ever absent and ever full of exciting lies.

Ichabod Crane's scientific talent is a continuation of his father's fear of the unconscious. He uses science to dismiss 'the black tide of mud' (to use Freud's expression), all the uncontrollable manifestations of the unconscious – instincts, hallucinations, phobias and other 'headless' phenomena. At the same time, as a scientist he moves far ahead of his father, leaving behind the medieval torture devices and improvable 'facts' of Christianity, and replacing them with exact instruments and scientific knowledge. His father's blind fanaticism and terrible practices (exorcising his wife, for instance) were the 'negative' incentives behind Ichabod's decision to look for the real answers to unsolved mysteries.

Edward Scissorhands retains the Inventor's talent for 'cutting new creatures out of rough materials' (the Inventor likes making cookies, and Edward was made from one of them) – but the 'inherited' abilities are not what made him what he is. Metonymically speaking, Edward *is* his hands; his character and behaviour are determined by the fact that he is 'not finished'. And he is not finished because the Inventor died before he had a chance to furnish his progeny with humanoid limbs. The Inventor is a far more positive character, and a better parent, than Ichabod's father, Willy Wonka's father or the freedom-loving Ed Bloom, but even he is prone to failure. He fails to be a perfect parent not by being too strict or, on the contrary, too loose, but by demonstrating the ultimate weakness, unacceptable for an ideal god-figure – by dying. Edward's god is dead, and this is what makes him disorientated, creative and, ultimately, angry.

The emergence of two other Burtonian 'monsters', Bruce Wayne and Oswald Cobblepot, also happens within the archetypal framework of the 'malfunction of god'. Batman's heroic abilities are born the moment his father is murdered by Jack Napier ('I made you, you made me first'). Unlike in some other Burton films, the shadow in *Batman* is split from the father figure, so the protagonist wrestles not with his 'wounding' parent, but with 'external' forces of evil.

Batman's principal enemy in the sequel, Oswald Cobblepot, has a lowbrow, tricksterish, infantile charisma which attracts the inhabitants of Gotham City. The Penguin's crowd-pleasing talents originate in his childhood. An ugly freak, he is discarded by his parents into the Gotham sewer. His attention seeking and will to power are inverted cravings for parental love, acceptance and attention. When Oswald does not get attention naturally, he thinks he can torture people into loving him.

The road to 'negative creativity' seem to go through the feeling of guilt: 'To be good is to be loved by one's own mother; you are bad because your mother does not love you' (Neumann, 2002: 87). Since, for the infant, the mother is thou, world and self in one, Neumann presumes, then,

> her defection transforms the world into chaos and nothingness, the thou disappears, leaving the child utterly lonely and forlorn, or becomes an enemy and persecutor, while the child's own Self is transformed into a representative of the Terrible Mother. In this mythological situation life, as the Great Mother, has turned away and nothing remains but death. Just as "absence" and "death" are identical in the child's experience, here the mother's nonexistence signifies the child's own death. [. . .] a child expelled from the primal relationship is expelled from the natural order of the world and comes to doubt the justification for its existence'.
>
> (2002: 87)

Such a correlation of guilt, misfortune and a sense of worthlessness is not confined to ontogenesis; on the phylogenetic level, Neumann continues, this desperate state is reflected in the book of Job (2002: 88). An attempt at reparation of the split in the primal relationship is usually accompanied by the immersion into the world of creativity, the realm of mythology and storytelling. The matriarchal world of mythological apperception helps the child to restore confidence and the sense of being protected:

That is why evening – bedtime – is the mother's time. With her stories, her songs, her sheltering tenderness she then becomes the Great Mother of the primal relationship. She confers a sense of security and shelteredness as Mother of the Night, and Goddess of the Inner World into which the child now enters. [. . .] His whole world, or in any case parts of it, are close to the unitary reality, and the garden in front of the house, the nearby woods, or some tree may represent a sheltering reality into which the child can withdraw. Here the primordial, archetypal experience of the world comes into its own, and forest, garden, or tree as symbol of the Great Mother becomes the Great Mother herself, ready to embrace the child in need of help.

(2002: 80)

The process of defamiliarising reality, translating its elements into the language of the parallel universe – the process which some people call art – cures the tortured, lonely soul, Neumann implies. True, the tree is the central symbol of Burton's creative universe, and the principal ingredient of his meticulously planned *mise-en-scène*. His protagonists seek shelter from the crowd in woods and gardens. Edward Scissorhands is a tree surgeon, and cultivates a beautiful garden in front of his castle. Metaphorically speaking, he 'tweaks' the raw material coming from the unconscious, to turn it into beautiful images. Victor from *Corpse Bride* walks into the woods at night, and accidentally 'marries' a tree when he puts the ring onto one of its branches. His fear of marriage makes him seek help from the 'Great Mother'. By releasing him at the end of the film, she (the mother, the unconscious, *anima*, Emily) gives him a chance to have a relationship in the real world, with a real woman. 'The tree of the dead' in *Sleepy Hollow* agrees to take back its bestial instinctuality in the form of the Headless Horseman (male aggression) and Lady Van Tassel (female sexuality), thus loosening its grip on Ichabod's heroic rationality. Edward Bloom is snatched, squeezed and nearly killed by a murderous tree in the fairy-tale forest. Ed Wood is shown, at the beginning of the film, carrying a tree in a pot to his studio. Willy Wonka has a garden where he 'cultivates' all kinds of sweet delicacies. His tasty inventions may be said to be 'growing on trees'. The tree is the symbol of imagination and vision; artists, like trees, feed their talent through their connection – their roots – in the unconscious. In Burton's world, talent is deemed to be melancholy because it gathers its materials in the depths of the Great Mother, who can be terrible (the absent mother; the mother of rejection) or good (the mother of creative reparation; the one who weaves stories), but she is always productive and never, ever short of fascinating material. To keep in touch with her, one must always remain a child. This is what Burtonian protagonists manage to do really well.

Following Neumann's path, we arrive at the explanation of the Gothic flavour of Burton's films as coming from the (personal or archetypal) parents' defection. Her rejection of the child brings out in him self-destructive rage, alienation from society, self-victimisation and fantasies of death. He feels 'abnormal' because he is expelled from the 'natural order of things'. Meanwhile, creativity, as a means of sublimating his inner darkness, helps him to stay alive.

At the highest level, Burton's films deal with the essence of the human condition; they attempt, albeit using popular and recycled cinematic material, to unravel the oldest dilemma of humanity – the dual nature of God. 'The primal relationship' in question is man's bond with the life-giving God who fails to provide his child with eternal Paradise, thus consigning him to a life of suffering, 'knowing', adaptation and personal development. Such a path, Burton assumes in his works, is murky and fraught with danger. Meanwhile, imagination is a lantern which helps humanity to find its way in the night.

'Too constrictive!'

Art and freedom in Ed Wood (1994)

Ed Wood was made mostly by committed fans. Certain aspects of the preparation stage recall Wood's own filmmaking habits: the 147-page script was written in just six weeks, it was hard to get off the ground, its budget was relatively small ($18 million) and Burton got most of the actors 'to do it for not a lot' (Salisbury, 2006: 129–136).

Burton's choice of black and white stock for Ed Wood, as homage to the title character, is not surprising. Normally, Burton explains, he does not do pure black and white films because the technique bears the mark of auteurism and pretentiousness, and he does not want 'to be perceived as pretentious' (Salisbury, 2006: 137). The monochromism of the film is part of Burton's 'postmodern nostalgia' – but it also emphasises Ed Wood's own nostalgic tendencies, and his habit, for lack of fresh ideas, to macerate, recycle and rework old B-oddities such as Bela Lugosi's Dracula and Maila Nurmi's Vampira. In Burton's words, he simply wanted to make a documentary about a passionate person; a guy who was 'doing *something*' (Salisbury, 2006: 134–141). Indeed, the most 'documentary' thing about Ed Wood is not the factual aspect; it is the emotional truth. Given that factual information about the characters is scarce, it is, at times, difficult to tell the difference between the real Ed Wood and the emotional imprint designed by Tim Burton.

Is the failed director Edward D. Wood Jr a suitable protagonist for a film about a tortured talent? Yes, if you want to show the tragicomic openness of a hopeful naivety; a futile overflow of youthful energy. To use Hillman's terminology again, if you decide to make a film about an open wound rather than a scar (the scar is Burton's usual way), Ed Wood is the ideal subject. Tim Burton is perfectly aware of the differences between his 'scar' protagonists and his 'open wound' characters: 'Edward was interior, this symbol come to life; Ed is more outgoing. It was interesting for me, after working with Johnny before, to explore a more open kind of thing' (Salisbury, 2006: 139).

Hillman writes about the bleeding puer:

> Openness and secrecy – so puer! The bleeding puer reveals his naked life and his soul is a sieve. It is all there for anyone to come and look; he will tell you all about himself. The puer influence in any complex lays out its wares in public, and passers-by are amazed that anyone can be so open, so unpsychological. This public display is enacted by writers, painters, performers, whose complexes compulsively insist on being widely published, hung upon the wall, or shown to large audiences.
>
> (Hillman, 1987: 114)

This paragraph brings to mind the scene from *Ed Wood*, in which Edward pitches the idea of *Glen or Glenda* to George Weiss. He really wants to direct the film. Upon being asked what makes him qualify for the job, Ed simple-mindedly mentions that he likes to dress in women's clothing. He fought in the Second World War, he adds, and was wearing women's undergarments under his uniform.

Wood's embarrassing frankness makes the authentic *Glen and Glenda* (1953) rather bizarre. The director Glen (played by Ed Wood himself) starts hyperventilating when he sees a fluffy angora sweater or a sheer black undergarment because he cannot wait to try them on. He often goes outside dressed as a woman, and at such times his name is Glenda. Glenda's character wears a blonde wig, black pencil skirt and high heels, and frequently stops near female clothes shops to sigh over window displays. The narrator confidently explains that transvestites should not be confused with homosexuals and therefore, he elucidates, Glen has a girlfriend and is planning soon to marry her. The problem is, Glen cannot decide whether to tell her about his 'other self' before, or after, the wedding. Eventually, he tells her, and together they seek psychoanalytic help. The doctor explains to Glen that he actually is in control of his 'double'; that he is the author of this 'fictitious character', and therefore has the right to kill Glenda off. Only by eliminating it, can Glen attain the happy ending and arrive at a successful family life, the psychiatrist concludes.

Wood's wound is in the film for everyone to gape at: 'Glen's father had no love for his son. His father wanted Glen to be a football hero or a baseball player, so that he could brag to his cronies at the corner saloon, just as his cronies bragged to him about their own sons. That's the root of Glen's fictitious character. He invented it when he could find no love from his mother or his father. His mother had hated her own father. Glen reminded her of her father. Therefore, she gave all her attention, love and affection to her daughter. 'Glen then decided also to become a daughter', explains the psychiatrist to the detective investigating the death of a transvestite.

Stylistically, *Glen or Glenda* is muddled; it is a mixture of clashing genres – exploitation, horror, documentary, educational film, melodrama, silent flick and even soft porn. It is full of pretentious but maladroit montage (Ed Wood thought of himself as following in the footsteps of Orson Welles), and crammed with half-digested philosophical, political, anthropological and psychoanalytic theories. Its extradiegetic music tracks, instead of being 'graceful', 'intricately conceived' and 'full of meaning', in truth are gauche and always out of place. Bela Lugosi's character (a sort of cruel, omniscient god) is entirely extraneous, the text he pronounces being so unadulteratedly symbolic that it does not have much sense. *Mise-en-scène*, far from appearing 'complex and conceptual', more often than not seems entirely disconnected from the characters. The principal female actress (Dolores Fuller, Ed Wood's girlfriend) cannot act; Ed Wood himself cannot act either.

The 'fetish footage', as the 'exploitation' producer George Weiss later admitted, was added to extend the picture's length to 70 minutes. In fact, the notorious scenes have nothing to do with Ed Wood, and were taken from an older film by the trash-horror-exploitation director Merle Connell (Grey, 1994: 48). Meanwhile, nothing was to be discarded and the crew had to utilise 'every bit of the footage that was shot because film was precious. That was the type of deal that all independents found themselves in' (Grey, 1994: 46). The notorious trashy style and 'cut and paste' method had often been the last resort for the threadbare filmmaker. He, as the *Plan 9 from Outer Space* actor Carl Anthony recalls,

> was always looking at available stock footage from film libraries, to see what he could tie together. He could see enough stuff and then he would start writing a script where he could incorporate a lot of stuff and then he wouldn't have to spend money on shooting. His mind could probably take all sorts of loose ends and make some sort of continuity out of it. He'd be the kind of guy, if a picture was halfway through the shooting and somebody ran out of money and somebody else was a quarter of the way through their picture and ran out of money, and somebody else again, he could probably pitch it all together and make something comprehensible out of it.
>
> He was undoubtedly the fastest writer and director in Hollywood, always hoping that he would get a chance to slow down and attend to details [. . .]
>
> (Grey, 1994: 54)

He continued to treat the sparse audiences to such films as *Bride of the Monster* (originally *Bride of the Atom*), *Plan 9 from Outer Space* and *Night of the Ghouls*, but eventually had to switch to pornography as a more predictable source of income. The big fan of angora sweaters died in 1978, destitute, suffering from alcoholism and utterly forgotten by Hollywood (Grey, 1994: 157–160). Enthusiasm, as Jung once said, can be 'a veritable gift of the gods, or a monster from hell' (CW11: para: 960).

It is, however, perfectly clear why Burton was fascinated by one of the trashiest directors of all times. Behind the pile of cinematic rubble one can glimpse a sensitive and imaginative but rather disorganised director who cannot, like many of Burton's other characters, pull the elements of his picture together; cannot make them work harmoniously. The fictionalised Ed Wood – a misunderstood artist with a double life, a penchant for fiends and freaks, and a tender filial love towards an old horror actor, inscribes himself perfectly into the body of Burton's work.

With his self-contradictory, confused, double personality, he was a typical split subject. His mother used to dress him in girls' clothes – a habit which he retained indefinitely, but which did not prevent him from displaying bravery and winning numerous medals in the Pacific and East Asia during World War Two (Grey, 1994: 16–17). During his military service, his wife remembers, he had lived through many horror stories, 'hated to kill, but . . . he did', and had nightmares about the first man he shot' (1994: 17). Some of Ed Wood's comrades knew that, underneath his marine uniform, he was wearing a pink bra and pink panties (1994: 20).

In his book *The Monster Show*, David Skal explains the return of 'old-fashioned ghoulishness' to the American comic industry, cinema and television during the post-war period:

> The new American prosperity of the early 1950s was won atop the largest bone pile in human history. World War II had claimed the lives of over 40 million soldiers and civilians, and had introduced two radical forms of mechanised death – the atomic bomb and the extermination camp – that seriously challenged the mind's ability to absorb, much less cope with, the naked face of horror at mid-century. And only five years after the fall of Germany and Japan, America was once again at war, this time "a police action" in Korea haunted by the spectre of the H-bomb, a looming necro-technology now shared uneasily with the Soviets. If America in the 1950s was filled with the smell of new cars, it was permeated by the stench of mass death, and the treat of more to come.
>
> (Skal, 1993: 229)

The 1950s was the decade when it was becoming clear that there soon would be changes in values in culture and the arts. Ed Wood, with his erratic vintage references, misarranged footage and lack of aspiration to make anything original, can be regarded as presaging the new era. His muddled techniques and deeply imperfect narratives reflect the undiluted essence of the postmodern taste. A war veteran, Ed Wood had stared horror in the face – both its physical and psychological aspects. No pink panties could prevent him from angrily stabbing the dead body of the Japanese soldier who had knocked out his front teeth (Grey, 1994: 20). Filtered through his mind, military nightmares, mutilated bodies, murders, atomic bomb scares (*Bride of the Atom*), the burgeoning questions of gender and ethnicity, and other issues pertaining to 'the other', all found their artless and crude expression in atomic monsters, alien gravediggers, and soldier drag-queens. In many ways, the wounds were all too real.

The puerile sincerity and cheap disorderliness of Wood's art was perfectly captured by Burton in the biopic. Unlike the general audience, Tim Burton grasps the essence of Ed Wood – he is that very man who wears 'bat ears'; the man with a profound sense of tragedy who, due to lack of training, patience and talent, fails to convey it to the viewer; the vulnerable man who openly displays the perplexing intimacies of his inner life; undresses his emotions. It is only logical that Wood ended up in the ultimate 'undressing' genre – pornography. He is the typical hapless, rejected, imperfect, Frankensteinesque freak of Burton's who unashamedly, melodramatically demonstrates his suffering: 'Do you think I care if I'm a millionaire? [. . .] What hurts me is the cruelty towards me. The way they want to deride me. They way they want to put me down and scoff at me. I'm only trying to do the best at what I feel. All this garbage I see, they praise, and me, they seem to love me and deride me' (Grey, 1994: 12). His wounds are open.

By being so inaptly expressed, the tragedy turns into the comedy, a run-of-the mill circus (and, for a while, Ed Wood had actually worked in a circus as a 'freak'). *Glen or Glenda*, for instance, touches upon a whole bunch of weighty philosophical, psychological and cultural issues: suicide; the categorisation of sexuality ('Glen is not a homosexual. Glen is a transvestite'); childhood complexes ('Glen's father had no love for his son'); society's normalising tendencies and rejection of difference; diversity of cultural discourses; male supremacy and gender politics ('It's predominantly who design your clothes, your shoes . . .'); instrumental rationality and its primacy of power; fear of the unconscious ('Beware of the big green dragon . . .'); and ultimately, the existentialist question of God's inadequacy and man's forsakenness ('People! All going somewhere. All with their own ideas, all with their own . . . personalities. [. . .] Pull the string!'). All these issues, however, are cancelled by the shameless exploitation stance adopted by *Glen or Glenda*'s creators and distributors. Wood's films do not display their maker's purity of intention; they are screaming: 'Watch me undress!'

Ed Wood's unstoppable desire 'just to tell stories' (as he explains to Sarah Jessica Parker's character, Dolores) is symbolically manifested in the 'palm tree' sequence at the beginning of Burton's biopic. Told to take a potted palm tree to the executive building, Ed grabs a palm among the various shrubs at the warehouse, and strolls along the very busy movie lot, stopping to talk to people and to admire the affluence of some movie sets ('Gosh, where do they get real camels?'). The tree, symbolising his connection with the unconscious, with the mother (the mythological 'Great Mother', and the personal mother who dressed him in girls' clothes) metaphorically represents the source of his artistic endeavour. Unfortunately, compared to other 'Hollywood trees' which have big sets, better ideas and lots of money, Ed's palm is only tiny and impermanent. He just can't make it big in Hollywood.

Burton's film, which takes the real Ed Wood's life as a base, stresses the connection between the protagonist's hermaphroditism and his infantilism. Johnny Depp's character keeps stealing, and wearing, his girlfriend's pink angora sweaters – the addiction which delineates his immaturity and the duality of his personality, alongside an embittered longing for the maternal. 'The creative man is "feminine" in his passive openness to the creative flow,' Erich Neumann writes (Neumann, 1974a: 29). Hillman's analysis of the wounded puer, written as a first-person narrative, is even more in keeping with Wood's fluffy passion: 'Hysterical regressions to the mother reveal my profound vulnerability, how utterly exposed I am, like an exaggerated wound, and I enter into my woundedness so that it may mother me. Instead of hysterically fleeing castration I am initiated by it. Here, the fantasy is wound = womb. Now, the womb is the right place, inside the deep belly, no longer wandering in hystericised woundedness, seeking help from friends, love in a restaurant, straws in the wind' (Hillman, 1997: 114).

Meanwhile, the usurped womb kept giving birth to monsters, vampires, flying saucers, Gothic pornography and suchlike unfiltered nonsense. Free from the constrictions of mainstream cinema, Wood's imagination produced images without boundaries; and without much sense.

Whereas Ed's mother is metonymically epitomised in Burton's film by pink sweaters and blond wigs, the father is represented by the ageing Bela Lugosi (played by Martin Landau, who received an Oscar for this role). Burton could personally relate to the creative–paternal relationship between Wood and Lugosi because it reminded him of his own connection with Vincent Price: '. . . there was an aspect of his relationship with Lugosi that I liked. He befriended him at the end of his life, and without really knowing what that was like, I connected with it on the level that I did with Vincent Price, in terms of how I felt about him. Meeting Vincent had an incredible impact on me, the same impact Ed must have felt meeting and working with his idol' (Salisbury, 2006: 131–134).

Burton and Landau depict Bela Lugosi as an idealised father figure – the father who Ed Wood had lost a long time ago, and now rediscovered. A good and devoted 'son', Ed reverentially listens to every word Bela utters ('Pull the strings!'), and watches every gesture he makes – like the hypnotic arm waving: 'Vampira! You will come under my spell! You will be my slave of love.' When Ed unsuccessfully attempts to copy Bela's gesture, the old man explains that, to achieve the desired 'scary effect', 'You must be double-jointed, and you must be Hungarian.' Attuned to his idol, Ed wants to imitate him in everything.

The real Ed Wood and Bela had a lot in common: Lugosi, who served as a lieutenant in the Austro-Hungarian Army in World War I, was twice wounded (Lennig, 2003: 26), and Ed Wood fought in World War II (Grey, 1994: 20). After the real, physical horrors of wartime, the plastic monsters and vampires of Hollywood must have seemed to them rather innocuous.

Both were creative people, who were used, reused and abused by the showbiz industry. Having stereotyped Lugosi, the industry persistently put him back into the coffin, up to the point where everybody thought he was already dead. In Burton's film, Bela finds his stereotypical position 'too constrictive'. This is how Ed feels, too, being unable to conform, or to restrain his disorganised vision. The film industry is Ed Wood's coffin.

The ultimate connection between the two characters is established in *Ed Wood* in the metaphor of the scarred arm. Bela's arm is covered in injection scars – the consequence of years of heroin abuse. Speaking symbolically, while Ed's wounds are still open, Bela's are closed. Ed's attempt to imitate Bela's hand gesture may be interpreted as coming from his readiness to close the wounds; as a sign of movement 'from bitterness and complaint to a taste for salt and blood' (Hillman, 1987: 115). Ed might be ready for a change of shift 'from focus upon the emotional pain of the wound – its causes, perimeters, cures – to its imaginal depths; from displacements of the womb onto women and "femininity" to its locus in one's own bodily rhythm' (1997: 115). Bela's scarred present is, possibly, Ed's more mature future.

Burton's *Ed Wood* has an intricate, typically postmodern Chinese-box structure: it is a film about films which are remakes of other films. The sheer heaviness and heterogeneity of this framework make *Ed Wood* a trifle cumbersome – that is probably why, despite unanimous critical acclaim and several important awards, it has never become a 'people's film' (Salisbury, 2006: 143). Nevertheless, behind the structural complexity (probably unintentional on Burton's part – he seems to be apologetic about any accidental auteurism occurring in his works), there is a psychologically truthful account of a creative mind in the post-catastrophe world. Burton's accentuation of Bela and Ed's friendship, albeit subjectively and idealistically presented, helps Ed's fans to understand their idol's confused mind. It also throws light on some of the strangest sequences in his films, like the decision to cut in stock footage of stampeding bulls in *Glen or Glenda*, or Lugosi's infamously meaningless 'green dragon' speech.

The 'green dragon' scene from *Glen or Glenda*, reconstructed in the biopic as one of the several scenes from Ed Wood's films, deserves a separate explanation. Sat amidst skeletons, bats and ghouls, Lugosi announces with an assumed air of self-importance: 'Beware. Beware! Beware, of the big green dragon that sits on your doorstep. He eats little boys! Puppy dog tails! Big fat snails! Beware. Take care. Beware!'

The first impression of the speech is that it sounds utterly unintelligible – either as a serious statement in Wood's original film, or reproduced in the warm ironic context of *Ed Wood*. Still, the notorious misplaced 'dragon' does make sense if we take into consideration Ed's veneration of the feminine, his and Lugosi's wartime experience, and the general feeling of uncertainty and doom which enveloped the world during, and around, the two world wars. Concerning the 'dragon of the unconscious', Erich Neumann wrote: 'As our daytime is devoured by the Terrible Mother, torn to pieces in the bloody rituals that are our wars, demonic, magical, and elementary irrationality invades us. The stream of libido flows inward, from the crumbling canon into the unconscious, and activates its latent images of past and future' (Neumann, 1974a: 118). As a result of this change, artists start producing 'a strange mixture', in which 'fragments of landscapes, cubes, circles, forms, colors, part of human figures, organic and inorganic components, curves, tatters of dreams, memories, deconcretised objects, and concretised symbols seem to float in a strange continuum' (1974a: 119).

Unfortunately, Ed Wood's 'strange continuum' is so incomprehensible that it is only understood by the chosen few.

'Family is not conducive to a creative atmosphere'

Charlie and the Chocolate Factory (2005)

Nowhere else does Tim Burton discuss the theme of 'fathers and sons' so openly, and so sentimentally, as in *Charlie and the Chocolate Factory* (2005). Here the director finally delineates the entire extent of the problem, and explains the issues clearly: a boy with an inadequate father may grow up to become a high-flyer – but all his achievements will be gained through pain, and marked with rebellious, and tricksterish, infantilism.

It was brave of the screenwriter John August and Burton to change the original story to incorporate this resounding father–son element; but it certainly worked. Whereas in Dahl's book Willie Wonka immediately agrees to allow Charlie to take his large family to live with him at the factory, Burton's Wonka is an artistic loner who thinks that relatives can only impede your talent because 'they're just telling you what to do, what not to do, and it's not conducive to a creative atmosphere'. The chocolatier's infantile complexes are so immense that he even has trouble pronouncing the word 'parents'. However, he changes his negative opinion about families and communal living after revisiting his estranged father, and making up with him. The film ends on a happy note of reconciliation and prosperity as Charlie's family gains the right to live at the factory together with their sweet-natured offspring.

The executive producer of the film and widow of the writer, Felicity Dahl, praised the narrative alteration: 'All books have to be changed for making a film. And these certainly enhanced the book' (DVD2/'Chocolate Dreams'). John August explained the change from his side: 'Script-wise, the biggest change that we made from the original book to our movie is sort of continuing the story on a little bit more at the end. As an audience, we know that Charlie's going to persevere and get the factory, but we need to add a little extra complication to that [. . .] It's *Charlie and the Chocolate Factory*, but it's also Tim Burton's *Charlie and the Chocolate Factory*, it takes place within the universe of his movies' (John August, DVD2/'Chocolate Dreams').

Indeed, visually and conceptually, it is very much a Burton film. It has the trademark contrast between monochrome and colour, the numerous retro references and parodies, and the strong musical element. Bearing in mind the director's cool attitude to the concept of cinematic narrative, musical numbers are a good way of creating the impression of a coherent whole. The various parts of *Charlie*, like the fragments of *The Nightmare Before Christmas, Corpse Bride* and later *Sweeney Todd* are glued together, and systemised, by the punctuation elements that are songs.

Burton's trademark contrast between the 'real' and 'fantasy' worlds, with colour as the demarcation line, had been previously utilised by him in *The Nightmare Before Christmas* and *Corpse Bride*. Burton commented on the decision to use the 'grey' palette in *Charlie*: 'One thing that we wanted to do was contrast the exterior factory, the town, black-and-white colour scheme – you remember in the *Wizard of Oz* when it's, like, black-and-white, and then you go into colour, it's an amazing moment' (DVD2/'Designer Chocolate').

Burton's love of contrasts and opposite clashes also finds its expression in the visual 'dialecticity' of the overall design. The world of 'common people' and Willie Wonka's factory differ not just in colour, but also in size. In fact, the 'castle looming over town' *mise-en-scène* had been used by Burton before, most notably in *Edward Scissorhands* and *The Nightmare Before Christmas*. The production designer Alex McDowell elucidates the ideas behind the set: '. . . the very first thing to do was to establish the polar opposites of the environment. One was the town, and one's the factory. The factory looms over it, and in a direct line from that, way down in the bottom of the hill, is a little crumbling house, which is also a unique structure in the town. All the rest of the town in between the Bucket house and the factory is basically identical generic housing' (McDowell, DVD2/ 'Designer Chocolate'). As Burton explains about the set, the town is neither American, not does it have an entirely 'British council estate' look. It is presented to the audience as an unnamed industrial town. The absence of a nationality and geographical location furnishes the set with 'a fable-like quality' (DVD2/'Designer Chocolate'). This visual decision presents the castle as a symbol of nonconformism and creativity, while the small house is a metaphor of humbleness and the very human gesture that is sacrifice. The geographical gap between the two buildings is filled with the ordinary lives of beings who are neither kind and modest, like Charlie, nor talented like the proud chocolatier.

Quite in line with Burton's 'hands-on' philosophy, real buildings were used whenever possible. The chocolate river, waterfall and grass were also all genuine and absolutely edible. In fact, the team went to great lengths to keep the film's *mise-en-scène* as 'physical' and handmade as possible. The special effects supervisor Joss Williams spent months in an attempt to establish the right texture for the chocolate river, into which the German actor Philip Wiegratz (Augustus Gloop) had to dive for real. Grass was made by confectioners, specially hired for this purpose. The squirrel army consisted of real animals, models and CGI squirrels. Actually, CGI was only used when there was no other option – as in the wide tunnel ride where Willie Wonka and his guests go down the tunnel towards the creative heart of the factory (DVD2/'Designer Chocolate'/'Under the Wrapper').

The 'monstrous physicality' of the set is counterbalanced by the usual absence of narrative realism. Even 'the real' part of the magic-realist world – i.e. the town with its grey terraces – is very stylised, sensational, hyperbolised, and therefore not terribly convincing (which was intrinsically Roald Dahl's intention). In true postmodern spirit, Burton includes visual references to famous films, such as Francis Ford Coppola's *Apocalypse Now* (1979) and Stanley Kubrick's *2001: A Space Odyssey* (1968). In a way, an allusion to *Apocalypse Now* was inevitable because of a number of intersecting themes: colonialism and 'the natives' (Oompa Loompas working for Willy Wonka), a mysterious river journey into 'the heart of darkness', etc. Augustus Gloop's surfacing after his fall into the chocolate river is a parodic carbon copy of Captain Willard's emergence from the water just before killing the renegade Colonel Kurtz. The reference to Kubrick's celebrated masterpiece is even more direct: the monkeys on screen in the TV room are the chimpanzees from the opening scenes of *2001: A Space Odyssey*.

There is even a joke about Ed Wood's angora obsession. On the tour of the factory, the visitors stumble upon Oompa Loompas shearing pink sheep. The host refuses to explain how pink wool can be utilised: 'I'd rather not talk about that one.' Apparently, the wool is needed for satisfying Wonka's passion for pink sweaters!

There are also musical allusions. Accompanying the chimps receiving their teleported bar of chocolate is Richard Strauss's tone poem *Also Sprach Zarathustra* – Kubrick's original choice for the extra-diegetic musical comment on the opening of his *Space Odyssey*. The songs written by Danny Elfman were intended by the author to be parodies of various 1970s and 1980s musical genres and styles (DVD2/'Sweet Sounds'). In truth, Willie Wonka himself can be regarded as a parody – of Michael Jackson. The similarities in appearance and behaviour have numerously been pointed out by fans and critics. For instance, Peter Travers's review for *Rolling Stone* describes Depp's portrayal thus: 'The Michael Jackson pallor. The unnaturally white teeth. The smile stretched with insincerity' (www. rollingstone.com). Another reviewer, Jim Emerson, expounds:

> It's kind of hard not to draw the comparison, given that Jackson's Santa Barbara County rancho notorious is named Neverland, and Depp just came off an Oscar-nominated performance in the best picture-nominated "Finding Neverland," in which he played the inventor of Peter Pan, a figure to whom Jackson has often been likened – and likened himself. [. . .]
>
> The physical details of Depp's performance, including the pale face, semi-pageboy haircut, tightly drawn lips, high whispery voice, effeminate demeanour, and semi-formal candy-dandy wardrobe (tarted-up traditional hats, velvet jackets, glam gloves – all with a fancified military and/or Victorian flavour), reminded many viewers of Jackson.
>
> (http://rogerebert.suntimes.com

But all the while, Depp denies looking to the notorious and reclusive singer for inspiration (Blitz and Krasniewicz, 2007: 96–97).

In a way, the comparisons with Michael Jackson were inevitable. The added narrative line about the stringent father suggested a link between adult infantilism and regression on the one hand, and childhood abuse on the other. The film was being shot and released at the time when the most high-profile case of such regression – the Michael Jackson ordeal of 2003–2005 – was being dragged through the international media. In several high-profile interviews (most notably with Oprah Winfrey in 1993, and with Martin Bashir in 2003) Jackson reluctantly revealed the dark truth about his childhood. The unnatural life of a star child was worsened by physical and emotional abuse at the hands of his father (Kincaid, 1998: 236). Both Jackson's family situation and the Burton/August/Depp rendition of Dahl's chocolatier invite similar comments on the origins of mad, immature creativity.

Back to *Charlie and the Chocolate Factory*: everything Wonka does seems to go back to the aborted relationship with his male parent (the mother is absent, as is the tradition with Burton's films). He cannot pronounce the heinous word 'parents'. He has recurring flashbacks, triggered by various free association words (such as 'kid' or 'parent'), about his father forbidding him to eat sweets and making him wear a horrendous piece of facegear (which, supposedly, is going to straighten out his teeth). He also thinks that the family is an impediment to the creative behaviour of the individual: 'A chocolatier has to run free and solo. He has to follow his dreams. Gosh darn the consequences!' When Charlie refuses his 'inheritance' offer, Wonka's creativity suddenly dries up. He only manages to unblock the source of his ideas after reconnecting with his father. As the audience, we are left to decide for ourselves whether his father is dead or alive, and whether their meeting is taking place 'for real', or is just happening in Wonka's head.

The father–son dynamic is similar to that outlined in *Edward Scissorhands* and *Big Fish*: the son 'loses' his father as an actual, positive, supportive father figure, but nevertheless retains his father's traits. His creative habits reflect, in a distorted, inside-out way, his parent's character and occupation. Indeed, Willie Wonka's profession is the negation of his father's career. The parental motivation he receives is negative motivation; a kind of 'achievement through anger'. Yet, Burton is also keen to stress that there is a connection between the two people, which is visually expressed in their gloved hands. Both Willie Wonka and his father have very physical, hands-on and hygiene-dominated professions. When they shake hands, they are wearing gloves. If we follow Burton's usual metonymic route, hands stand for whole vulnerable personalities and represent broken hearts. Wonka's hands (in Depp's version) also serve as surrogates for facial expressions, because his hurt inner puer is safely concealed underneath a frozen, introvertedly inexpressive façade.

Hands are also means of physical and emotional contact. Within a radius of the hands = personality metonymy, gloves covering hands equal a mask hiding a face; they signal the presence of what Jung called 'persona' – the protective outer padding, the mask, the official (or artificial) façade one shows to the world. Sometimes such a mask can, in the words of Jolande Jacobi, '"grow on" so rigidly that it can no longer be laid aside', while the real personality, with its swarm of personal inadequacies, peevishness and infantilism is firmly locked underneath (Jacobi, 1973: 29). However hard Wonka and his father want to hide their inner vulnerabilities from each other, they are still deeply connected. 'To the hands', James Hillman writes, 'belong two distinct spiritual functions – creative and authoritative, the wand and the mace' (Hillman, 1987: 104). The wand and the mace, Wonka and his father, resemble each other so much that they cannot be further apart.

There is also a dark edge to Wonka's creativity, which is an intrinsic ingredient in Dahl's book. This bent has perfectly suited Burton's needs. He says: '[Roald Dahl] was, to me, one of the first writers who captured the mixture of light and dark and humorous and being politically incorrect, and all those things you kind of love as a child and as an adult' (DVD2/ 'Designer Chocolate'). This edge is reflected in Wonka's aloofness, his tricksterish qualities, weird hobbies, his introverted, unnatural behaviour; and reaches its striking visual culmination in the image of the factory host welcoming his guests with scissors in his right hand, and a cane in his left. Wonka is Edward who has acquired a mask but still has not learnt how to deal with frustration and pain, the emotional legacies of inadequate (celestial or personal) parenting. At the same time, he certainly makes an effort to 'pull himself together'. His destructive hobbies (such as, for instance, the ritual melting and subsequent repairing of wax dolls) are counterbalanced by his enormous creative output. Whenever he falls to pieces, he seeks consolation in his occupation. His desire to create, to 'join the pieces', comes via the route of overcoming the pain, and healing the inner split. The destructive gives birth to the creative.

Charlie and the fairtrade chocolate factory?

The father–son psychological dimension, added to the original story of Willy Wonka, has elucidated certain parts of the existing narrative; for instance, the origins of the chocolatier's talent, his reclusiveness and, most significantly, his conflict with the proverbial 'crowd'. Wonka's faith in humankind is shattered when spies hired by other firms steal secrets of his amazing products. Interestingly enough, Willie Wonka is unusually idealistic for a proprietor. His response to the industrial espionage story is naïve and childish. He regards this deed as 'something that only bad people can do', as a true betrayal, a breach of trust. In that, Wonka's reaction to the loss of his treasure is similar to Pee Wee's childish anger, sadness and confusion when his precious bike gets stolen. Willie Wonka prefers to generate his own ideas rather than purloin somebody else's. People who steal intellectual property are lacking creativity; they are people without imagination – grey, common people. Wonka asks Grandpa Joe at the gates of his factory if he was one of those despicable spies who tried to steal his life's work, and sell it to the parasitic copycats. And when the old man gives a negative answer, the chocolatier puts his smiley mask back on, and welcomes everyone inside. Wonka does not like those who do not observe the fair principles of copyright.

Yet, both Wonka and Pee Wee are 'contradictions in terms'. They learn how to protect their idealised private property in the cruel capitalist world, but do not mind getting involved in serious business ventures. Pee Wee's story ends on the happy note of him selling his adventure to Hollywood. An oxymoronic idealistic industrial capitalist, Wonka's mind is supposedly unspoilt, whereas the people outside are gripped by greed and envy.

There is also a dark tint to his chosen mode of production. The environment inside his factory consists of a series of sterile and impersonal rooms, while the workers are all similar-looking Oompa Loompas (played by one actor, Deep Roy) from Loompaland. In the original text they are described as pygmies from 'the very deepest and darkest part of the African jungle, where no white man had ever been before' (McCann and Woodard, 1972: 112). They come to work at the factory because they worship coco-beans, and their wages are also paid in this edible currency. The parodic recreation of the bathing scene from Coppola's *Apocalypse Now* serves as a veiled supporting reference to the barely visible theme of exploitation and colonialism.

The Oompa Loompas' identical appearance, apart from the classic 'those natives all look alike' attitude, alludes to the replaceability of the workforce within the impersonal production apparatus. This, in its turn, brings about the whole Marxist question of alienation in capitalist society; for, in the last instance, it is Willie Wonka who owns the factory and controls the production process. He is the brain behind the enterprise. This alienation allusion can even be placed into a wider metaphorical context. Le Blanc and Odell suggest that Burton's Oompa Loompas are 'cuddly' answers to the Martians from *Mars Attacks!* (Le Blanc and Odell, 2005: 134). Wonka's workers might as well be compared to the green creatures because they are entirely alien to their surroundings.

The industrial capitalist dimension is further supported in the film (and the book) by the scenes depicting two other industrial giants, the toothpaste factory and the nut factory, which belongs to Veruca Salt's father. Mr Bucket has a repetitive job putting the caps on tubes. Eventually, he loses his position and is replaced by a much faster machine, but then returns to the factory in a new role – as a machine repairer. He has no power at the workplace – in stark contrast to Mr Salt, the owner of a plant called 'Salt's Nuts', where he has the utmost control over his workers. On his cue, they stop shelling nuts and start shelling chocolates in order to find a golden ticket for his capricious daughter.

The thread about industrial capitalism, exploitation and mass production adds another angle to Burton's observations on modernity, postmodernity and their transgressions. It also fits into his favourite pool of themes: man and machine, creativity versus mass production, the complex relationship between the inventor and the invented, and, ultimately, contemporary man and his search for God. *Charlie and the Chocolate Factory* is an optimistic film in that it asserts that capitalism with a human face exists, and that the case of modernity is not lost. The recipe for the ideal capitalist concoction seems to include one creative person, a number of mechanisms and contraptions, one dead father, a pinch of darkness, a dash of guilt, and a human face – that of a child. Charlie, for instance. The boy is the redeeming element in this mix; he is the one who, by choosing tradition (his family) over profit (Wonka's offer), liberates Wonka from his guilt. Charlie is also the one who 'resurrects' the father, and who keeps the whole machine going. And finally, as a gesture of hopeful faith in the ideas and achievements of modernity, he gets to inherit the factory.

In Wonka's quest for individualism and originality in the age of mass production, common humanity appears to be the key ingredient. Even in Burton's own industry, humanity is the key to the contentious issue of auteurism versus mass-orientated cinematic products. Rather than falling into one of these two categories – mass-appeal or greater independence – Tim Burton chooses to make films that are warm, emotionally and intellectually accessible yet, at the same time, meaningful and profound.

Chapter 5

The maniac

A harmless psycho or a harmful psycho? The trickster versus the shadow

All Burton's 'maniacs' – Betelegeuse, the Joker, Sweeney Todd – cross the line between infantile rage and adult aggression, as well as between childhood playfulness and deliberate harm. This can be analysed in view of Jung's theory of the shadow and the trickster. The 'maniacs' occupy different positions on what I call the trickster–shadow spectrum, or the scale which 'measures' the degree of malevolence in the character's playfulness (or is it the degree of playfulness in the character's malevolent actions?). But first, let us explain the difference between the two terms.

Of all the archetypes Jung outlined, the trickster and the shadow are probably the most directly related to the problem of the 'second personality'. In mythology and popular culture, including cinema, they are often depicted as the so-called 'double' (discussed in the Introduction and Chapter 2) – an unmanageable second self who, akin to Stoker's Dracula, or Stevenson's Mr Hyde, comes out at night-time and commits the unspeakable acts which would never come into the head of its wholly decent and law-abiding carrier. The double hijacks the 'daytime' personality, subverting the individual's control over his or her own actions and thoughts.

Despite mapping the outlines of the archetypes of the shadow and the trickster in detail, Jung does not closely study the crossing of the boundary between them. As Susan Rowland rightly points out, although Jung groups the 'trickster qualities' with Native American myth, and assigns the shadow to Western discourse, he struggles to bring the two together (Rowland, 2005: 188).

the trickster   the shadow

Figure 5.1

Like all archetypal images, they can be regarded as both mythical figures and inner psychic experiences. However, there exists a generic divergence between the two types of the double. Whereas the trickster is more 'unconscious', playful and benign, the shadow's actions are conscious and deliberate. At the highest analytical level, they represent the different attitudes of human consciousness towards the concept of evil – both in the psyche, and in the external environment. The owner of the inner trickster 'does not notice' evil because he or she does not perceive himself as detached from nature and the world of instincts, whereas the shadow is a fruit of guilt, the atavistic, animalistic burden of the civilized person. As such, the shadow is a place of negativised projections, and a waste bin for the unwanted parts of the self.

The trickster figure, much favoured in pre-industrial societies, has been analysed by social anthropologists such as Paul Radin (who studied the Winnebago Indians trickster cycle), Thomas Belmonte and Adolf Bandelier, as well as by Carl Jung and the analytical psychologist-cum-literary critic William Willeford. Jung defines the trickster figure as the wise fool, the clown, the delight-maker who has a dual nature: half-animal, half-divine. Trickster subverts the hierarchic order, is capable of changing shape and is famous for his frisky tricks and pranks. Jung also mentions the strong link between the trickster figure and the carnival culture, where the devil appeared as *simia dei* – the ape of God (Jung, 1954, CW9/I: paras. 456–486). A good example of the trickster archetype in mythology is the many-faced deity Hermes/Mercurius[1], while the Shakespearean jester (Touchstone, Trinculo, Yorick, the Fool in *King Lear*) is probably the most famous illustration of the trickster in literature.

Phylogenetically and anthropologically, he represents the dawn of civilisation and the origins of human consciousness; ontogenetically he symbolises a pre-conscious child, a creature who cannot be held entirely responsible for what he does because he does not yet possess a full moral code to define his actions. As Jung writes, in his clearest manifestations the trickster 'is a faithful reflection of an absolutely undifferentiated human consciousness, corresponding to a psyche that has hardly left the animal level' (CW9/I: para. 465). No longer the animal but not yet the human, the trickster is stuck in a sort of developmental *purgatorio*. On the one hand, he is 'superior to man because of his superhuman qualities, and on the other hand inferior to him because of his unreason and unconsciousness'. Yet, he is 'no match for the animals either, because of his extraordinary clumsiness and lack of instinct. These defects are the marks of his human nature, which is not so well adapted to the environment as the animal's' (CW9/I: para. 473). In fact, the trickster is a playful 'goodbye' to the natural animalism of man.

1 This example was used by many anthropologists, including Jung, Karl Kerenyi and the Russian folklorist and cultural theorist Eleazar Meletinskii.

This fascinatingly subversive and ever-changing character has an unsurpassed ability to captivate audiences. The most popular contemporary variant of him is the clown figure which has its origins in the Italian *commedia dell'arte* and the French mime tradition. The clown's behaviour amuses the child whose psyche has reached a higher level of maturation than that of the trickster. Comparing themselves to the clown, children can see that his actions are obviously senseless and silly. But some serious and perfection-seeking adults, far from being fascinated, 'may feel very queerly indeed when confronted by the figure of the trickster' (CW9/I: para. 471). Apparently, a fully fledged trickster is not to everyone's liking.

I have always envisaged the trickster and the shadow as forming a continuous spectrum rather than being two separate archetypes. There are a number of transitory stages where the boundary between mischievousness and hostility becomes blurred. This can be best illustrated using examples from popular cinema. At the peak of his career in the middle of the 1990s, Jim Carrey was typecast as a trickster – light-headed, dumb, inadequate, and therefore compulsively, hysterically, almost therapeutically funny. He created a spectrum of amazingly infantile characters: Ace Ventura (*Ace Ventura: Pet Detective*, 1994; *Ace Ventura: When Nature Calls*, 1995), Stanley Ipkiss (*The Mask*, 1994), Lloyd Christmas (*Dumb and Dumber*, 1994) and Fletcher Reede (*Liar Liar*, 1997). However, even the highly idiotic Lloyd Christmas has a dark side: for instance, he inadvertently kills an ulcer-plagued gangster by feeding him a spicy burger. In yet another uncanny moment Lloyd is struck by a sudden inspiration to glue his dead parrot's head back onto the body in order to sell it to a blind boy. However cruel this scene may sound in theory, Lloyd's silly parrot-selling decision was not purposefully hurtful, and did not harbour an evil intention. It is a half-digested joke – because the joker does not possess the mental capacities necessary for analysing his actions. The presence of a large number of primitive 'toilet humour' jokes in Carrey's films only highlights his trickster connection. Preoccupation with inferior bodily functions, and the lack of 'civilised fear and disgust' towards them is typical for mythological tricksters.

The body of the delight maker is flexible, transmutable and guilt-free, Jung postulates: 'He is so unconscious of himself that his body is not a unity, and his two hands fight each other. He takes his anus off and entrusts it with a special task. Even his sex is optional despite his phallic qualities: he can turn itself into a woman and bear children. From his penis he makes all kinds of useful plants' (CW 9/I: para. 472). He will remain in this state of 'excretion naivety' until he starts to realise, speaking ontogenetically, that certain functions are better hidden from the public eye. In other words, when the process of cognition starts, and a sense of guilt emerges in relation to biological functions.

The trickster archetype stands for the connection with the source of creativity in the human psyche. His entertaining qualities come from his proximity to the unconscious. As Jung writes, trickster mythology has an interesting therapeutic effect: 'It holds the earlier low intellectual level before the eyes of the more highly developed individual, so that he shall not forget how things looked yesterday' (CW 9/I: para. 480). Jung also admits that he cannot explain why such an unconscious figure can be so attractive for the contemporary civilised public, but reproduces Radin's words: 'Viewed psychologically, it might be contended that the history of civilization is largely the account of the attempts of man to forget his transformation from the animal into a human being' (quoted in Jung, CW 9/I: para. 480). Put simply, the trickster reconnects the viewer to the 'uncivilisedness' of the natural world, and the unconscious. This brings us back to the question already explored in the last chapter, about the Genius: the Burtonian child is 'dark' because of proximity to the unconscious, and he is also creative because of this proximity. Creativity, infantilism and the unconscious are the trio that defines and shapes Burton's principal characters.

The thin line dividing the archetypes of the trickster and the shadow can also be explained using the example of the circus culture. The circus is a basic form of entertainment, aimed at satisfying the simpler tastes of the crowd. Some of the traditional circus acts, such as those involving animals, trapeze artists and clowns, and, in the past, freak shows, may seem inappropriate to contemporary audiences. In the Western world today cruelty to animals is unacceptable, freak shows are politically incorrect, and balancing, trapeze and other acrobatic acts are deemed unsafe. Meanwhile, clowns, probably because of the implied duplicity of the mask, are often perceived by many people as menacing rather than amusing. The clown's motley appearance and showmanship reflect the vulgarity of crowd entertainment, and hints at his menacing side – that is, the cruel and senseless joker. Depending on your perception, circus culture can be seen as dazzling, amusing and delightful – or as the shadow of civilisation. The thin line divides rough tastes and primitive drives from the rational, civilised conscience.

Following Paul Radin's research on the Winnebago hero myth, Joseph Henderson argues that the trickster cycle forms the base of this myth. In the evolution of the archetype of the delight maker, there is a phase when he begins to transform into a more mature being; when he becomes a hero. Henderson writes: 'At the end of his rogue's progress he is beginning to take on the physical likeness of a grown man' (Jung and von Franz, 1964: 104). In the Winnebago hero myth this stage is called Hare, or the Transformer. It shows the mischievous child as 'becoming a socialised being, correcting the instinctual and infantile found in the Trickster cycle' (1964: 165). The trickster may mature into the hero – or the shadow, or even both (like Batman), forever poking his soul for signs of evil, and trying to heal the split. Mythologically speaking, the end of innocence and the beginning of consciousness is also the end of paradise. This is when the shadow is born.

The actor who is often typecast in shadow roles (and indeed, is very good in them) is Jack Nicholson. As the shadow grows out of the trickster, it can retain its subversiveness, playfulness and even a counterfeit light-hearted attitude. Nicholson's most devilish roles – Jack Torrance (*The Shining*, 1980), Daryl Van Horne (*Witches of Eastwick*, 1987), Jack Napier – are characterised by mischievousness and unpredictability. The foolishness of Nicholson's tricksters, however, is fake. These characters are clever, their actions are deliberate, and their thinking is shrewd – albeit evil and mad. And it is this insane, menacing unpredictability that is scary about Jack Torrance or even the rebellious Randle Murphy from *One Flew Over the Cuckoo's Nest* (it is symbolical that the mercurial Murphy is eliminated by the cold, impersonal, tyrannical rationality of the mental institution).

Behind the silly mask (either perceivable or imaginary) there is always a sinister intention, and the mask itself becomes the symbol of the madness of the unconscious. The shadow is the enemy of the individual because it drags them back into the unthinking collectivity; it is individual, independent traits that are at stake in the conflict between nature and civilisation. The shadow, Jung keeps reminding his reader everywhere in his works, is dangerous if undifferentiated, and explosive when totally neglected and left to brood inside the owner's psyche. And things can go even worse when personal shadows merge to form an aggressive system of beliefs such as fascism, communist totalitarianism or other, much smaller thought-epidemics.

Jung linked the emergence of the collective shadow in the war-ridden twentieth century to the psychological effects of industrialisation and the new urban lifestyle. He argued that late modernity made the individual feel powerless and confused. Burdened with the feeling of deep inadequacy, the individual is prone to being suddenly whirled into a mass movement or becoming the victim of the latest psycho-bug:

> As I have said, the uprush of mass instincts was symptomatic of a compensatory move of the unconscious. Such a move was possible because the conscious state of the people had become estranged from the natural laws of human existence. Thanks to industrialization, large portions of the population were uprooted and were herded together in large centres. This new form of existence – with its mass psychology and social dependence on the fluctuation of markets and wages – produced an individual who was unstable, insecure and suggestible. He was aware that his life depended on boards of directors and captains of industry, and he supposed, rightly or wrongly, that they were chiefly motivated by financial interests. He knew that, no matter how hard he worked, he could still fall a victim at any moment to economic changes which we utterly beyond his control.
>
> (Jung, 1952, CW10: para. 453)

This lack of orientation, and the sense of losing control over one's destiny, is not limited to individual members of society. Personal shadows have a tendency to merge into collective evil, Jung warned. This is precisely what happened in Germany prior to, and during, World War II: 'The individual's feeling of weakness, indeed of non-existence, was thus compensated by the eruption of hitherto unknown desires for power. It was the revolt of the powerless, the insatiable greed of the "have-nots" [. . .] Thus the avalanche rolled on in Germany and produced its leader, who was elected as a tool to complete the ruin of the nation' (CW10: para. 454).

The collective shadow is a relatively simple and useful term to show the demarcation line between 'a group of individuals' and 'a mass of people'. Jung saw it as defined by collective projection – as a summation of individual 'hatreds', directed against another group of individuals, a culturally and socially different 'enemy'. Like the personal shadow, the collective version works like a mirror in that it reflects a bouquet of undesirable qualities of a group of people who are unaware of them. The 'shadow qualities', meanwhile, are 'looking' for a 'host', a victim, someone to blame for one's own mistakes, weaknesses and imperfections. Paradoxically, the shadow is both 'inside' and 'outside' of one's psyche, always on the lookout for a new enemy. Jung says of the dynamics of 'demonic forces' that possess the mob:

> There is indeed reason enough for man to be afraid of the impersonal forces lurking in the unconscious. We are blissfully unconscious of these forces because they never, or almost never, appear in our personal relations or under ordinary circumstances. But if people crowd together and form a mob, then the dynamisms of the collective man are let loose – beasts or demons that lie dormant in every person until he is part of a mob. Man in the mass sinks . . . to an inferior moral and intellectual level, to that level which is always there, below the threshold of consciousness, ready to break forth as soon as it is activated by the formation of a mass'.
>
> (Jung, 1938/1840, CW11: para. 23)

In the case of the collective shadow, society's negative traits – aggression, exploitative tendencies, weaknesses and self-indulgences – can be projected onto various political, social and cultural scapegoats: the Jewish population of Europe during World War II, indigenous American Indian tribes in colonial America, and 'witches' in Medieval Europe. Projection can also be mutual, when each conflicting side regards the other as a terrorising demon whose actions are always wrong, for instance, the USA and the Soviet Union during the Cold War; or the mutual mistrust and religious stand-off between Anglo-Saxon capitalism and the Arab world today.

The most dangerous aspect of the shadow, thus, is its ability to seize control of the mind – or minds. The shadow problem is closely related to the issues surrounding the development of the individual: the tyranny of nature, the tyranny of the collective, lifestyle pressures of industrial and post-industrial society. On all sides, the small man gets squashed by these biological, psychological, political and economic giants. It is not surprising that Tim Burton, whose films are about the fate of the individual in contemporary society, has authored several prominent shadows (and two most charming tricksters, Betelgeuse and Jack Skellington). Burton's shadow stories – *Batman, Batman Returns, Sweeney Todd* – are about anger, survival, paranoia, the existential void, the schizophrenic multiplicity and borderline emptiness in contemporary Western culture and politics. He does not, however, provide any answers, or give prescriptions to the cultural maladies depicted in his films. He only states what he sees.

'It's show time': the way of Burton's trickster

Beetlejuice (1988) and The Nightmare Before Christmas (1993)

Tim Burton's *Beetlejuice*, despite its visual and narrative shabbiness, became a trend-setter in the world of popular cinema. It sparked a fashion[2] for trickster films, which burned brightly throughout the 1990s, and produced a string of truly funny comedies such as *Drop Dead Fred* (1991), directed by Ate de Jong and starring Rik Mayall, *The Mask* (1994), *Dumb and Dumber* (1994), *Ace Ventura: Pet Detective* (1994), *Ace Ventura: When Nature Calls* (1995) and *Liar Liar* (1997). *The Mask* even contained direct allusions to the trickster figure – in the scene where Dr Neuman explains to Stanley Ipkiss that the green mask is the mask of Loki, the Norse god of mischief, but that it should be taken as a metaphor, and not literally.

Beetlejuice is a film in which the spirit of the trickster is present at every level. For a start, it was rather tricksterish and vengeful of Tim Burton and the scriptwriter Michael McDowell to send an ordinary American couple, with a suburban house and plans to have kids, into an alternative parallel world, where they are compelled to behave in an abnormal, paranormal and generally unnatural way.

Also, the film's visual ambitions and supernatural content commanded the creative team to summon all the inner tricksterism in order to finish the

2 In fact, Jim Carrey had effectively hijacked the trend because nobody could 'outtrickster' him. The genre expired towards the end of the decade, when the king of delight makers Carrey shifted to the darker scale of the archetype (Cable Guy, Riddler), and then began to experiment with more 'human' characters altogether (*The Truman Show, The Majestic, Bruce Almighty, Eternal Sunshine of the Spotless Mind*).

film within the limits of the $13 million budget. The visual effects supervisor Alan Munro remembers:

> The crew on the principal photography was very uncomfortable a lot of times with our approach to certain shots and with what we'd show up with on the set. There weren't a lot of believers when we were actually working on the film. The big advantage was that most of us came from that same school of low-low-budget filmmaking, so everybody had a lot of experience throwing stuff together on the fly.
>
> There are a lot of shots where the backgrounds are fiddled together with little shapes, little pieces of paper, a little spray-paint, a little cardboard and a little glue . . . None of us had any fear, but occasionally people on the production would come over to where we were shooting and give us that 'you-gotta-be-kidding' look when they'd see how unbelievably wanky some of this stuff looked on the set.
>
> (White, 1989: 68)

Some of the techniques, Munro admits, were genuinely vintage, and 'have been used in motion pictures since the earliest days of moviemaking': '. . . there are a couple of scenes we shot during old-style mirror effects, rather than the more readily accepted and standard Blue Screen' (White, 1989: 68). The film's nearly 300 effects necessary to depict the complex interaction between the worlds of the living and the dead (including live action and stop-motion for bigger monsters), were completed for $1 million (Matthews and Smith, 2007: 63).

All these efforts, despite being slightly 'edwoodian', eventually paid off, proving that a film about a silly masked maniac can be a big hit with the viewers. *Beetlejuice* took $32 million in its first two weeks, eventually grossing more than $73 million (Salisbury, 2006: 68). It even won an Oscar for make-up – a truly magical occurrence for a movie which could have easily gone the other way.

Before the entrance of the title character in the middle of the narrative, *Beetlejuice* is dominated by the very boring and normal Adam and Barbara Maitland. They are, as Burton defines them, 'the bland characters [that] need to be goosed a little; they need to get their blood going a little bit' (Salisbury, 2006: 69). Their main task is to balance the mad, hallucinatory 'afterlife', and the white-faced, dishevelled outcast whose behaviour is so radical that the underworld red tape altogether refuses to deal with him. The bio-exorcist, as Betelgeuse (or Beetlejuice – in the simplified version) calls himself, is hired by the Mailtlands in the hope that he will scare off the horrible Deetzes – the irritating upper-middle class new owners of the house. The Deetzes family incorporates a pseudo-artistic 'boho' mother with a penchant for making ugly, creepy sculptures (Catherine O'Hara), her subservient husband (Jeffrey Jones) and a gothically minded daughter,

Lydia (Winona Ryder), a teen drama queen who writes suicide letters and wears oversized black hats. The renowned bio-exorcist, however, is not terribly successful in chasing the weird trio out of the house. The Maitlands end up sharing the home with the Deetzes, and even help them with Lydia's education and upbringing.

The main message of *Beetlejuice* is as ancient as the world itself, and the one that Tim Burton is very fond of affirming. Every family, even the most decent-looking, boring and suburban, has a ghost or two in the closet. There is always in his films an alternative universe, inhabited by creatures who appear monstrous to those who do not understand them. As such, the worlds of 'light' and 'darkness' are not so far removed from each other as some 'normal' people hasten to proclaim. Tim Burton seems to like to make sure that these two dimensions in his films intersect and 'contaminate' each other. The meek and boring Maitlands, for instance, are less ghoulish than the supposedly proper Deetzes, with their suspicious acquaintances, frightening sculptures and lack of moral principles. The 'abode of the dead' has waiting rooms and receptions to rival any 'real world' bureaucratic and civic obsession with paperwork and form-filling. An anarchist or a marginalised rebel with alternative principles does not stand a chance there – just as he would have not stood a chance in real life.

The radicality of the trickster, Paul Radin reminds us, is ingrained in his character type. No ethical values exist for him, Radin writes (Lambek, 2002: 246). The folklorist Barbara Babcock-Abrahams defines him as a challenger of 'normality', the one in charge of the 'tolerated margin of mess': 'He is positively identified with creative powers, often bringing such defining features of culture as fire or basic food, and yet he constantly behaves in the most antisocial manner we can imagine. Although we laugh at him for his troubles and his foolishness and are embarrassed by his promiscuity, his creative cleverness amazes us and keeps alive the possibility of transcending the social restrictions we regularly encounter' (Babcock-Abrahams, 1975: 147).

The worst of all boundaries, of course, is the 'cage' in which the tricksters are initially locked – the metaphorical representation of 'being repressed in the unconscious'. Beetlejuice, for instance, is relegated to a small model of town, which is, obviously, too constrictive for him. In a way, he is the precursor of Burton's two other 'big fish in a small pond' – Jack Skellington who runs out of creative steam because he feels stifled within a small space, and Edward Bloom whose native town of Ashton is not big enough for his ambition. Because of this 'repressed' position, the trickster principle accumulates intensive potentiality, which explodes upon contact with 'conscious reality'. When they break free from their stifling cages, cinematic tricksters wreck havoc on the stale world of 'reality'. Breaking free, however, is not an easy operation. Beetlejuice, for instance, can only be released if someone ignorant enough agrees to pronounce his name three times.

The trickster's name (or names) is his passport into the world. Michael Keaton's character has two names: Betelgeuse and (its phonetic pronunciation) Beetlejuice. Paul Radin links the process of naming, and the notion of the name, to the individual's status in his or her community. Radin shows why the Winnebago trickster Wakdjunkaga takes much interest in his name, which translates as 'a foolish one'. 'In Winnebago society,' he writes, 'a child has no legal existence, no status, until he receives a name' (Lambek, 2002: 247). The marginalised trickster Beetlejuice can only get himself 'legitimised', and break out from his tiny patch of land into the 'big world' by making people pronounce his name. Similarly, the Penguin proclaims himself a human being when he announces, after discovery of his parentage, 'I am a man! I have a name! Oswald Cobblepot.' The acts of acquiring a name, hatching out of the vacuum, breaking the constraints of the local, making others pronounce your name, also stand for making oneself known and becoming famous.

Jack Skellington, too, feels imprisoned within the conventions of locality. He has a natural talent for entertaining and organising events, and is seen as a big fish in his native town of Halloween. But locally acclaimed 'delight-making' is not enough for him. He laments the 'emptiness in his bones' and complains that he has acquired 'a longing he has never known'.

Although his trickster status is completely legitimate, and even celebrated, in the small dark world to which he belongs, this does not stop him from trying to 'widen his horizons' by wandering into a forest and finding a tree with a door which leads to the parallel town of Christmas. Having observed many new traditions and habits in the defamiliarised 'normal world', Jack comes back full of enthusiasm and new ideas. He decides to improve Halloween's existing holidays by adding Christmas to the list. He plans to lighten up the gloomy spirit of the town. He wants to be the new 'Sandy Claws'. He asks his fellow-citizens to make presents for the children of the Christmas town – which they duly accomplish, wrapping up dead scorpions, rubber ducks with bleeding stigmata, giant sock snakes, scowling pumpkins and suchlike beauties for the little ones to enjoy. Jack transgresses the boundaries of two cities, breaks the limits of two different traditions, and, as a consequence, pays dearly for his daring actions. But, Burton implies, he could not have done otherwise. Overstepping and pushing the boundaries is a very important condition of creativity. One cannot make anything new without disregarding the old. To transgress is a trickster's way – but this is also the way of the artist.

There are other boundaries, too – social, physical, moral. None of them exist for Betelgeuse, who has a truly fluid relationship with his surroundings. As the trickster archetype designates the budding psyche for which the border between the self and the outer world does not yet exist, the trickster mythology is invariably preoccupied with transgressing and trespassing. For instance, having grabbed and kissed Barbara, Betelgeuse proceeds to enquire of her shocked husband: 'Am I overstepping my bounds? Just tell me.' This is an anarchic way of challenging the 'civilised' notion of social norms, as well as the accepted rules of emotional and physical contact. His lack of respect for authority is radical even for the world of the dead, where he is treated with great suspicion.

But forget the hypothetical boundaries – Betelgeuse also rejects the physical frontiers, the very base of 'reality'. He is capable of transforming into a 'Great Mother' snake; or gatecrash Otho's occult party dressed in a mad carousel hat and wearing giant hammer-weight arms. He floats in and out of things, changes shape, and yet, while he can play magical tricks on other people, he is not aware of his own body. In a scene in the mini-graveyard with the Maitlands, Betelgeuse is fumbling in his pockets for a business card but cannot find it. Instead, he finds a live mouse, and hands it to the terrified Barbara, then takes a dip into the other pocket, grabs a fistful of dirty dollars, and gives them to Adam. It could have been the inspiration for a similarly structured scene in *The Mask*, in which two policemen search Stanley Ipkiss's masked double, and find various rubbish in his pockets – big sunglasses, bike horn, bowling pin, mousetrap, rubber chicken, a bazooka, etc. Meanwhile, the Mask appears nonchalant, as if he does not know how all these objects, including a picture of Lieutenant Kellaway's wife, found their way into his pockets.

A genuinely silly trickster is not supposed to have full control over his body. Wakdjunkaga from the Winnebago trickster cycle is always in confrontation with different parts of his physical self. They are so alien to him that he talks to them as if they are entirely separate beings – and even eats them (they eventually regenerate)! In one of the episodes, Paul Radin recalls, Wakdjunkaga wakes from his sleep and realises that his blanket is missing:

> He sees it floating above him, and only gradually recognizes that it is resting on his huge penis erectus. Here we are brought back again to the Wakdjunkaga whose right hand fights with his left, who burns his anus and eats his own intestines, who endows the parts of his body with independent existence and who does not realize their proper functions, where everything takes place of its own accord, without his volition. 'This is always happening to me' – he tells his penis.
>
> (Lambek, 2002: 248)

Betelgeuse encounters a very similar problem when his head spontaneously starts spinning on his shoulders. 'Don't you hate it when that happens?!' he asks the astonished Maitlands.

This 'loss of control' theme is pervasive throughout the film suggesting, optimistically rather than pessimistically, that there are forces that are beyond human control. Even the bland Adam and Barbara catch the trickster bug and learn how to play a joke or two. In the celebrated sequence, they brighten up the Deetzes' stuffy dinner reception by making everyone possessed by a Harry Belafonte recording. The hosts and the guests cannot help but mime and move to the banana-boat song 'Day-O'. Again, the scene could have inspired the famous 'mass possession' sequence in Jim Carrey's first real hit – *The Mask* (1994). In it, Stanley Ipkiss's green-faced double, dressed as a Latino dancer, hypnotises a crowd of policemen and women into singing and dancing to Desi Arnaz's *Cuban Pete*.

Lydia – the drama-queenly, sadness-infected teenager – could have been Vincent Malloy's elder sister. She likes the liberating, uncontrollable influence of the subliminal world and is prepared to trade control over her body for a few minutes of liberating bliss. She regards the world of the unconscious not as a terrifying underworld with dim waiting rooms and expressionist-style corridors, but as a place where her tortured spirit will finally 'come to rest'. In one scene, tearful and dressed in black, she is writing a suicide note: 'I am . . . alone. I am . . . *utterly* . . . alone. At the time . . . you read this . . . I will . . . be gone. Having jumped [crosses out] . . . having *plummeted* off the Winter River Bridge'.

Her longing for a return to the unconscious metaphorically culminates in her agreeing to marry the trickster and become a kind of 'corpse bride'. From this marriage of inconvenience she is rescued by Barbara, who ingeniously finds a monster to rival the strength of Betelgeuse – the glut-tonous 'dune snake' from the psychedelic desert outside the house. After-wards, Barbara and Adam agree to satisfy Lydia's thirst for 'darkness' and 'hypnotic control', and occasionally make her float to the ceiling and sing another of Harry Belafonte's masterpieces, 'Jump in the Line'. The dosage of the unconscious has to be carefully measured out. Such a vast thing as this has to be administered in small portions. 'The strange and unusual' Lydia is prohibited from the crime of 'not growing up', but is at least allowed to stay a little immature.

Beetlejuice affirms and celebrates the state of powerlessness – and the various states of being severed, burnt, disjointed, torn, split and ruptured. Burton's hallmark visual metonymisation strategy would look a little too grisly in the film if it had not been executed so cheaply and grotesquely. The Maitlands find it easy to transform their bodies into various monstrous shapes. The waiting room in the underworld is full of disfigured clients such as the magician's assistant who is sawn in half, the three-fingered recep-tionist, or the burnt victim of smoking in bed. The parallel universe, as is the habit in Tim Burton's films, is full of fragmented creatures. Diversity, rather than uniformity, is celebrated.

In *The Nightmare Before Christmas*, there is a whole town inhabited by such diversely abnormal creatures, headed by a lenient mayor and a trickster, who is in charge of their ghoulish festivities. The witches, skeletons, horrible clowns, corpses and other crumbling-and-reassembling creatures exist on the aforementioned 'margins of the mess', where mad imagination reigns.

This is transformation *à la* Tim Burton – at first sight, a negative event, a process leading to an internal or external disintegration of the character (or, rather, internal disintegration metonymised as an external episode). However, despite the ghoulish picture he delivers, the impression from films like *Beetlejuice* and *The Nightmare Before Christmas* is surprisingly life-affirming. Looming over the grotesque gruesomeness in the movie is Burton's own role as a magician, an inventor, someone who can create a moving story out of a mass of disjointed junk. This is, undoubtedly, the highest transformative achievement of creative tricksterism.

John Izod writes that '. . . the trickster can be thief, prankster or cheat, but at the same time has the power to bring revelation and with it the reconciliation of the opposing elements of a personality' (Izod, 2006: 141). Although the bio-exorcist Betelgeuse behaves in a destructive manner, the result of his pranks and seemingly cruel stunts is positive. After he is eaten by the 'dune snake', the two families resolve their differences – or, to translate the metaphor, the Deetzes accept the skeletons in their closet, and the Maitlands learn to be more mischievous because being such nice, boring people is as good as being dead. The opposites – the gloomily creative and occult family, and the totally uncreative family, are ironically compelled to share a house together. Lydia, too, learns her lesson. She realises that she does not have to withdraw from the world of the living in order to become happier.

The trickster is swallowed by the mother-snake; he is sacrificed, reclaimed by the unconscious for the sake of the unity of the opposites. In *The Nightmare Before Christmas*, Jack, too, has to 'die' (if one can use such expression with regard to a skeleton) and become 'resurrected' before the two towns, and their respective perspectives on what constitutes a true festivity, can be reconciled.

The trickster is an important archetype because, anarchic and mad as he is, he is about challenging the perceived set of 'norms' and removing the stagnant elements of the existing social order. He is the one who keeps society alive. On yet another level, Burton's tricksters are rebels and breakers of convention. Jack Skellington is not a 'prince of horror' – he is the king of marginality, and so is Betelgeuse. They break free from their 'small town' metaphors because stagnation is death, and transgression – ironically – is the only way to move on and stay alive.

Shadow within, shadow without

Batman (1989) and Sweeney Todd: The Demon Barber of Fleet Street (2007)

'I am the world's first fully functioning homicidal artist', announces the Joker to his 'prospective' girlfriend, Vicki Vale, during their 'meeting' at the

Flugelheim museum. Whereas Betelgeuse's talent, despite its perceptible darkness and danger, is chiefly about transformation, the Joker is about destruction. Betelgeuse, when asked to assist in ousting an irritating couple from the house, after a series of mishaps and lopsided wizardry, ends up bringing the two couples together and endorsing peace rather than war. Inadvertently, he creates. For the Joker, nothing is inadvertent and everything is well-planned in advance. When he wants to kill, he kills. Burton himself justifiably linked Betelgeuse and the Joker, stating that they are connected via the ideas of marginality, insanity and freedom (Salisbury, 2006: 80).

Like a trickster, the Joker wears a mask. Like a trickster, he possesses an unsettling, disturbing creativity. Like a trickster, he belongs to the underworld (in his case, the world of crime), despises authority and readily breaks boundaries. There is one trait, however, which sets him apart from the trickster figure – the Joker is too aware of himself. His evil deeds are more deliberate than accidental. His childlikeness, his love of toys, his pranks and tricks are all tainted by violence and aggression. His jokes are no longer silly; they are intentionally cruel. Although looking like a trickster, on the *doppelgänger* scale the Joker is moving towards the shadow pole. No amount of clowning can hide the fact that, speaking psychologically, he is a shadow.

The Joker's creative habits are murderous – or, as he puts it, 'I make art . . . until someone dies.' Ironically, he is not the 'shadowiest' of Burton's maniacs. At least, he still possesses a sense of ghoulish humour, and wears a smile – albeit superficial and artificial. He even coins a rhyme in which he admits that his laughter is artificial ('my smile is just skin deep') and invites everyone to 'join him for a weep'.

The offshoot of Edward Scissorhands, Burton's version of Benjamin Barker/Sweeney Todd, like the Joker, 'makes art until someone dies'. The difference is, he makes it with a really serious face. Although he adopts a new personality, he does not have to wear a 'visible' mask. His mask is the face distorted by existential anger and a lifetime of pain. Underneath Sweeney Todd's hardened, tortured, grimly maniacal countenance there is an ex-human being who is 'really crying', and who is inviting his fellow-creatures to 'join him for a weep'. The only treatment which a deeply flawed world like this deserves is bloody, vengeful annihilation. Londoners will eventually join Sweeney Todd for a weep, and weep they will – with bloody tears.

The ruthless barber is a 'full-time' shadow; the Joker is a shadow with pronounced trickster elements, but the two are united by the idea which often crops up in Burton's films – that of the demonic, possessed, dark urban environment. Neither of the films has a definitive time-scale, but their dark colour palette and cluttered, Gothicised, dilapidated *mise-en-scène* produce a profound impression of an urbanised hell.

Before becoming Tim Burton's film, the story of the demon barber went through various artistic transformations – it had been an urban legend, a penny dreadful, several plays, numerous film and TV adaptations, and Stephen Sondheim's famous musical. The original penny dreadful, *The String of Pearls*, was set in 1785 and published in 1846. However, Burton did not want to assign Sweeney Todd any concrete time-slot. Ever an impressionist and expressionist, he was after emotional effect and not historical accuracy:

> It kind of goes back to sort of old horror-movie stuff where we didn't really want . . . to have a thing like 'London, 1953', or whatever; just to kind of keep it in the fable London, you know, it's Victorian. Tried to make it sort of not too late, kind of in the middle where things were still developing, where there was, you know, probably a little bit more crime. Again, more slightly expressionist, kind of, movie London, sort of horror-movie London, and not, you know, be so literal.
>
> (Disc 2/Special Features/'Sweeney Todd is Alive')

Victorian London, with its mighty criminal underworld, substandard living conditions for the poor, diseases, pollution, industrialisation, dreary urban landscape and vulgar entertainments is an archetypal match for the temporally later metropolis that is Gotham city. They are the ultimate breeding places for mass infections – be it physical or moral. Moving along the scale of modernity, Burton refuses to discern between the human psychology of its 'earlier' and 'later' phases. People of contemporary New York (or Gotham City, if you like) are as prone to mind control as the inhabitants of Victorian London. Certain moments in the film refer, narratively as well as visually, to Robert Wiene's *The Cabinet of Dr Caligari*, which endorses these issues. For example, the barber contest scene in *Sweeney Todd* is comparable, in essence, to *Caligari*'s carnival scene in which the doctor is exhibiting the hypnotised Cesare as an attraction. In a way, Sweeney Todd also hypnotises and subdues his victims before murdering them. It is easy to lose control and fall prey to the shadow in the isolating, disempowering atmosphere of the urban environment.

Actually, both Sweeney Todd and the Joker mock and despise the urban population's stupidity and facelessness. Benjamin Barker calls London 'a great black pit' inhabited by 'vermin of the world' and ruled by 'the privileged few'.

For his part, before puncturing the gas-filled balloons at the Gotham City two-hundredth Anniversary Parade, the Joker announces to his 'subjects': 'Now comes the part where I relieve you, the little people, of the burden of your failed and useless lives. But, as my plastic surgeon always said: if you gotta go, go with a smile'.

One thing the Burtonian collective shadow seems to target is the integrity of the body. Both Sweeney Todd and the Joker position themselves as 'beauticians'. Sweeney Todd's art is rather rough: he lures men into his parlour, slits their throats, and hands the corpses over to Mrs Lovett, who then proceeds to mince them and serve them up in meat pies. This image has gone further than the notorious metaphorical fragmentation of the modern/postmodern subject. This is the ultimate destruction, maceration, elimination of the subject; swallowing up and digestion of the individual by other individuals. Sweeney Todd is the collective shadow of society in which 'dog eats dog' is still the principal law of existence behind the enlightened façade.

The Joker's 'beauty secrets' are more subtle. He controls the cosmetics industry. Rather than dissecting the body, he summons poisoned cosmetic products to erode it from the inside and the outside. After all, the Joker explains throughout the film, he is an artist, and therefore cannot use openly crude methods. Every defaced picture and every defaced face (like that of Alicia, for instance), is his unique creation.

Ideologically, Sweeney Todd the shadow is rooted in modernity and industrialism; and Burton's Joker is the product of postmodernity and post-industrial lifestyle. But the two are invariably connected via the idea of the plastic, dismantleable body. In her essay '"Material Girl": The Effacements of Postmodern Culture', the feminist philosopher Susan Bordo explicates the roots and blossoms of this paradigm:

> In a culture in which organ transplants, life-extension machinery, microsurgery and artificial organs have entered everyday medicine, we seem on the verge of practical realization of the seventeenth-century imagination of the body as machine. [. . .] In the early modern era, machine imagery helped to articulate a totally determined human body whose basic functionings the human being was helpless to alter. The then dominant metaphors for this body – clocks, watches, collections of springs – imagines a system that is set, wound up, whether by nature of God the watchmaker, ticking away in a predictable, orderly manner regulated by laws over which the human being has no control.
>
> (Rivkin and Ryan, 2001: 1099)

However, as modernity progressed, the image of a helpful, watchful and orderly God was gradually being dissolved and replaced by the gods of medicine and science. When, during the twentieth century, corporeal adjustability entered the mass market as a viable product, the boundaries between natural and artificial physicality were permanently effaced. No longer dependent on God, but rather on the human creator, the Frankenstein monster has now truly come to life. As Bordo argues, in place of God the Almighty, we now have ourselves, 'the masters and sculptors of the plastic':

Pursuing this modern, determinist fantasy to its limits, fed by the currents of consumer capitalism, modern ideologies of the self, and their crystallization in the dominance of 'American' mass culture, Western science and technology have now arrived, paradoxically but predictably . . . at a new, 'postmodern' imagination of human freedom from bodily determination. Gradually and surely, a technology that was first aimed at the replacement of malfunctioning parts has generated an industry and an ideology fuelled by fantasies of rearranging, transforming and correcting, an ideology of limitless improvement and change, defying the historicity, and indeed, the very materiality of the body.

(Rivkin and Ryan, 2001: 1099–1100)

Technology is an important subject in the works of Tim Burton. For example, he repeatedly introduces the conveyor-belt assembly metaphor into his films as designating an idealistic paradisiacal state of long-lost godly order (Hillman's 'repaired puer', 1987: 104). This metaphor is present in *Frankenweenie, Pee Wee's Big Adventure, Edward Scissorhands* and *Charlie and the Chocolate Factory*. Pee Wee, Edward, Willy Wonka and Victor Frankenstein all have childlike qualities. Speaking mythologically, they are child-gods, and their youthful creativity is fresh – albeit imperfect. They designate the trickster phase where creativity and imperfection are still glued to each other, and are ideally matched to generate new ideas. And although their creative habits invariably have an edge – Pee Wee is odd, Victor resurrects dead bodies, Edward has dangerous blades, Willy Wonka is mysterious and can be rather unmerciful with badly behaved children – their 'evil' side is not yet fully fledged. They do not deliberately use their edge to destroy the hateful, unthinking masses. Their 'industrialism' is still productive in the sense that making pancakes, chocolate, cookies and patched-up dogs is much better than mincing people up by the dozen.

In *Sweeney Todd* and *Batman*, however, the industrial image of the assembly line transmutes into a homicidal horror. The opening credits of *The Demon Barber* show a *disassembly* line consisting of various pieces of pie-making equipment, machinery and underground pathways – an unfailing system for the disposal of dead bodies and the resulting litres of blood.

The Joker's, too, is a 'disintegrating' industry. He does not cut and mince – he burns and dissolves instead. After the death of his former boss, Jack Napier is left in charge of Gotham's industrial empire, and establishes

control over the city by chemically modifying cosmetic and hygiene products. People get poisoned by using certain combinations, rather than
individual products. With his acid-induced smile, the Joker is the chemical
industry personified.

Cosmetics and chemicals is the kind of occupation and ownership that
truly befits a tarnished trickster. Napier's acid jokes and pranks form a
valid metaphor for the trickster's hallmark dissolution of boundaries. The
fluid Joker, using his tricksterish ability to transcend borders and limits,
moves into, and amongst, the crowd. What in *Beetlejuice* used to be the
humorous theme of mind control via catchy Caribbean songs, in *Batman*
transmutes into the idea of mass possession by an individual with an evil
mind. And whereas Lydia finds the state of powerlessness liberating,
creative and illuminating, the Joker's mind-controlling tricks are far less
innocuous. Moreover, they are invariably connected to the traditionally
metropolitan issues of money, power, and political corruption. Although
these issues may look simplified in the contemporary mytho-parable that is
Batman, their psychological importance and emotional power are not to be
overlooked.

Taking up a trickster's stance, the Joker positions his 'acid art' as a form
of creative challenge, a phenomenon that alters the stagnant order of things
and thwarts the vulgar tastes of the crowd. 'Gentlemen, let's broaden our
minds!' he announces to his henchmen, effectively asking them to trash the
museum. He also says to Vicki Vale at the fateful meeting: 'We mustn't
compare ourselves to regular people. We are artists.' And: 'You will join me
in the avant-garde of the new aesthetic.'

The Joker's vision of the new bourgeois aesthetic is reminiscent of Eric
Neumann's description of modernist paintings as 'having a sinister quality'
because they depict the world that is 'torn to pieces': 'The dissolution of the
outside world, of form and the individual, leads to a dehumanization of art'
(Neumann, 1974a: 118–119).

Whereas Neumann's position regarding physical and artistic fragmentation is modernist, in the sense that he is deeply concerned with what he
perceives as a deplorable state of the human psyche, Tim Burton's *Batman*
depicts the postmodern world that celebrates and even glorifies
fragmentation. The Joker's splintered mind tirelessly dissects reality into
pieces: here the bird's eye camera shows him dancing amongst photograph
clippings, there his image is multiplied by the media and appears on all
television screens. He is the king of this world (he actually has his own
throne at the city parade), and the ultimate shadow of the plastic society.
He represents the postmodernist end point of what previously had been the
determinist fantasy of modernism.

The shadowy side of the beauty industry is, of course, the possibility that
an operation or a procedure can always go wrong. Revealing Alicia's
disfigured face, the Joker explains to the onlookers that 'she is just a sketch,

really.' His comparisons of vivisectory activities to art is not far removed from one real-life piece from *Details* magazine, cited by Susan Bordo in her article:

> Dr Brown is an artist. He doesn't just pull and tuck and forget about you . . . He did liposuction on my neck, did the nose job and tightened up my forehead to give it a better line. Then he took some fat from the side of my waist and injected it into my hands. It goes in as a lump, and then he smoothes it out with his hands to where it looks good. I'll tell you something, the nose and neck made a big change, but nothing in comparison to how fabulous my hands look. The fat just smoothed out all the lines, the veins don't stick up anymore, the skin actually looks soft and great. [But] you have to be careful not to hang your hands.
>
> (*Details*, quoted in Rivkin and Ryan, 2001: 1100)

This is the supreme example of Neumann's 'dissolution of form and the individual' in a world which no longer deems such dissolution harmful, and where it is the norm rather than a sign of some collective psychic obsession.

Luckily for Gotham City, there is one hero who is prepared to fight the shadow, and thus save the individual quickly drowning in the dark, anonymous, high-tech collectivity of the contemporary metropolis. The Joker discovers that the biggest breaker of boundaries in today's world is the media, where one can 'multiply' himself and get into the minds of Gotham's citizens. Batman hijacks his adversary's attempts to dominate the press. He also thwarts Napier's mass poisoning plans by cracking the product compatibility code. Finally, Wayne spoils Jack's most glorious and creative scheme of mass murder – the gas poisoning at the parade – by taking away the inflatable toys. Batman saves the crowd even though his opinion of them is not much higher than that of the Joker.

The finale of the cathedral scene reveals the true nature of Jack Napier's tricksterism. From an overhead angle, the camera focuses downward until nothing is left on the screen but the Joker's blood-stained yet sinisterly smiling face. Meanwhile, his laughter remains audible until the chief policeman extracts a 'laughing device' from the inner pocket of the Joker's suit. This closing metonymy – laughter separated from the body – asserts that Batman's enemy, and his plastic ideology, still had the final laugh. The trickster, it transpires, was fake.

Trickster is a creature prone to metonymisation. His constant 'falling apart' comes from his 'unconsciousness', his ability to attain psychic 'wholeness'. He lacks the 'conscious' backbone which would allow him to keep pieces of himself together, in order and under control. However, unlike Beetlejuice's or Jack Skellington's reversible tricksterish grotesquerie, the death of the Joker is final. His 'brokenness' is irreversible – like the chemical damage to his face or his botched plastic surgery. He cannot be rebuilt from fragments because he is already too 'conscious' and too darkly human to become 'resilient' in the true trickster fashion. Whereas 'true' tricksters can afford to deny physical reality, with its restrictions and boundaries, the Joker becomes confined within the limits of the human form.

But the moral is simple. Any society that takes itself too seriously, and that has forgotten the trickster, ends up being swallowed by the shadow.

Chapter 6

The monstrous society

Despite his films gravitating towards social and cultural critique of modernity, Tim Burton has so far had little success in producing critically and commercially successful works with an openly political stance. His films that exclusively explore the problems of society rather than the drama of the mental and physical isolation of the male protagonist – *Mars Attacks!* and *Planet of the Apes* – do not seem to work as well as those predominantly concentrating on the individual's struggle with the oppressive forces of society. When he removes the 'personal element', the suffering hero, the emotional quality of his films subsides. In other words, for some reason, the brilliance of his perception dims when he 'infiltrates' the collective shadow from the inside, and attempts to understands its working principles.

The much-criticised *Mars Attacks!* (1996) and *Planet of the Apes* (2001) are not built around the struggle with the personal *doppelgänger* of the main character, but are about the dark, brutal and inhuman side of society in general, and American society in particular. In both these films, the collective shadow takes the form of an outside invader (Martians in *Mars Attacks* or humanoid apes in *Planet of the Apes*), and attempts to eliminate the human race. Surprisingly, the films' narratives, *mise-en-scène*, editing and sound do not seem to work together, clashing and leaving gaps in diegetic continuity rather than forming a coherent whole. Instead of the panoramic picture of Western society's ills, we get a disjointed, very general attempt at social criticism.

The apes and the Martians serve as a collective projection – they represent the deep-seated militaristic, aggressive, masculine qualities of American politics and culture. They are 'external' invaders who, in fact, come from the 'inside', they are society's self-destructive forces. The apes and the Martians are metaphors for colonial behaviour, a basic aggressive strategy concealed as an enlightened and 'enlightening' campaign. In their extended form, the metaphors become allegories, and the films themselves parables of oppressive political conduct.

The hairy alien

Planet of the Apes (2001)

Burton's *Planet of the Apes* (2001) is a remake of a 1968 science fiction film directed by Franklin J. Schaffner. The original film was loosely based on the dystopian novel *La Planète des Singes* (1963) by French author Pierre Boulle. Schaffner's version was moodily dark and, despite the sci-fi genre and improbable subject matter, painfully realistic. Three American astronauts on a scientific mission crash-land on an unknown planet. Taylor, Landon and Dodge walk through what looks like a barren, unpopulated land, wondering whether the planet can sustain any life. They also take time to plant an American flag into the dry soil of the desert. A line of weird scarecrow figures, possibly indicating a border, does not prevent them from taking a dip in an oasis lake. But soon the situation begins to change and the astronauts' initial supposition that the planet is uninhabited is disproved. First they spot a group of wild, mute humans, and then a group of militant apes on horseback. The apes attack and seize some of the humans; they also kill Dodge, and capture Landon and Taylor. In the Ape City Landon is lobotomised, and Taylor is put into a cage and treated for a throat wound. He is given a mute human female, Nova, for 'reproductive purposes'. Although he cannot speak, a progressive chimpanzee scientist, Zira, and her fiancé, Cornelius, believe that he is different from the rest of the human slaves. Dr Zaius, a 'keeper of the faith', is convinced that Taylor is a dangerous animal, and must be emasculated. After a string of failed attempts to prove to the ape rulers that Taylor is a visitor from another planet, the astronaut, Nova, Zira and Cornelius flee to the Forbidden Zone (the desert with scarecrows). They go to the cave where, some time ago, the rebellious archaeologist Cornelius stumbled upon proof that humans had lived on this planet long before the apes. Dr Zaius and his band of gorillas find them and decide to blow up the cave in order to eliminate the last traces of human civilisation because the Simian Bible warns that it was a doomed, aggressive and self-destructive civilisation. Dr Zaius then lets Taylor, who intends to start a new life with Nova in the desert, walk away. The 'keeper of the faith' famously says: 'Don't look for it, Taylor. You may not like what you find.' In the final scene Taylor discovers the remains of the Statue of Liberty half-buried in the sand. Taylor reacts to the scene by shouting bitterly: 'You Maniacs! You blew it up! Ah, damn you! God damn you all to hell!'

Planet's producer Richard Zanuck did not believe that the film would be successful until the end of the preview: 'If we could get by the first scene of talking apes and the audience did not laugh hysterically, I knew we'd be OK,' he recollects (Woods, 2002: 164). Contrary to his pessimistic initial predictions, *Planet* was a remarkable critical and commercial success. The film owes its cult status to its existentialist subject-matter, which perfectly reflected the key political moments of the turbulent 1960s: the Cold War and nuclear threat ('You blew it up!'; the barren no-go area – a euphemism for the 'dead' nuclear radiation zone); race riots and the civil rights movement (the themes of slavery, chauvinism and the right to speak as opposed to 'lacking a voice'); and the Vietnam War (the themes of invasion, occupation, flag planting, as well as political and religious propaganda).

Taylor, an American explorer (a euphemism for 'invader') comes to another planet to find himself and start a new life there, but what he actually finds is his own shadow, first in the collective allegorical form of the narrow-minded, bigoted ape society, and, in the final scenes of the film, in the form of the decayed symbols of Western civilisation – a talking doll and the damaged Statue of Liberty.

Pierre Boulle's dystopian novel was informed by his own bitter life experiences: he worked as a supervisor on a rubber plantation in Kuala Lumpur, and joined the French army in Singapore in 1939. As a secret agent, he was involved in helping the resistance movement in China, Burma, and French Indochina. He had a genuine 'heart of darkness' quality to him – first-hand experience of the demise of white European civilisation as it was gradually swallowed up by it own inner darkness. Symbolically, in 1943 he was captured by Vichy loyalists when he was floating down the Mekong river in a bamboo raft (cf. Captain Willard from *Apocalypse Now* is sent up the allegorical Nung River, a stand-in for Mekong, on a US Navy patrol boat). Boulle was subjected to forced labour but managed to escape in 1944.

With a biography like this, it is not surprising, then, that Boulle, like his favourite author Joseph Conrad, was concerned with colonisation and its consequences – both for the coloniser and the colonised. In his fiction he explores 'the darkness of the heart', the inner 'brute' of the coloniser who 'exterminates' and seizes while thinking of his activities as 'liberating' and 'enlightening'. Franklin J. Schaffner's film truly captures the existentialist spirit of the novel, mercilessly revealing the shameful, shadow qualities of human nature. The Simian Bible in the film contains the indictment of humankind expressed in the following lines: 'Beware the beast man for he is the devil's pawn. Alone among God's primates he kills for sport, or lust, or greed. He will murder his brother to possess his brother's land.' Sam Keen, an American philosopher, academic and author expresses the same idea in slightly different words:

We human beings are *Homo hostilis*, the hostile species, the enemy-making animal. We are driven to fabricate an enemy as a scapegoat to bear the burden of our denied enmity. From the unconscious residue of our hostility, we create a target; from our private demons, we conjure a

public enemy. And, perhaps, more than anything else, the wars we
engage in are compulsive rituals, shadow dramas in which we con-
tinually try to kill those parts of ourselves we deny and despise'

(Abrams and Zweig, 1991: 198)

No doubt, Burton had all these eternal themes in mind when he was
planning his film. After all, the unfathomable darkness of one's own heart
is his favourite topic. Shaffner's film is a highly symbolic, dark, magnificent
allegory which clearly delivers its apocalyptic political vision. Burton, too,
specialises in fable-like structures, distinctly artificial visuals and well-
defined symbolism. But, as one reviewer, Jonathan Romney, writes, 'there's
no image in the world that a literal-minded remake can't drain of its
mythical power' (Woods, 2002: 169). The elements of Burton's remake just
refuse to function as a logical whole. The *mise-en-scène* (which is usually
his best feature as he is primarily an artist, and only then a cinematographer) in most shots looks artificial and 'plastic', like bad theatre props.
Danny Elfman's music – in itself as fine as ever – nevertheless fails to
engage with the other cinematic codes; I would even say it is so good that it
sounds incongruous as a background score for some really bad acting and
unnatural action sequences. The acting, as most critics noted, is generally
bad. According to David Denby from the *New Yorker*, Mark Wahlberg,
who plays the protagonist, 'moves well, but . . . belongs in a specific
neighbourhood, like the Bronx or South Boston – he doesn't have enough
going on in his face to carry a movie alone, and the women at the
screening, bored, began hoping he would be reduced to a loincloth, as
Charlton Heston was thirty-three years ago' (www.newyorker.com).
Another reviewer notes that Davidson's female companion, played by
Estella Warren, is 'a pure waste of space, pouting vacantly in the skimpy
buckskin last modelled by Raquel Welch in *One Million Years BC*'
(Woods, 2002: 169).

Just like Schaffner's film, Tim Burton's version wanders deeply into the
zone of political. Here are the premise and the plot: a group of scientists on
board a spaceship work with live chimpanzees. One of them, Pericles, fails
to come back after being sent into open space in a small space-pod as part
of an experiment. One of the 'human' team, Leo Davidson, feels that it is
his responsibility to rescue the animal, and flies off in pursuit.

He does not find the chimp but crash lands on an unknown planet, and
is captured by its inhabitants – humanoid apes. Together with a 'wild' girl
named Daena (Estella Warren), he is bought by a kind female ape, Ari
(Helena Bonham Carter), who falls in love with him. Leo plans to free the
human slaves and escape into the Forbidden Area. He also manages to
convince Ari to join their cause. The apes, led by general Thade, the
dictator of Ape City, organise a chase, which results in a battle between
the humans and the apes in the middle of the desert. At the height of the

battle the lost chimp Pericles lands in the middle of the desert in his pod. The apes are appeased because they take Pericles for their god Semos. According to their scriptures, it was he who founded the ape race. In the end, Leo flies back to Earth in Pericles's pod. He lands in Washington DC only to discover that the Lincoln Memorial is now a monument in honour of Thade.

The script, loosely based on Boulle's novel, underwent numerous changes prior to and during the filming. Many of these changes had to do with the parameters of the film's budget. The original scriptwriter, William Broyles, was at some point joined by Tim Burton who became the script's co-author. 'I think it was starting to drive him crazy', Burton admits (Fraga, 2005: 160). Broyles left before the project's production begun, and was replaced by Lawrence Konner and Mark Rosenthal. They were supposed to make the necessary budget-minded changes to the script (i.e. cut the budget by $200 million), as well as fine-tune and simplify it (Woods, 2002: 165). Some of the alterations were done concurrently with shooting on location. In Burton's words, 'Larry Konner was on the set every day doing new pages as the shoot progressed, because dialogue that might sound good in a story conference isn't necessarily going to sound great when you get people in make-up saying it' (Fraga, 2005: 160).

Having been patched and repatched by four writers, the script of the *Planet*'s remake is one of its biggest failures. The final scenes are completely muddled; the story suddenly begins to speed up but the events, in the sequence that they appear, do not look terribly plausible – even for a sci-fi plot. During post-production it was even rumoured that several endings has been shot, but this information was disproved by Burton (Matthews and Smith, 2007: 272). Leo gathering his wild human 'army' and telling them to go away and hide, while he would stay to face Thade and his apes ('I'm the one they want'), is one of the film's worst scenes. There are gaps, incongruities and pauses within the scene, slightly ameliorated by the extra-diegetic score, which at least links the shots into some kind of 'emotional story'. 'Look, you gotta make your people understand, it's over, there's no help coming,' says the gasping Leo Davidson to Daena, while the lovesick, forlorn Ari is watching them from a distance. The close-up of Estella Warren answering him with some seriously contrived ardour and adulation, 'You came', is the final nail in the script's coffin. Many reviewers also criticised the lazy *deus ex machina* climax, with Pericles landing in the Forbidden Zone in the midst of the human–ape combat. On his arrival a sudden unexpected peace breaks out. Attar, an enormous gorilla, proclaims: 'We'll leave the graves unmarked. No one who comes will be able to tell apes from humans. They'll be mourned together . . . as it should be, from now on.' Leo happily surrenders his favourite chimp to the apes 'for religious purposes' ('Take good care of him, OK?'), and dutifully flies home, leaving behind both his female companions, Ari and Daena, as well as his human tribe. This anticlimax just renders Leo's whole quest pointless. As a hero on a quest he did not learn anything, did not gain an '*anima*', and did not solve 'the shadow problem' – in fact, he is defeated by his culture's shadow back on Earth. He failed even as an existential hero (for whom a negative, futile ending to a quest would be an adequate outcome) – since he lacks the necessary aggression, the Hamletian acid anger, the existential rebel's trademark profound dissatisfaction with the way the world is organised. He simply does not possess the bravery and determination to confront the world's 'careless Creator'.

However, the bad narrative base is not the main determining factor in the film's debacle. For Burton, the script is never the main feature of the film; visuals are. He even self-confessedly abandoned storyboarding in order to keep his options open (Fraga, 2005: 82). He also admits that editing is not his primary concern (Fraga, 2005: 33; 2005: 83).

In *Planet of the Apes*, neglect of order and pattern leads to the disintegration of the film's underlying narrative structure, and with the basic structure so badly eroded, the non-verbal cinematic codes are automatically going to suffer. Even such peripheral cinematic codes as colour and lighting feel the strain. The film's colours are invariably dark and moody throughout a number of completely different backdrops, from the misty forest where Leo crash-lands and the empty landscape of the Forbidden Area, to the dimly lit houses and slave dungeons of the Ape City. Owen Gleiberman observes that most of the film is shot 'in monotonous woodland darkness' (Woods, 2002: 168), while Le Blanc and Odell note that the *Planet*'s 'overall look rejects contrast in favour of a dank, leaden landscape of depression and misery' (Le Blanc and Odell, 2005: 117).

Another problem is that Tim Burton is not an action director. The *action* Burton is trying to express is more of a psychological than a 'real' phenomenon. Even on the visual level, the 'quest' motif in his films, along with its principal battles and challenges, lacks the 'physicality', brutality and (pseudo)realism of traditional action movies. It is the 'inner', not the 'outer' movement that Burton is trying to convey. The 'action' parts of Burton's films are invariably upstaged by the psychological depth (always embodied in visually powerful symbolism) of the hero-quest. For instance, in *Batman* (1989) the emphasis is clearly shifted from the 'real' to the 'symbolic/fantastic', and from 'physically killing the bad guys' to 'redeeming the world from the universal evil'. Speaking about his relationship with the *action comics* genre, Burton admits,

> There's a zillion great directors and I'm not one of them. Yet this is the genre. On this new thing [*Batman Returns*], I feel better about the action. It's not James Cameron. There are a few people that can jack things up to that kind of level, and why try? I feel like, in the second one, I tried something a bit more representative of myself. I do feel

better about it than I did about the first. The action feels more like a
part of the movie, as opposed to: here's the movie, and here comes
some action, and I've seen better action in my day.

(Fraga, 2005: 78)

The biggest action build-up in *Planet of the Apes* happens towards the end
of the film, in the human–ape battle scenes. On the surface, all the ingredients of a good action movie are present and should, in theory, function
together: the two mighty armies, fast cutting, (Neanderthal) period costume, Rick Heinrichs's production design, Rick Baker's amazing ape make-
up, Danny Elfman's evocative music score, and an inspiring 'shadow'/
'universal evil' theme (a tried-and-tested accompaniment to many a sci-fi
movie that works every time).

But however good the separate ingredients are, they refuse to fuse
together to form a smooth, fast, mass of physical action. Burton is certainly
right when he says that action sequences are not his strongest asset. A good
action sequence is not just about fast, rhythmic cutting, a variety of angles
or well-designed decorations. It principally entails an understating of the
emotional impact of a shot as part of a fast-moving sequence; a vision of
the most impressive, representative moments of an action. By contrast,
Burton's vision, although deep and symbolic, is static. The rhythm of action
editing is irregular. Action sequences, which have always been Burton's
weakest point, and are traditionally rescued by his ingenious *mise-en-scène*,
in *Planet* cannot be saved by any such means. The seams are too visible for
the sequences to be believable. The human–ape battle loses pace; at times it
slows down so much that it looks like a bad rehearsal. Even moments with
significant emotional weight – like Daena pulling back Ari's hand bandage
and discovering a fresh slave mark on her palm – seem to be incongruous
and misplaced. The scene's emotional value, which is built on contrast
('although an ape, she bears the stigmata of a human slave') and its
semantic weight (the themes of rivalry, suffering for love's sake, etc.) do not
in any way strengthen the battle panorama's visual and semantic structures.
Ari's bandaged hand, which is supposed to express the pain of being
human, is emotionally void compared to the poignancy of Edward's blades
or the bleeding hand of Ichabod Crane.

There are a few big symbols in the film – big both physical size-wise and
meaning-wise – that provide a good frame for the crumbling narrative and
mis-edited action sequences. These iconic images form a bridge between
the protagonist's technologically advanced native culture on the one hand,
and the brutal habits and atavistic lifestyle that are the norm on the ape
planet on the other. The spiky remains of Leo's space station in the middle
of the Forbidden Area are reminiscent of the collapsed Statue of Freedom's
crown from the original movie; but the crumbled statue itself, as a metaphor for the demise of American culture, is replaced in Burton's version

with the transformed Lincoln Memorial – another wrecked symbol of democracy and freedom.

Nevertheless, Burton's 'American dream' ruins do not provide a sufficiently iconic base for the film to work as 'one piece'. Despite their size, isolated as they are, the space station and the Thade memorial in the film's finale do not ensure the smooth archetypal functioning of *Planet*. The bitter political message, which worked so well in the original film, and which redeemed Charlton Heston's overacting and cheap special effects, in the 2001 remake falls apart. 'We don't get into the nuclear thing too much because we weren't attempting to remake the original,' explains Burton in an interview with Kristine McKenna (Woods, 2002: 158). But what is it that the allegory – and a classical one, with animals behaving as humans involved – was trying to convey? The most obvious answer is that, when a society cannot control its shadow, the shadow gradually takes control of its political affairs, and that the collective shadow is an ideology is war. This is a valid message; a very good point indeed. Unfortunately, most of it was 'lost in translation', or, to use the Jacobsonian communication model, 'lost in communication'. Whole parts of the message fell off somewhere on the way from the *addresser* to the *addressee* – like debris from Leo's team's space station. The glorious remains of the grand initial idea can barely hold the narrative together – comparable to the station's spiky skeleton, whose looming presence in the background provides minimal visual, symbolic or semantic support for the otherwise meaningless mess of the human–ape conflict. Apparently, the message was 'shaped' by too many *addressers*, each with his own vision of the situation, and no standardisation procedures took place. Looking at what is left of it, one might as well exclaim: 'You maniacs! You blew it up! Ah, damn you! God damn you all to hell!'

The green alien

Mars Attacks! (1996)

Personally, I think that *Mars Attacks!*, a black comedy B-movie spoof, is a more successful attempt at social criticism. At least it boasts a pleiad of stars who deliver a tolerable comedic performance – Jack Nicholson as the President of the United States, Pierce Brosnan as Professor Donald Kessler, and Tom Jones as, erm, himself. Sarah Jessica Parker plays a fashion show host whose head is cut off by the Martians in a weird experiment, and then placed on the tiny body of her lapdog. *Mars*'s comedic value lies in its anarchic, subversive power, a kind of tricksterish, Beetlejuice courage to turn the world upside down, and then expect that everyone else will be filled with glee over the idea. This kind of energy does not come from nowhere. The film's scriptwriter, Jonathan Gems, used to be an actual punk, so he is a bona fide expert in the theory and practice of subversion: 'There is a certain kind of joy in the way that the Martians just come and smash everything up. I was a punk in London and we always used to do pranks. So here you get the Martians taking the p*ss out of society' (Woods, 2002: 134).

A self-confessed outsider and rebel who used to listen to punk as a teenager, Burton liked Gem's idea of sabotaging popular culture and scandalising the Hollywood establishment: 'I just thought it would be fun to see big stars getting blown away' (Woods, 2002: 134). At the same time, there is a discernible political undercurrent in the contemptuous, anarchic tone of *Mars Attacks!* Burton's choice of material was dictated by an uneasy feeling about America at the time: 'I connected to the whole thematic idea of "Things aren't what they seem". I was feeling really strangely about things at the time, about America – everything just seemed really off-kilter to me, and I think that was a partial dynamic of what I liked about the material. I was just feeling more anarchic, and that was the energy I liked in it – I saw that in the Martians' (Salisbury, 2006: 146).

The movie is a perfect representative of its genre and follows the classic 'alien invasion movie' fabula (or storyline): an army of evil, ugly extraterrestrial creatures land on Earth in a flying saucer, and use their super-powerful and technologically advanced weapons to eliminate the population and destroy buildings. They do not, however, manage to expropriate the planet thanks to the heroic behaviour of several brave individuals.

Whereas the fabula level does not reveal any deviations from the genre norm, the plot (or *sujet*, to use the classic formalist division) shows a number of 'inverted' elements characteristic of a parody; and not just any parody – a political spoof. It becomes known that a number of skull-headed, big-brained Martians are planning to land in the US, and the President, James Dale, uses the event as a photo opportunity. Professor Kessler – Pierce Brosnan – who advises him on the issue of extraterrestrial life, has the view that advanced civilisations are amicable and non-violent. At first, it looks like the Martians indeed intend to be friends with the human race, but they suddenly change their minds when a hippie sends a white dove of peace into the sky. Bearing in mind that the script was written by a punk, it is not at all surprising that the Martian representative incinerates the dove with the Martian version of a heat-ray gun. The aliens then proceed to burn the American ambassador, US army soldiers, useless journalists and panicky gapers from the crowd. Later on, they reduce the entire Congress to smouldering fluorescent red and green skeletons and eliminate entire chunks of the urban and rural population of the United States. The key political figures, however, are not simply burned; they are killed inventively, and with a certain kind of humour: the President's wife dies when the Nancy Reagan chandelier falls on her; Donald Kessler's body is literally dismantled during an experiment; and the belligerent fan of atomic warfare General Decker is reduced to a blabbering thing the size of a mouse. Luckily, all ends well for humankind when country boy Richie realises that the green invaders can be killed by Slim Whitman's music. His favourite grandma is a big devotee of the singer. When the Martians are just about to incinerate the unsuspecting old lady with a complex device suspiciously looking like a radio-locator, her headphones become unplugged, and the aliens are subjected to Whitman's piercing yodelling. Ironically, the song she was listening to was called 'Indian Love Call'. It turns out to be lethal to the Martians as on hearing it their heads explode.

Visually and conceptually, *Mars Attacks!* is based on bubble-gum trading cards of the same name, first released by Topps in the 1960s, and re-printed in the mid 1990s. The first edition of the cards was not extremely popular because many customers found the content to be too gory and unnecessarily anarchic. The cards, as Chuck Wagner writes, were 'the ultimate evocation of leftover late Fifties paranoia' (Woods, 2002: 127), i.e. the famous/infamous UFO-sighting craze which started in the 1940s and persisted throughout the 1950s.

Many researchers have pointed out the psychological nature of the UFO phenomenon, among them Carl Gustav Jung. In his essay, *Flying Saucers: A Modern Myth of Things Seen in the Sky* (1958), Jung relates UFO-sightings to the quest for the unity of the self. He suggests that the spaceship might represent a unity symbol deeply seated in the unconscious (especially with the demise of Christian religious symbolism in the West after World War II), which is projected onto the outside world in the guise of 'flying saucers'. Jung explains the round shape of alien spaceships in terms of universal religious symbolism; in his view, 'the circular symbols have played an important role in every age [. . .] There is an old saying that "God is a circle whose centre is everywhere and circumference nowhere". God in his omniscience, omnipotence and omnipresence is a totality symbol *par excellence*, something round, complete, and perfect. [. . .] On the antique level, therefore, the UFOs could easily be conceived as "gods"' (Jung, 2002: 17).

By the 1950s 'flying saucers' had already become a collective dream image, with people reporting cases of seeing flying saucers, being abducted by aliens, or aliens sharing wisdom with them. In Jung's view, even after the two world wars, there was still a belief in people's intrinsic goodness and the power of human consciousness ('the power of man'). This belief 'thrust itself to the forefront in the form of a symbolic rumour, accompanied and reinforced by the appropriate visions' and therefore activated an archetype 'that has always expressed order, deliverance, salvation and wholeness', that is, the 'masculine' qualities (Jung, 2002: 18). Jung wrote in 1958 that in contemporary Western society 'consciously rationalistic enlightenment predominates' and that 'belief in this world and in the power of man has, despite assurances to the contrary, become an . . . irrefragable truth' (Jung, 2002: 18). The technological guise of the 'saviour' symbol fits well into the position of a masculine principle representation as it inherits the aura of enlightenment and the rational through its relation to structure and empirical knowledge. The UFOs became a powerful mass dream image also partly because, in Jung's words, 'anything that looks technological goes down without difficulty with modern man' (Jung, 2002: 18).

A 'higher' (or 'enlightened', as Professor Kessler would have called it) civilisation as the new representation of the masculine principle, a kind of collective version of 'God the Father', is a logical conclusion to the gradual cultural shift from religion to science in the West in late modernity. Unfortunately, as any 'divinity', technology is two-faced; it has a dark side alongside the beneficial one. Narratives produced at the dawn of information-age anxiety, following in the footsteps of H G Wells, seriously tainted the image of the alien in B-movies and in science fiction, endowing extraterrestrial visitors with a number of destructive qualities. For instance, sometimes they plan to infiltrate human bodies with the intention of replacing the entire human race (*Invasion of the Body Snatchers*, 1958); sometimes they create zombies out of humans (*Plan 9 from Outer Space*, 1959); often they simply land on Earth and attack the human race (Orson Welles's scandalous radio version of *The War of the Worlds*, 1938); but the more sophisticated of them swallow up people and structures (*The Blob*, 1958).

Not all aliens were bad, though. In the film *The Day the Earth Stood Still* (1951), which can be read as a post-World War II allegorical warning against political mass hysteria, visitors from another planet are sent to Earth to deliver the message of peace.

There is also an uncanny link between the notion of parenthood and the figure of the alien. Although the Topps Cards Martians physically do not resemble aborted foetuses, the cultural imagination has always linked the UFO myth to 'horrors of reproduction'. Aliens, like the vicious parasites in Ridley Scott's *Alien* (1979), are creatures who infiltrate and break apart the human body. The horror film historian David Skal describes how, in post-war horror cinema, the reproduction process became entirely Franken-steinesque – monstrous or demonic: 'Women would become pregnant by demons or computers, tinkered with by genetic engineers. Pregnancy was an act of war, a violent invasion by the enemy. These fearful images were rarely part of the debate over reproduction technology and abortion rights, but they provided a persistent subtext worth examination' (Skal, 2001: 294). Films like Roman Polanski's *Rosemary's Baby* (1968), David Lynch's *Eraserhead* (1977), David Cronenberg's *The Brood* (1979) and many other, less high-profile films, presented the monster as the indescribable, defamiliarised 'other'; an abnormal, aborted, misshapen creature.

The post-war horror metaphors of failed parenthood – an aborted baby who comes back to life to haunt his creators, or the myth of alien abduction or infestation, were the disturbing signs of the crisis of faith and reason in the Western world. The baby's rage was the man's existential rage at the 'inadequacy of his care' by the parent. Peering into the Camusian black hole of the absurd, the individual was horrified by the fact that the universe lacked order, and that the Creator was gone – or worse, has never existed. Fascism not only 'destroyed God' – it also uncovered a full-scale identity crisis in the midst of the orderly cosmos ruled by instrumental rationality. Freed from the tenets of blind faith, the man was entrusted with a burden of responsibility for his destiny and decisions. And, worst of all, the disappearance of God also meant the disappearance of his nemesis – the devil. Which inevitably meant that the concept of 'evil' had to follow the suit of its counterpart, 'the good', and go back to reside in the human soul, just as Nietzsche predicted. Suddenly, the ordinary human being became the carrier of the disease, and the unwilling owner of a small alien dwelling somewhere in his psyche, ready to erupt any minute.

Extraterrestrial invasion is truly a good all-purpose metaphor. The alien figure possesses distinct characteristics: he is mysterious, intelligent, all-powerful, assertive, speaks a different language, and is firmly in control of all human–alien communication processes. These features render themselves especially well to the stock sci-fi themes of mind control, conspiracy and paranoia – the traditional sublimation of political fears of such diverse scope as totalitarian communist governments, capitalist mind-manipulation, colonialist occupation, the hidden power of the media, secret service conspiracies, and other forms of 'Big Brother' control and surveillance. David Skal explains how World War II changed the face of horror entertainment in the United States: 'Most Americans found it easier not to face the invasion/annihilation anxieties directly; they found indirect expression in McCarthyism, UFO hysteria, and perhaps, most pointedly, in the popular medium of lurid and sensational comic books that had been growing steadily since the end of World War II'. The terrible war gave creative industries new imagery, themes and symbolism because it 'had introduced two radical new forms of mechanized death – the atomic bomb and the extermination camp' (Skal, 1993: 229–230).

Where art critics speak of sublimation, psychotherapists speak of projection. The end of Enlightenment rationality, of progressive, linear history, of faith in the power of reason, and other quintessential tokens of modernity, caused an epidemic of psychological disturbance in the West, UFO sightings being one of its numerous manifestations. Jung explains in *Flying Saucers*:

> We would be . . . inclined to think of the possibility of *psychic* disturbances and interventions, especially as our psychic equilibrium has become something of a problem since the last World War. In this respect there is an increasing uncertainty. Even our historians can no longer make use of the conventional techniques in evaluating and

explaining the developments that have overtaken Europe in the last few decades, but must admit that psychological and psychopathological factors are beginning to widen the horizons of historiography in an alarming way.

(Jung, 2002: 13)

'The little green man' can host a number of conspiratorial projections and cultural anxieties grounded in the semantic fields of authority, invasion and occupation. Technology, that child of rationality, becomes a metaphor for the worst 'testosterone qualities': power, aggression, control and military conflict. The 'rational' and 'protecting' science of the Enlightenment cannot be seen in a totally positive light any more – not after the two world wars, not after Auschwitz and Hiroshima. Scientific progress in the cultural mind is not 'the saviour' of the masses, but his binary opposite – a weapon of mass annihilation. In the course of projective-metaphorical transformation, the army of green aliens becomes a mirror for humankind's vices.

The story of invasion of extraterrestrial creatures as a parody on American international politics is an interesting but controversial idea. A successful rendition of such an idea would require a degree of cultural sensitivity and understanding on the part of both the director and the scriptwriter. However, it appears that what Burton was truly interested in in Gem's script was not its risky political undertones, but its retro character, teeming as it was with opportunities for the exploration of B-movie references and other cinematic memorabilia. Indeed, as far as cinematic citations are concerned, *Mars Attacks!* was a real 'treasure chest' for Burton who often uses pre-existing materials and techniques (especially the ones he admired as a child). In his movies he recycles traditional monster figures (Frankenstein and Godzilla), pays tribute to Ray Harryhausen's visual aesthetics and uses elements of well-known B-movie plots. *Mars Attacks!* is no exception; apart from the obvious borrowings from Topps sketches, there are references to the Godzilla movies ('the running robot'), narrative elements from Ed Wood's *Plan 9 from Outer Space* (the human–Martian 'interpreting machine'), imitation of Ray Harryhausen's stop-motion techniques (the appearance and trajectory of the Martians' spaceships, reminiscent of Harryhausen's *Earth vs the Flying Saucers*), and even self-references (Poppy the Chihuahua, Burton's own dog, is 'experimented on' by the Martians. The motif of 'zombie-dog' has appeared before in *Vincent, Frankenweenie, The Nightmare Before Christmas* and *Corpse Bride*).

The opuses of Burton's childhood heroes – Ed Wood, Ray Harryhausen, James Whale – are recreated with an understandable degree of sentimentality. However, that is not to say that anything else in the movie is sentimental. Burton's handling of the film's main conflict is far from Stephen Spielberg's treatment of human characters as 'fallible but redeemable' in *War of the Worlds* (2005). Being a parody, *Mars Attacks!* does not promote pity for the inhabitants of planet Earth. There are only a few likeable characters in the film, and they are the ones who are lucky to be spared the fate of becoming green fluorescent skeletons: the slow but nice donut-shop worker Richie (Lukas Haas), his senile grandma Florence (an outstanding comedic performance by Sylvia Sidney), Taffy the President's daughter (Natalie Portman), the black boxer Byron (Jim Brown) and his family, Tom Jones (himself), and the recovering hippy-alcoholic Barbara (Annette Benning). The good heroes win without glory, while the bad and immoral ones are killed off without pity. In his interviews Burton has always been very specific about whose side he is on in conflicts between monsters and people – monsters, of course, because they have 'much more heartfelt souls than the human characters around them' (Salisbury, 2000: 3). True to its genre, *Mars Attacks!* endorses the 'lost in translation' theme – the Martians' actual intentions, motives and culture remain equally mysterious for the extradiegetic and intradiegetic spectators. In order to show the 'otherness' of the Martians' lifestyle, the traditional 'defamiliar-isation' (or 'estrangement') stylistic device is used, i.e. their culture and behaviour are represented in a way that we do not recognise, as a completely odd phenomenon. Some elements of their cultural code can be comprehended by comparing them to the 'human equivalents'. For example, one can guess by the Martians' dress that they have ranks; it is also possible to vaguely distinguish 'chunks' of semantic content in their 'aaak' utterings. When the Martians shoot the 'dove of peace', Professor Kessler is confident that a 'cultural decoding error' has occurred: apparently, unlike in Western civilisation, where birds are generally regarded positively, and doves as symbols have a particularly good reputation, the signifier 'bird' in the Martian culture has a 'sinister' signified attached to it. The true meaning of this signified, together with other 'visible' elements of the extraterrestrial culture, is left undeciphered; it remains within the circle of 'estrangement'.

Whereas in *Batman* and *Edward Scissorhands* communication breakdown and failure of language is presented as a deeply tragic state of affairs, *Mars Attacks!* openly celebrates this carnival of misunderstanding. Uniquely for Burton, instead of his unusual emotional connection, he delivers a purely postmodernist message about the joys of disconnection. Neither the audience, nor the human characters of the film, receives access to the secrets of the Martians' lifestyle; all they can see is a 'defamiliarised' stream of obscure signs and symbols. In the case of the burned 'symbol of peace', the two audiences – the 'internal' and the 'external' do not even know whether the 'communication mistake'/'bird fear' was genuine. It could as well have been a convenient premise for starting the war, or simply a manifestation of a peculiar Martian sense of humour.

At the same time, unlike extraterrestrials from traditional examples of the 'alien invasion' genre (*War of the Worlds* (1953); *Earth vs the Flying Saucers*

(1956); Stephen Spielberg's version of *War of the Worlds* starring Tom Cruise, 2005), Burton's Martians are not exactly a 'faceless enemy'. They do have a face, and this face is not completely unfamiliar to the society of individuals portrayed in *Mars Attacks!* As Jung puts it, explaining the meaning of the shadow archetype, 'whoever looks into the mirror of the water will see first of all his own face. Whoever goes to himself risks a confrontation with himself' (CW9/I: para. 43). The strategy of defamiliarisation is employed in the film for metaphorical purposes. One can draw a certain parallel between the stylistic device of estrangement (the cinematic version of estrangement, of course, which is enriched and extended by the 'visual' cinematic codes), and the concept of split-off unconscious materials. This concept is widely used by different branches of psychoanalysis and psychology. In its Jungian version, the repressed materials in question can be archetypes (inhabiting the collective part of the unconscious) and complexes (residing it its 'personal' part – the part which owes its existence to personal experience) (CW9/I: paras. 88–89).

Analysed from the Jungian point of view, the Martians represent the American collective shadow; an ugly set of aggressive characteristics that has been 'split off' from the glorious 'civilising missionary' image of the United States. The shadow is often split off, repressed or denied because, as Jung argues, 'the meeting with ourselves belongs to the more unpleasant things that can be avoided as long as we can project everything negative into the environment' (CW9/I: para. 43). Although Jung is talking here about the personal shadow, his comment is as true of the collective *doppelgänger*. A nation, a group or a crowd would have more difficulties in admitting its own weaknesses than a single individual as 'all human control comes to an end when the individual is caught in a mass movement' (Jung, 1953: CW 10: para. 243). Put into a metaphor, society's negative traits become unrecognisable – and indeed, they do look totally unfamiliar in the form of hyper-brained, technologically advanced 'enlightened' (Professor Kessler's term) Martians, with their green bodies and 'aaak' language. The extraterrestrial lifestyle represents an inversion, a mockery, a reflection of the West's obsession with rationalism, scientific progress and technology. In the film they even try to 'copy' the West's 'cultural shadows' – for instance, when they ogle a blond big-breasted model in an erotic magazine.

Aliens 'exist' because, as Sam Keen maintains, 'the body politic mass produces hatred while remaining unconscious of its own paranoia, projection and propaganda: The problem in military psychology is how to convert the act of murder into patriotism. For the most part, this process of dehumanising the enemy has not been closely examined. When we project our shadows, we systematically blind ourselves to what we are doing' (Abrams and Zweig, 1991: 199). The song that kills the Martians is called 'Indian Love Call', an indirect reference to a murky chapter of US history – the European colonisation of America. The real enemy is inside, not

outside; but the crowd perceives it in its external, 'dehumanised' form –
alien yet distinctly, and suspiciously, recognisable. 'Indian Love Call', and
its mass-hypnotising potential, is reminiscent of *Beetlejuice's* 'Day O' and
'Jump in the Line'.

Mars Attacks! contains a truly rebellious message: the 'monsters' –
Burton's favourites – destroy the emblems of the American way of life in all
its diversity, from blind suburban patriotism (Billy Glenn) and the militar-
ism of the top political circles (Generals Casey and Decker), to the headless
vanity of the fashion industry (Nathalie Lake) and the callousness and
futility of the gambling business (Art Land, Rude Gambler). An American
film critic, Jim Hoberman, writes: 'Personal and anarchic where
Independence Day is corporate and patriarchal, *Mars Attacks* has an even
purer hatred of politicians – and of adult authority in general' (Woods,
2002: 141). Burton, invariably happy to teach 'common people' a lesson,
puts on his 'monster' guise and gleefully cuts off the head of a fashion show
host, uses a ray gun to burn an American general till there is only a glowing
skeleton left, and enthusiastically kills off a bunch of the richest investors in
the world. He sets ablaze the entire US Congress together with its members,
drops a huge chandelier lamp onto the head of Marsha Dale (the image-
obsessed President's wife), and incinerates affluent LA casinos. One can
easily trace Burton's – and the Martians' – destructive mirthfulness to his
childhood obsession with Gothic 'body transformation' movies (Whale's
Frankenstein series, various Draculas, or quasi-Frankenstein sci-fi like *The
Brain that Wouldn't Die*, 1962). This is his sublimated way of criticising the
norms, the accepted and the established – by 'blowing up' an entire
society's structure.

Interestingly, Burton's 'personal' films – stories of outcasts and misunderstood monsters – are warm and empathic. The director tends to
identify with the main character, turning the narrative into a sublimated
exploration of the causes of rejection, unhappiness and loneliness. The main
character is usually highly likeable in his eccentricity – Edward Scissorhands, Ed Wood, Edward Bloom, Batman – and the audience (consisting
mainly of common people, by the way!) ends up sympathising with him.

By contrast, the main atmosphere of *Mars Attacks!* is chillingly cold. An
army of ugly, cruel, bulge-eyed extraterrestrials, in place of Burton's usual
'loveable monster', are not exactly charming. Some scenes and narrative
threads in the film are debasingly cruel and insensitive in the worst postmodernist manner. A notable example of this is the burning of the US
militaristic patriot Billy Glenn (Jack Black), with his parents, back in their
trailer, watching the live footage of his death. The subsequent spoof of a
US military funeral is an even more disturbing choice of material. The Billy
Glenn narrative thread was supposed to be a critique of grassroots militar-
ism and cheap patriotism, and on the surface it looks like a good political
message. However, the soldier funeral scene transgresses all acceptable

boundaries of postmodernist self-reflectivity, decenteredness and parodic emptiness. For the America of the post-Gulf era, the death of military servicemen is not joke material.

The narrative of *Mars Attacks!* is a good example of what the American political theorist Fredric Jameson called 'pastiche', a worn-out, useless travesty – a true reflection of the ever-changing images of consumerist society (Malpas, 2001: 25–26) (this was discussed in detail in Chapter 1). *Mars Attacks!* fits into the pastiche framework surprisingly well. The film's main message, despite its strong political undertones, is nevertheless lost in the midst of colourful details and carefully reproduced retro-references. For most of the audience, the message is 'lost in translation' – similar to the Martian communications, when they are misinterpreted (or even worse – interpreted correctly!) by Dr Zeigler's imperfect 'translator device'. *Mars Attacks!* delivers a confusingly controversial message; like the Martians' 'Don't run, we are your friends' it erases itself in a weird suicide stunt.

The film is so self-centered, so obsessed with itself, so full of self-admiration that it is 'too busy' to promote any idea that goes beyond the logic of its inner structure. One could foreground the political message more, or at least try to wrap it in a 'softer', more 'humane' packaging (the way Spielberg did it in his *War of the Worlds* – showing the dialectics of human tragedy and human fallibility). *Mars Attacks's* warning of the dangers of mainstream thinking is delivered in a careless and unsympathetic manner. There is a handful of positive, obligatorily misfit characters, and they are the force that keeps the movie alive. But apparently, for American audiences this was not a good enough incentive to fall in love with the film, even with a happy end sewn on to the Martian invasion theme like the tail to a Frankenstein dog. Kim Newman rightly notes that *Mars Attacks!* 'is the sort of thing that alienates far more people than it converts' (Woods, 2002: 145).

Mars Attacks! was destined to be unpopular, especially in the United States, where it was probably regarded as a cinematic 'spit in the nation's face'. The movie is unanimously considered Burton's second-worst movie and his first flop. Most reviewers picked up the film's campness, its parodic value as an alien invasion movie, and its tricksterish qualities. But, as a film critic Ken Feil writes, '*Mars Attacks!* privileges irony, self-parody, and carnivalesque carnage to the exclusion of straight-forward entertainment and affirmative social messages' (Feil, 2006: 106). Many reviewers preferred not to mention the film's political undercurrent at all as if it was completely irrelevant to the film's inner structure because Burton failed to – or did not want to – put an emphasis on it. For instance, Janet Maslin of *The New York Times* takes notice of the film's 'groundless pastiche' quality; in her view, '"Mars Attacks!" is just a parade of scattershot gags, more often weird than funny and most often just flat' (http://movies.nytimes.com). The review published in the *New Yorker* mentions 'a strong whiff of self-destructiveness' which makes the film 'a kind of anti-entertainment' (Woods, 2002: 140). The punkish, tricksterish habit of rubbing one's defects into one's face does not make viewers more aware of their 'shadow'. It makes them angry.

Mars Attacks! does not exactly fall apart the way *Planet of the Apes* does (at least it possesses some kind of visual unity), but there is a sense of emptiness to it, which sets it apart from Burton's 'dark hero' films. Its political aura can be easily overlooked, 'lost in translation', very much like the anti-colonisation message in *Planet of the Apes*.

One can only applaud attempts at social criticism by a big-budget Hollywood director, but in Burton's case both attempts did not come off terribly well. *Mars Attacks* is dispassionately, mindlessly anarchic, while *Planet of the Apes*, as Jonathan Romney notes, is 'impersonally opulent' (Woods, 2002: 170). By contrast, the anarchy of his personalised tricksters – Beetlejuice is charismatic; and the Gothic romantic opulence of his 'personal' *doppelgängers* – Edward Scissorhands, Bruce Wayne, Willy Wonka – at times might look naïve and smack of teenage posturing, but are never quite annoyingly artificial.

The success appears to be hidden in the deeply felt personal attachment to the material. In order to be successful, Burton's material has to be based on the subject of the protagonist's individuation, and not around social issues. It repeatedly salvages Burton's sloppy editing and bulky, uneven scripts. Whereas personalised monsters are emotionally accessible, defamiliarised monsters are aloof and detached. I suppose, the secret of Burton's art lies in the following schemata: singling out a protagonist, making him the focaliser, and concentrating on his personal problems on the one hand, and his grievances against society on the other. Meanwhile, society, and all that is normal and accepted, should be estranged, and look entirely 'new'. There is one condition, however. When the protagonist's enemies are aliens, it does not seem to work. His real enemy is common people. The camera belongs to the monster.

Conclusion

> Heretics are the only (bitter) remedy against the entropy
> of human thought
>
> (Evgeny Zamyatin, in Stacy, 1974: 141)

Tim Burton's popularity as a director and visionary, which comes despite his films being marginal, overtly Gothic and otherwise nonconformist, is not surprising. His depiction of the individual as a fragile creature whose integrity is being threatened by the unthinking collectivity, and the decisions of those few who have the power to influence the direction of mass thinking, is acutely relevant in the contemporary post-industrial, globalised capitalist world.

The threat to the individual does not always come wrapped up in a red flag, and carrying hammers, sickles, scythes and other symbols of communal work, collective life and uniformed thinking. Evgeny Zamyatin, the author of *We* (1921), the famous anti-utopia which would later inspire George Orwell to write his *1984*, based his book in equal parts on his experiences of living in Bolshevist Russia and working as an engineer in England during World War I.

However stifling and oppressive communist ideologies can be, the Western brand of instrumental rationality is not entirely free from the horrors of conformity and depersonalisation. In fact, the word 'mass' firmly dominates contemporary political, cultural and economic discourses. Every day we hear about weapons of mass destruction, mass production, mass media, mass market and mass unemployment. At times, instrumental rationality can be scarier than the militant uniformity of communal existence because capitalist ideologies are subtler, and therefore more pervasive (here we are going back to the Joker's chemical charm, boundary-dissolving fluidity, PR talents and his love affair with the media).

Without resorting to openly political statements, Burton's films reflect the psychological dangers of a whole cluster of issues that come with modernity and postmodernity: an excessively materialist and utilitarian view of the world and physical processes; efficiency and technology at the expense of humanity; the rationalisation and professionalisation of private life; and even – ironically, given the general individualistic stance of Burton's *oeuvre* – loss of communal and familial ties. After all, the artistic–capitalistic loner Willie Wonka in *Charlie and the Chocolate Factory* restores the connection with his estranged father, and acknowledges, following Charlie's advice, the importance of community in the life of the individual.

Looking at the web of Burton's works, one cannot fail to notice how his characters, figuratively speaking, exchange genetic material. Edward Scissorhands's touching, helpless desperation transmogrifies into the apocalyptic existentialist disillusionment of Sweeney Todd. Edward's dead Inventor transmutes into Will Bloom's missing father, and then becomes Willie Wonka's unfeeling parent. Vincent's dead bride finally materialises in Victor Van Dort's wedding nightmare. The world is too small a place for Jack Skellington's ambition, and also for Ed Bloom. Pee Wee's comical 'breakfast production line' turns into Wonka's grand factory. The methodical prophet of budding modernity, Ichabod Crane, finds dissection of bodies a justified, serious and scientific activity; meanwhile, the shadow of technological progress, Jack Napier, regards manipulating people's bodies and photographic images as a meaningless, but nonetheless pleasant, pastime. Ichabod's fighting with chaos and absurdity, and gaining a temporary victory, is reignited in Batman's battle for meaning in the absurdity of the fluid postmodern world. And, most disturbingly – in the ever-serious, ever-professional, over-regulated Western society, the genuinely rebellious scowl of Betelgeuse metamorphoses into the fake, consumable and detachable laughter of the Joker.

I deliberately eschewed extensive use of the psychobiographical approach because, in a way, Tim Burton's art and his vision are bigger than any number of childhood complexes he may harbour. *Edward Scissorhands, Batman* and *Sweeney Todd*, far from reflecting a narrowly personal set of problems, map out the psychological face of the contemporary world. Burton's rebellious child, having proclaimed himself the next god, is nevertheless anxiously, and helplessly, peering into the chaos in the hope of discerning a definite structure, distinguishing a centre; catching a glimpse of sense. Being an individual, he resists division. The audience, who is peering into the dark mirror together with him, knows that he will eventually succeed.

And finally, a little disclaimer: because the body of Burton's work is loose – at times broken up, at times patchy and uneven – it was not easy to pull the pieces together. I used my utmost monster-building abilities to sew it into a unified framework. Please forgive me for the occasional tears and holes.

Filmography

Vincent (1982)

Director: Tim Burton
Producer: Tim Burton
Screenplay: Tim Burton
Cinematography: Victor Abdalov
Narrated by Vincent Price

Frankenweenie (1984)

Production Company: Walt Disney
Producer: Julie Hickson
Director: Tim Burton
Screenplay: Lenny Ripp, based on an original idea by Tim Burton
Cinematography: Thomas Ackerman
Editor: Ernest Milano
Art Director: John B. Mainsbridge

Pee Wee's Big Adventure (1985)

Production Company: Aspen Film Society-Shapiro/Warner Bros.
Executive Producer: William E. McEuen
Producers: Robert Shapiro, Richard Gilbert Abramson
Director: Tim Burton
Screenplay: Paul Reubens, Phil Hartman, Michael Varhol
Cinematography: Victor J. Kemper
Editor: Billy Webber
Music: Danny Elfman
Production Designer: David L. Snyder

Beetlejuice (1988)

Production Company: The Geffen Company
Producers: Michael Bender, Larry Wilson and Richard Hashimoto
Director: Tim Burton
Screenplay: Michael McDowell and Warren Skaaren
Cinematography: Thomas Ackerman
Editor: Jane Kurson
Music: Danny Elfman
Production Designer: Bo Welch

Batman (1989)

Production Company: Warner Bros.
Executive Producers: Benjamin Melniker, Michael Uslan
Producers: Jon Peters, Peter Guber, Chris Kenney
Director: Tim Burton
Screenplay: Sam Hamm and Warren Skaaren
Cinematography: Roger Pratt
Editor: Ray Lovejoy
Music: Danny Elfman
Production Designer: Anton Furst

Edward Scissorhands (1990)

Production Company: Twentieth Century Fox
Executive Producer: Richard Hashimoto
Producers: Denise Di Novi, Tim Burton
Director: Tim Burton
Screenplay: Caroline Thompson, story by Tim Burton and Caroline Thompson
Cinematography: Stefan Czapsky
Editor: Richard Halsey
Music: Danny Elfman
Production Designer: Bo Welch

Batman Returns (1992)

Production Company: Warner Bros.
Executive Producers: Jon Peters, Peter Guber, Benjamin Melniker, Michael Uslan
Producers: Denise Di Novi, Tim Burton
Director: Tim Burton

Screenplay: Daniel Waters, story by Daniel Waters and Sam Hamm, based on characters created by Bob Kane
Cinematography: Stefan Czapsky
Editor: Chris Lebenzon
Music: Danny Elfman
Production Designer: Bo Welch

Tim Burton's The Nightmare Before Christmas (1993)

Production Company: Touchstone Pictures
Producers: Denise Di Novi, Tim Burton
Director: Henry Selick
Screenplay: Caroline Thompson, story and characters by Tim Burton, adaptation by Michael McDowell
Cinematography: Pete Kozachik
Editor: Stan Webb
Music: Danny Elfman
Art Director: Deane Taylor

Ed Wood (1994)

Production Company: Touchstone Pictures
Executive Producer: Michael Lehmann
Producers: Denise Di Novi and Tim Burton
Director: Tim Burton
Screenplay: Scott Alexander, Larry Karaszewski
Cinematography: Stefan Czaspsky
Editor: Chris Lebenzon
Music: Danny Elfman
Production Designer: Tom Duffield

James and the Giant Peach (1996)

Production Company: Walt Disney Pictures, Allied Filmmakers, Skellington Productions
Producers: Tim Burton, Denise Di Novi, Jake Eberts
Director: Henry Selick
Screenplay: Steven Bloom, Karey Kirkpatrick, Jonathan Roberts
Novel: Roald Dahl
Cinematography: Pete Kozachik, Hiro Narita, Eric Swenson
Editor: Stan Webb
Music: Randy Newman
Art Directors: Bill Boes, Kendal Cronkhite, Blake Russell, Lane Smith

Mars Attacks! (1996)

Production Company: Warner Bros.
Producers: Tim Burton, Larry Franco
Director: Tim Burton
Screenplay: Jonathan Gems
Cinematography: Peter Suschitzy
Editor: Chris Lebenzon
Music: Danny Elfman
Production Designer: Wynn Thomas

Sleepy Hollow (1999)

Production Company: Paramount Pictures/Scott Rudin Productions/ Mandalay Pictures
Executive Producers: Larry Franco, Francis Ford Coppola
Producers: Scott Rudin, Adam Schroeder
Director: Tim Burton
Screenplay: Andrew Kevin Walker
Cinematography: Emmanuel Lubezki
Editor: Chris Lebenzon
Music: Danny Elfman
Production Designer: Rick Heinrichs

The World of Stainboy (2000)

Written and directed by Burton for shockwave.com (http://atomfilms. shockwave.com/)

Planet of the Apes (2001)

Production Company: Twentieth Century Fox/Zanuck Company
Executive Producer: Ralph Winter
Producer: Richard D. Zanuck
Director: Tim Burton
Screenplay: William Broyles Jr, Lawrence Konner and Mark Rosenthal
Cinematography: Philippe Rousselot
Editor: Chris Lebenzon
Music: Danny Elfman
Production Designer: Rich Heinrichs

Big Fish (2003)

Production Company: Columbia Pictures/Cohen Company/Zanuck Company
Executive Producer: Arne L. Schmidt
Producers: Richard Zanuck, Bruce Cohen, Dan Jinks
Director: Tim Burton
Screenplay: John August, based on the novel by Daniel Wallace
Cinematography: Philippe Rousselot
Editor: Chris Lebenzon
Music: Danny Elfman
Production Designer: Dennis Gassner

Corpse Bride (2005)

Production Company: Warner Bros.
Executive Producers: Joe Ranft, Jeffrey Auerbach
Producers: Tim Burton, Allison Abbate
Director: Tim Burton, Mike Johnson
Screenplay: Caroline Thompson, John August, Pamela Pettler
Cinematography: Peter Kozachik
Editor: Jonathan Lucas
Music: Danny Elfman
Production Designer: Alex McDowell
Art Director: Nelson Lowry

Charlie and the Chocolate Factory (2005)

Production Company: Warner Bros., Village Roadshow, Zanuck Company
Executive Producers: Felicity Dahl, Patrick McCormick, Michael Siegel, Graham Burke, Bruce Berman
Producers: Brad Grey, Richard Zanuck
Director: Tim Burton
Screenplay: John August, based on Roald Dahl's book
Cinematography: Philippe Rousselot
Editor: Chris Lebenzon
Music: Danny Elfman
Production Designer: Alex McDowell

Sweeney Todd: The Demon Barber of Fleet Street (2007)

Production Company: Warner Bros./DreamWorks Pictures/Zanuck Company

Producers: Richard D. Zanuck, John Logan, Walter F. Parkes, Laurie MacDonald
Director: Tim Burton
Screenplay: John Logan, Stephen Sondheim, Hugh Wheeler and Christopher Bond
Cinematography: Dariusz Wolski
Editor: Chris Lebenzon
Music: Stephen Sondheim
Production Designer: Dante Ferretti

Bibliography

Abrams, Jeremiah and Zweig, Connie (1991) *Meeting the Shadow: The Hidden Power of the Dark Side of Human Nature*, New York: Jeremy P. Tarcher/Putnam.

Aers, David, Cook, Jonathan and Punter, David (1981) *Romanticism and Ideology: Studies in English Writing 1765–1830*, London: Routledge.

Alister, Ian and Hauke, Christopher (eds.) (1998) *Contemporary Jungian Analysis: Post-Jungian Perspectives from the Society of Analytical Psychology*, London: Routledge.

Avins, Mimi (1993) 'Ghoul World', in Christian Fraga (ed.) (2005) *Tim Burton Interviews*, Jackson: University Press of Mississippi, pp. 95–101.

Babcock-Abrahams, B (1975) 'A Tolerated Margin of the Mess: The Trickster and his Tales Reconsidered', *Journal of the Folklore Institute*, 11, pp. 147–186.

Barnaby, Karin and D'Acierno, Pellegrino (eds.) (1990) *C. G. Jung and the Humanities: Towards a Hermeneutics of Culture*, London: Routledge.

Baudrillard, Jean (2000) *Simulacra and Simulation*, London: Routledge.

Baumlin, James S., Baumlin Tita French and Jensen, George H. (2004) *Post-Jungian Criticism: Theory and Practice*, New York: State University of New York Press.

Bazin, André (1967). *What is Cinema? Vol. 1* (translated and edited by Hugh Gray), Berkeley: University of California Press.

—— (1971) *What is Cinema? Vol. 2* (translated and edited by Hugh Gray), Berkeley: University of California Press.

Belmonte, Thomas (1990) 'The Trickster and the Sacred Clown: Revealing the Logic of the Unspeakable', in Pellegrino D'Acierno and Karin Barnaby (eds.), *C. G. Jung and the Humanities: Towards a Hermeneutics of Culture*, London: Routledge, pp. 45–66.

Berger, P. and Luckman, T. (1967; 1966) *The Social Construction of Reality*, New York: Random House.

Bertens, J. W., Bertens, Hans and Fokkema, D. W. (eds.) (1997) *International Postmodernism: Theory and Literary Practice*, Amsterdam: John Benjamins Publishing Co.

Bertens, Hans (1997) 'The Detective', in J. W. Bertens, Hans Bertens and D. W. Fokkema (1997), *International Postmodernism: Theory and Literary Practice*, Amsterdam: John Benjamins Publishing Co., pp. 195–202.

Biodrowski, Stephen (1991) '*Edward Scissorhands*', in Paul A. Woods (ed.), *Tim Burton: A Child's Garden of Nightmares*, London: Plexus, pp. 70–71.

Blitz, Michael and Krasniewicz, Louise (2007) *Johnny Depp*, Orlando, FL: Greenwood Publishing Group.

Bordo, Susan (2001; 1993) '"Material Girl": The Effacements of Postmodern Culture', in Julie Rivkin and Michael Ryan (eds.), *Literary Theory: an Anthology*, Oxford: Blackwell, pp. 1099–1115.

Botting, Fred (1993) 'Powers in the Darkness: Heterotopias, Literature and Gothic Labyrinths', *Genre* 26, 2–3, pp. 253–282.

—— (1996) *Gothic*, London: Routledge.

Boulle, Pierre (2001; 1963) *Planet of the Apes*, New York: Del Rey.

Branigan, Edward (2006; 1992) *Narrative Comprehension and Film*, London and New York: Routledge.

Breskin, David (1991) 'Tim Burton', in Christian Fraga (ed.) (2005) *Tim Burton Interviews*, Jackson: University Press of Mississippi, pp. 37–88.

Brown, Blain (2002) *Cinematography: Theory and Practice*, London and New York: Focal Press.

Burgoyne, R. Flitterman-Lewis, S. and Stam, R. (1992) *New Vocabularies in Film Semiotics*, London: Routledge.

Burton, Tim (1997) *The Melancholy Death of an Oyster Boy and Other Stories*, New York: HarperEntertainment.

www.cameraguild.com/index.html?magazine/stoo1199.htm~tcp.man_hp

Campbell, James (2008; 1968) *The Hero with a Thousand Faces*, Novato, CA: New World Library.

Caughie, John (ed.) (1981) *Theories of Authorship*, London: Routledge.

Chesterton, G. K (2006; 1902) *The Defendant*, Teddington: The Echo Library.

Clark, John (1994) 'The Wood, the Bad and the Ugly', in Paul A. Woods (ed.), *Tim Burton: A Child's Garden of Nightmares*, London: Plexus, pp. 111–118.

Clarkson, Petrûska (ed.) (1997) *On the Sublime in Psychoanalysis, Archetypal Psychology and Psychotherapy*, London: Whurr.

Coleman, David (1983) *'Vincent'*, in Paul A. Woods (ed.), *Tim Burton: A Child's Garden of Nightmares*, London: Plexus, p. 13.

Corliss, Richard (1992) 'Battier and Battier', in Paul A. Woods (ed.), *Tim Burton: A Child's Garden of Nightmares*, London: Plexus, pp. 77–80.

Cotterell, Arthur (ed.) (1999) *Encyclopaedia of World Mythology*, London: Paragon.

Dahl, Roald (1998) *Charlie and the Chocolate Factory*, London: Puffin Books.

Davies, Oliver (2004) 'Theorizing Writerly Creativity: Jung with Lacan?', in James S. Baumlin, Tita French Baumlin and George H. Jensen (2004) *Post-Jungian Criticism: Theory and Practice*, New York: State University of New York Press, pp. 55–75.

Denby, David (1989) 'Babes in Cinema Land', in Paul A. Woods (ed.), *Tim Burton: A Child's Garden of Nightmares*, London: Plexus, pp. 37–39.

—— (2001) 'Misanthropes', in *The New Yorker*, http://www.newyorker.com/archive/2001/08/06/010806crci_cinema, downloaded on 16 May 2009.

Eagleton, Terry (1997; 1996) *The Illusions of Postmodernism*, Oxford: Blackwell.

—— (2003) *After Theory*, London: Allen Lane and Penguin.

Edelstein, David (1988) 'Mixing *Beetlejuice*', in Christian Fraga (ed.) (2005) *Tim Burton Interviews*, Jackson: University Press of Mississippi, pp. 9–15.

—— (1990) 'Odd Man In', in Christian Fraga (ed.) (2005) *Tim Burton Interviews*, Jackson: University Press of Mississippi, pp. 31–36.

Eliot, T. S (1988; 1940) *The Waste Land and Other Poems*, London: Faber and Faber.

Elliot, David (1985) 'Is America Ready for a Nut Who's a Genius?', in Paul A. Woods (ed.), *Tim Burton: A Child's Garden of Nightmares*, London: Plexus, p. 26.

Emerson, Jim (2005) 'Is Willy Wonka Wacko Jacko?', http://rogerebert.suntimes.com/apps/pbcs.dll/article?AID=/20050718/EDITOR/50718002, downloaded on 16 May 2009.

Faris, Wendy B. and Zamora, Louis Parkinson (1995) *Magical Realism: Theory, Hostory, Community*, North Carolina: Duke University Press.

Feil, Ken (2006) *Dying for a Laugh: Disaster Movies and the Camp Imagination*, Middletown, CT: Wesleyan University Press.

Felpern, Leslie (1994) 'Animated Dreams', in Paul A. Woods (ed.), *Tim Burton: A Child's Garden of Nightmares*, London: Plexus, pp. 102–107.

Ferrante, Anthony C. (1997) 'Hidden Gems', in Paul A. Woods (ed.), *Tim Burton: A Child's Garden of Nightmares*, London: Plexus, pp. 129–131.

Fraga, Kristian (ed.) (2005) *Tim Burton Interviews*, Jackson: University Press of Mississippi.

Fredericksen, Don (1979) 'Jung/Sign/Symbol/Film', in Ian Alister and Christopher Hauke (eds.) (2005) *Jung and Film: Post-Jungian Takes on the Moving Image*, London: Routledge, pp. 17–55.

French, Lawrence (1994) 'A Meeting of Minds: Tim Burton's *Ed Wood*', in Christian Fraga (ed.) (2005) *Tim Burton Interviews*, Jackson: University Press of Mississippi, pp. 102–107.

Fuller, Graham (1990) 'Tim Burton and Vincent Price', in Paul A. Woods (ed.), *Tim Burton: A Child's Garden of Nightmares*, London: Plexus, pp. 14–16 and 59–61.

Garfield, Simon (1988) 'Beetle Mania', in Paul A. Woods (ed.), *Tim Burton: A Child's Garden of Nightmares*, London: Plexus, pp. 34–37.

Giddens, Anthony (1991) *Modernity and Self-identity: Self and Society in the Late Modern Age*, Chicago: Stanford University Press.

Gleiberman, Owen (2002) 'Planet of the Apes', in Paul A. Woods (ed.), *Tim Burton: A Child's Garden of Nightmares*, London: Plexus.

Graves, Robert (1998; 1955) 'Theseus and Ariadne', in David Adams Leeming (ed.) (1998) *Mythology: The Voyage of the Hero*, Oxford: Oxford University Press.

Greer, Germaine (2007) 'Yes, Frankenstein really was written by Mary Shelley. It's obvious – because the book is so bad', in *The Guardian*, 9 April 2007, p. 28.

Grey, Rudolph (1994; 1992) *Nightmare of Ecstasy: The Life and Art of Edward D. Wood, Jr.*, London and Boston: Faber and Faber.

Goldenberg, Naomi R. (1990) 'A Feminist Critique of Jung', in Robert L. Moore and Daniel J. Meckel (eds.), *Jung and Christianity in Dialogue: Faith, Feminism and Hermeneutics*, Mahwah, NY: Paulist Press.

Hanke, Ken (1992–1993) 'Tim Burton', in Paul A. Woods (ed.), *Tim Burton: A Child's Garden of Nightmares*, London: Plexus, pp. 81–95.

—— (1999) *Tim Burton: An Unauthorized Biography of the Filmmaker*, Los Angeles: Renaissance Books.

Hauke, Christopher (1996) 'The Child: Development, Archetype, and Analytic Practice' in *The San Francisco Jung Institute Library Journal*, 15 (1), pp. 17–38.

—— (1997) 'The Phallus, Alchemy and Christ: Jungian Analysis and the Sublime', in Petrûska Clarkson (ed.), *On the Sublime in Psychoanalysis, Archetypal Psychology and Psychotherapy*, London: Whurr, pp. 123–144.

—— (2000) *Jung and the Postmodern. The Interpretation of Realities*, London and Philadelphia: Routledge.

Hauke, Christopher and Alister, Ian (eds.) (2001) *Jung and Film*, London and New-York: Routledge.

—— (2005) *Human Being Human: Culture and the Soul*, London: Routledge.

Henderson, Joseph L. (1978; 1964) 'Ancient Myths and Modern Man', in Carl Jung and M.-L. von Franz (eds.), *Man and His Symbols*, London: Picador, pp. 96–156.

Hillman, James (ed.) (1977) 'Puer Wounds and Ulysses Scar', in *Puer Papers*, Dallas: Spring, pp. 100–128.

—— (1987; 1979) *Puer Papers*, Dallas: Spring.

Hoberman, J. (1995) 'Ed Wood . . . Not', in Paul A. Woods (ed.), *Tim Burton: A Child's Garden of Nightmares*, London: Plexus, pp. 118–123.

—— (1999) 'Heads or Tails', in Paul A. Woods (ed.), *Tim Burton: A Child's Garden of Nightmares*, London: Plexus, pp. 160–161.

—— (2002) 'Pax Americana', in Paul A. Woods (ed.), *Tim Burton: A Child's Garden of Nightmares*, London: Plexus, pp. 138–143.

Hockley, Luke (2001) *Cinematic Projections: The Analytical Psychology of C.G. Jung and Film Theory*, London: University of Luton Press.

Hoffmann, E.T.A. (2001; 1819) *Klein Zaches genannt Zinnober*, Chestnut Hill, MA: Adamant Media Corporation.

Holquist, Michael (2004) 'Detective Films and Images of the Orient: A Post-Jungian Reflection', in James S. Baumlin, Tita French Baumlin and George H. Jensen (eds.) (2004) *Post-Jungian Criticism: Theory and Practice*, New York: State University of New York Press.

—— (1971) 'Whodunit and Other Questions: Metaphysical Detective Stories in Post-War Fiction', *New Literary History*, 3, 1, pp. 135–156.

Irving, Washington (2008; 1820) *The Legend of Sleepy Hollow*, Charleston, South Carolina: Forgotten Books.

Izod, John (2001) *Myth, Mind and the Screen: Understanding the Heroes of our Time*. Cambridge: Cambridge University Press.

—— (2006) *Screen, Culture, Psyche: A Post-Jungian Approach to Working with the Audience*, London: Routledge.

Jacobi, Jolande (1942; 1973) *The Psychology of C. G. Jung* (8th edn), trans. Ralph Manheim, New Haven and London: Yale University Press.

—— (ed.) (1953) *Psychological Reflections. An Anthology of the Writings of C.G. Jung*, London: Routledge and Kegan Paul.

—— (1964) 'Symbols in an Individual Analysis', in Carl Gustav Jung and Marie-Louise von Frantz (eds.) (1964) *Man and His Symbols*, London: Picador, pp. 323–374.

Jameson, Fredric (2001; 1985) 'Postmodernism and Consumer Society', in Simon Malpas (ed.), *Postmodern Debates*, London: Palgrave.

—— (1975) *The Prison-House of Language: A Critical Account of Structuralism and Russian Formalism*, Princeton, NJ: Princeton University Press.

Jones, Alan (1987) '*Pee Wee's Big Adventure*', in Paul A. Woods (ed.), *Tim Burton: A Child's Garden of Nightmares*, London: Plexus, pp. 27–29.

—— (1989) '*Batman*', in Christian Fraga (ed.) (2005) *Tim Burton Interviews*, Jackson: University Press of Mississippi, pp. 16–30.

Jung, C. G. Except where a different publication was used, all references are to the hardback edition of C. G. Jung, *The Collected Works* (CW), edited by Sir Herbert Read, Dr Michael Fordham and Dr Gerhardt Adler, and translated by R. F. C. Hull, London: Routledge.

Jung, C. G. (1958; 2002) *Flying Saucers*, London and New York: Routledge.

—— (1963; 1995) *Memories, Dreams, Reflections*, London: Fontana.

—— (1975) *Letters, II, 1951–1961*, Gerhardt Adler (ed.) in collaboration with Aniela Jaffé, trans. R. F. C. Hull, Princeton, NJ: Princeton University Press.

Jung, Carl Gustav and von Franz, M.-L. (eds.) (1978; 1964) *Man and His Symbols*, London: Picador.

Kant, Emmanuel (1784) 'An Answer to the Question: What is Enlightenment?', in James Schmidt (ed.) (1996) *What is Enlightenment?*, CA: University of California Press.

Keen, Sam (1991) 'The Enemy Maker', in Jeremiah Abrams and Connie Zweig (eds.) (1991) *Meeting the Shadow: The Hidden Power of the Dark Side of Human Nature*, New York: Jeremy P. Tarcher/Putnam, pp. 197–202.

Kinkaid, James Russell (1998) *Erotic Innocence: The Culture of Child Molesting*, Durham, NC: Duke University Press.

Koningsberg, Ira (1996) 'Transitional Phenomena, Transitional Space: Creativity and Spectatorship in Film', in *Psychoanalytic Review*, 83(6) December, pp. 865–869.

Lambek, Michael (ed.) (2002) *A Reader in the Anthropology of Religion*, San Francisco and Indianapolis: Wiley-Blackwell.

Leeming, David Adams (1998) *Mythology: The Voyage of the Hero*, Oxford: Oxford University Press.

Lennig, Arthur (2003; 1974) *The Immortal Count*, Lexington, KY: University Press of Kentucky.

Lizardi, Tina and Frankel, Martha (1990) 'Hand Job', in *Details*, February 1990, p. 38.

Lynch, David (2006) *Catching the Big Fish: Meditation, Consciousness and Creativity*, London and New York: the Penguin Group.

Lynette, Rachel (2006) *Tim Burton: Filmmaker*, San Diego, CA: Kidhaven Press.

Malpas, Simon (ed.) (2001) *Postmodern Debates*, London: Palgrave.

Maslin, Janet (1996) 'The Moral: Be Careful of Aliens', in *The New York Times*, 13 December 1996, p. 5.

Matthews, Clive J and Smith, Jim (2007) *Tim Burton*, London: Virgin Books.

Mayo, Michael (1985) '*Frankenweenie*', in Paul A. Woods (ed.), *Tim Burton: A Child's Garden of Nightmares*, London: Plexus, pp. 18–21.

McCann, Donnarae and Woodard, Gloria (1972) *The Black American in Books for Children: Readings in Racism*, Lanham, MD: Scarecrow Press.

McGough, Roger (1989) *Selected Poems, 1967–1987*, London: Cape.

McHale, Brian (1992) *Constructing Postmodernism*, London and New York: Routledge.

—— (1997) *Postmodernist Fiction*, New York and London: Methuen.

McKenna, Kristine (2001) '*Playboy* Interview: Tim Burton', in Christian Fraga (ed.)

(2005) *Tim Burton Interviews*, Jackson: University Press of Mississippi, pp. 155–175.

McMahan, Alison (2005) *The Films of Tim Burton*, London and New York: Continuum.

Mellor, Anne K (1988) *Mary Shelley: Her Life, Her Fiction, Her Monsters*, London: Methuen.

Metz, Christian (1974) *Film Language: A Semiotics of the Cinema*, New York: Oxford University Press.

Miles, Robert (1993) *Gothic Writing 1750–1820: A Genealogy*, London: Routledge.

Miller, Karl (1985) *Doubles: Studies in Literary History*, Oxford: Oxford University Press.

Mills, David (2002) 'One on One: Tim Burton', in Paul A. Woods (ed.), *Tim Burton: A Child's Garden of Nightmares*, London: Plexus.

Milton, John (2003; 1667) *Paradise Lost*, London: Penguin Classics.

http://movies.nytimes.com/movie/review?res=9F04EEDA173EF930A25751C1A 960958260

Nashawaty, Christopher (1998) 'A Head of Its Time', in Christian Fraga (ed.) (2005) *Tim Burton Interviews*, Jackson: University Press of Mississippi, pp. 128–133.

Natale, Richard (2002) 'Remaking, not Aping, an Original', in Paul A. Woods (ed.), *Tim Burton: A Child's Garden of Nightmares*, London: Plexus.

Novel-Smith, John (1981; 1967) *Visconti* (extract), in John Caughie (ed.) (1981), *Theories of Authorship*, London: Routledge, pp. 136–137.

Neumann, Erich (1969; 1949) *Depth Psychology and a New Ethics*, trans. Eugene Rolfe, London: Hodder & Stoughton.

—— (1970; 1949) *The Origins and History of Consciousness*, trans. R. F. C. Hull, Princeton: Princeton University Press.

—— (1974a; 1959) *Art and the Creative Unconscious: Four Essays*, Princeton: Princeton University Press.

—— (1974b; 1955) *The Great Mother*, trans. Ralph Manheim, Princeton: Princeton University Press.

—— (2002; 1973) *The Child: Structure and Dynamics of the Nascent Personality*, London: Karnac.

Newman, Kim (1988) '*Beetlejuice*', in Paul A. Woods (ed.), *Tim Burton: A Child's Garden of Nightmares*, London: Plexus, pp. 32–34.

—— (1989) '*Batman*', in Paul A. Woods (ed.), *Tim Burton: A Child's Garden of Nightmares*, London: Plexus, pp. 54–57.

—— (1994) 'Tim Burton's *The Nightmare Before Christmas*', in Paul A. Woods (ed.), *Tim Burton: A Child's Garden of Nightmares*, London: Plexus, pp. 108–109.

—— (1995) '*Ed Wood*', in Paul A. Woods (ed.), *Tim Burton: A Child's Garden of Nightmares*, London: Plexus, pp. 123–125.

—— (2000) 'The Cage of Reason', in Paul A. Woods (ed.), *Tim Burton: A Child's Garden of Nightmares*, London: Plexus, pp. 156–160.

—— (2002) 'Mars Attacks!', in Paul A. Woods (ed.), *Tim Burton: A Child's Garden of Nightmares*, London: Plexus, pp. 143–145.

http://www.newyorker.com/archive/2001/08/06/010806crci.cinema

Odell, Colin and Le Blanc, Michelle (2005) *Tim Burton: Pocket Essentials*, Harpenden: Oldcastle Books.

O'Sullivan, Charlotte (2001) 'Numb and Number', in Paul A. Woods (ed.), *Tim Burton: A Child's Garden of Nightmares*, London: Plexus.

Page, Edwin (2007) *Gothic Fantasy: The Films of Tim Burton*, London and New York: Marion Boyars.

Pizzello, Stephen (1999) 'Head Trip', in Christian Fraga (ed.) (2005) *Tim Burton Interviews*, Jackson: University Press of Mississippi, pp. 134–141.

Poe, Edgar Allan (1991) *The Raven and Other Favourite Poems*, Mineola, NY: Dover Editions.

Poe, Edgar Allan and Barger, Andrew (ed.) (2008) *Edgar Allan Poe Annotated and Illustrated Entire Stories and Poems*, Memphis, TN: Bottletree Books LLC.

Punter, David (1996; 1980) *The Literature of Terror: A History of Gothic Fictions from 1765 to the Present Day*, Vols 1 & 2, Longman Group Ltd.

Radin, Paul (1956a) *The Trickster: A Study in American Indian Mythology*, New York: Schocken Books.

—— (1956b) 'The Winnebago Trickster Figure', in Michael Lambek (ed.) (2002) *A Reader in the Anthropology of Religion*, San Francisco and Indianapolis: Wiley-Blackwell, pp. 244–257.

Resner, Jeffrey (1992) 'Three Go Mad in Gotham', in Paul A. Woods (ed.), *Tim Burton: A Child's Garden of Nightmares*, London: Plexus, pp. 73–77.

Rivkin, Julie and Ryan, Michael (eds.) (2001) *Literary Theory: An Anthology*, Oxford: Blackwell.

Rogers, Pauline, 'Headless Horror: Emmanuel Lubezki, ASC Puts a Twisted Look on the Macabre Myth of *Sleepy Hollow*', in *International Cinematographers' Guild*, http://www.cameraguild.com/index.html?magazine/stoo1199.htm~top.main_hp, downloaded 16 May 2009.

http://rogerebert.suntimes.com/apps/pbcs.d11/article?AID=/20050718/EDITOR/50718002

http://www.rollingstone.com/reviews/movie/6152042/review/74469897/charlie_and_the_chocolate_factory_movie_review

Romney, Jonathan (2002) 'Don't Monkey with a Great Ape', in Paul A. Woods (ed.), *Tim Burton: A Child's Garden of Nightmares*, London: Plexus.

Rose, Frank (1991) 'Tim Cuts Up', in Paul A. Woods (ed.), *Tim Burton: A Child's Garden of Nightmares*, London: Plexus, pp. 62–70.

Rowland, Susan (2005) *Jung as a Writer*, London: Routledge.

—— (1999) *C.G. Jung and Literary Theory: The Challenge from Fiction*, London: Palgrave Macmillan.

—— (ed.) (2008) *Psyche and the Arts*, London: Routledge.

Salisbury, Mark (2000) 'Graveyard Shift', in Paul A. Woods (ed.), *Tim Burton: A Child's Garden of Nightmares*, London: Plexus, pp. 150–155.

—— (2001) 'Gorillas Just Want to Have Fun', in Christian Fraga (ed.) (2005) *Tim Burton Interviews*, Jackson: University Press of Mississippi, pp. 141–154.

—— (ed.) (2006; 2000), *Burton on Burton*, London: Faber and Faber.

Samuels, Andrew (1993) *The Political Psyche*, London: Routledge.

—— (1985) *Jung and the Post-Jungians*, London: Routledge.

Samuels, Andrew, Shorter, Bani and Plaut, Fred (1992) 'Trickster', in Richard P. Sugg (ed.), *Jungian Literary Criticism*, Evanston, Illinois: Northwestern University Press, pp. 273–274.

Sarris, Andrew (1968) *The American Cinema: Directors and Directions 1929–1968*, California and New York: Da Capo Press.

Sartre, Jean-Paul (1993; 1943) *Being and Nothingness: A Phenomenological Essay on Ontology*, trans. Hazel E. Barnes, Washington DC: Washington Square Press.

Schmidt, James (ed.) (1996) *What is Enlightenment?*, CA: University of California Press.

Schwartz, David (1992) 'Dark Knight Director', in Christian Fraga (ed.) (2005) *Tim Burton Interviews*, Jackson: University Press of Mississippi, pp. 89–94.

—— (2003) '*Big Fish*: American Museum of the Moving Image', in Christian Fraga (ed.) (2005) *Tim Burton Interviews*, Jackson: University Press of Mississippi, pp. 176–187.

Shapiro, Mark (1988) 'Explaining *Beetlejuice*', in Christian Fraga (ed.) (2005) *Tim Burton Interviews*, Jackson: University Press of Mississippi, pp. 3–8.

Shelley, Mary (1999; 1818) *Frankenstein*, Ware, Hertfordshire: Wordsworth Classics.

Skal, David J. (1993; 2001) *The Monster Show: A Cultural History of Horror*, New York: Faber and Faber.

Spines, Christine (2002) 'Men are from Mars, Women are from Venus', in Paul A. Woods (ed.), *Tim Burton: A Child's Garden of Nightmares*, London: Plexus.

Stacy, Robert H (1974) *Russian Literary Criticism*, Syracuse, NY: Syracuse University Press.

Steegmuller, Francis (ed. and trans.) (1982) *The Letters of Gustave Flaubert*, Cambridge, MA: Harvard University Press.

Stein, Murray (ed.) (1995) *Jung on Evil*, London: Routledge.

Sugg, Richard P. (ed.) (1992) *Jungian Literary Criticism*, Evanston, IL: Northwestern University Press.

Tarkovsky, Andrey (1989; 1986) *Sculpting in Time: Reflections on the Cinema*, Austin: University of Texas Press.

Thomas, Kevin (1988) 'Gleeful Grand Guignol of *Beetlejuice*', in Paul A. Woods (ed.), *Tim Burton: A Child's Garden of Nightmares*, London: Plexus, pp. 31–32.

Travers, Peter (2005) 'Charlie and the Chocolate Factory', in *Rolling Stone*, http://www.rollingstone.com/reviews/movie/6152042/review/7469897/charlie_and_the_chocolate_factory_movie_review, downloaded on 16 May 2009.

Vasileva, Lena (2008) 'The Father, the Dark Child and the Mob that Kills Him: Tim Burton's Representation of the Creative Artist', in Susan Rowland (ed.) (2008) *Psyche and the Arts*, London: Routledge, pp. 87–95.

Vassilieva, Elena (2004) 'Gothic Archetypes in Hollywood: The Trickster and the Double in *Batman* and *The Mask*', in *Anglophonia, French Journal of English Studies*, 15 (2004), pp. 199–207.

Vogler, Christopher (2007; 1998) *The Writer's Journey: Mythic Structure for Writers*, CA: Michael Wiese Productions.

von Franz, Marie-Louise (1964) 'The Process of Individuation', in Carl Gustav Jung and Marie-Louise von Franz (eds.) (1964) *Man and His Symbols*, London: Picador, pp. 159–254.

—— (1973; 1970) *An Introduction to the Interpretation of Fairytales'*, Zurich: Spring Publications.

Waddell, Terry (2006) *Mis/takes: Archetype, Myth and Identity in Screen Fiction*, London and New York: Routledge.

Wagner, Chuck (2002) 'Martian Inspiration: The Bubblegum Cards', in Paul A. Woods (ed.), *Tim Burton: A Child's Garden of Nightmares*, London: Plexus.

Walker, Stephen F. (2002) *Jung and the Jungians on Myth*, New York and London: Routledge.

Warren, Bill (1997) 'Tim Burton Attacks!', in Christian Fraga (ed.) (2005) *Tim Burton Interviews*, Jackson: University Press of Mississippi, pp. 108–116.

White, Taylor L. (1989a) '*Pee Wee's Big Adventure*', in Paul A. Woods (ed.), *Tim Burton: A Child's Garden of Nightmares*, London: Plexus, pp. 24–25.

—— (1989b) 'The Making of Tim Burton's *Beetlejuice* and his other Bizarre Gems', *Cinefantastique*, 20, 1/2, pp. 64–85.

Wollen, Peter (1969–1972) *Signs and Meaning in the Cinema*, London: Secker and Warburg.

Wollstonecraft, Mary (1993; 1792) *A Vindication of the Rights of Woman*, London: Penguin.

Woods, Paul A. (2002) (ed.), *Tim Burton: A Child's Garden of Nightmares*, London: Plexus.

Wright, Elizabeth (ed.) (1989) *Psychoanalytic Criticism. Theory in Practice*, London and New York: Routledge.

Young-Eisendrath, Polly and Dawson, Terence (eds.) (1997) *The Cambridge Companion to Jung*, Cambridge: Cambridge University Press.

Zamyatin, Yevgeny (1992) *A Soviet Heretic: Essays by Yevgeny Zamyatin*, Evanston, IL: Northwestern University Press.

DVD, video and film

Charlie and The Chocolate Factory (2-disc deluxe edition), Disc 2 – Special Features, 2005 [DVD] New York: Warner Brothers.

Sweeney Todd: The Demon Barber of Fleet Street (2-disc edition), Disc 2 – Special Features, 2005 [DVD] New York: Warner Brothers.

Index